JUST BALLIN'

THE CHAOTIC RISE OF THE NEW YORK KNICKS

MIKE WISE AND FRANK ISOLA

SIMON & SCHUSTER

New York   London   Sydney   Singapore

SIMON & SCHUSTER
Rockefeller Center
1230 Avenue of the Americas
New York, NY 10020

Copyright © 1999 by Mike Wise and Frank Isola
All rights reserved,
including the right of reproduction
in whole or in part in any form.

SIMON & SCHUSTER and colophon are registered trademarks
of Simon & Schuster, Inc.

Designed by Bonni Leon-Berman

Manufactured in the United States of America

10   9   8   7   6   5   4   3   2   1

Library of Congress Cataloging-in-Publication Data is available.
ISBN 0-684-87220-X

Photo Credits

AP/Wide World Photos: 3, 4, 5, 6, 7, 8, 12, 13, 16
Linda Cataffo/New York *Daily News:* 1, 9
Howard Simmons/New York *Daily News:* 2, 10
Corey Sipkin/New York *Daily News:* 11
Mike Albans/New York *Daily News:* 14
Barton Silverman/NYT Pictures: 15
Keith Torrie/New York *Daily News:* 17

ACKNOWLEDGMENTS

The authors would like to first thank Jeff Neuman. As our editor and point guard the last few months, he always saw the big picture and made the right decisions. We would also like to thank Andrew Cohen at Simon & Schuster, our intrepid agent David Vigliano, and Mark Reckeweg.

A special acknowledgment goes out to Carl Nelson for his insight, direction, and friendship.

Also, our editors at the New York *Daily News* (Barry Werner, Leon Carter, Teri Thompson, and John Gruber) and the *New York Times* (Neil Amdur, Bill Brink, Kathleen McElroy, Jay Schreiber, Joe Sexton, Mike Hale, and Tom Jolly), some of America's smartest—and most tolerant—newspaper people.

We also owe appreciation to some of our colleagues: at the *Daily News,* Mark Kriegel, Mitch Lawrence, Filip Bondy, Ohm Youngmisuk, and Darren Everson; and at the *Times,* Harvey Araton, Chris Broussard, and Selena Roberts, whose seminal writing and reporting proved invaluable to the project.

A debt of gratitude also goes out to the people with whom we covered the Knicks and the NBA over the past five years, friends, associates, or both who kept us honest and in our place: Barbara Barker, Shaun Powell, Dave D'Alessandro, Chris Sheridan, Steve Adamek, Steve Popper, Kevin Kernan, Thomas Hill, Cliff Brown, Greg Logan, Barry Rubinstein, Mike Del Negro, Mike Dougherty, and John Jeansonne.

To Martin McNeal, Ian O'Connor, Adrian Wojnarowski, Matt Steinmetz, and David Steele, whose stories also made the project possible.

We also could not have written this book without the cooperation of Dave Checketts, Ernie Grunfeld, Ed Tapscott, and Jeff

6   ACKNOWLEDGMENTS

Van Gundy. The help of Dennis D'Agostino, Barry Watkins, Chris Weiller, Lori Hamamoto, and their assistants also was vital and greatly appreciated.

Finally we would like to thank the players, past and present Knicks. In the end, they not only gave us something to write every day, but on certain nights, when Madison Square Garden was full of magic and noise, they also made us realize how lucky we are to cover the NBA for a living.

For my father, Roger Wise, whose ink-stained hands turned out to be contagious, and Catharine, whose grace and smile made the tough times disappear.

—Mike Wise

For Tonja, Liam, and Gabrielle, the most loving and patient family a man could know.

—Frank Isola

CONTENTS

"I valued a player who cared for others and could lose himself in the group for the good of the group. Understanding that the good of the group comes first is fundamental to being a highly productive member of a team."

—*John Wooden, legendary UCLA basketball coach*

"I'm just ballin'. That's when basketball is fun, going up and down. At this point of my career, I'm not going to change."

—*Latrell Sprewell, New York Knicks guard*

JUST
BALLIN'

1

THE INTERROGATION

They were sitting across from the most notorious villain in professional sports, four men with the same thought:

Was Latrell Sprewell going to help us or kill us?

For more than a year, Sprewell had been branded as America's Thug. A self-described loner, he had developed a reputation on the court as a malcontent, and his career was scarred by violent altercations with those who were supposedly on his side.

His team, the Golden State Warriors, was going nowhere and Sprewell was feuding with his coach. His frustration and anger boiling inside him, on December 1, 1997, Sprewell had lost his mind and control of his senses. He assaulted P.J. Carlesimo during a practice, grabbing his coach around the throat and threatening to kill him.

This reckless incident set off incendiary reactions from network television and national radio commentators and newspaper columnists. Sprewell was the subject of dinner table conversations from Portland to Poughkeepsie.

The National Basketball Association acted swiftly, banning Sprewell for a year. Now, thirteen months after taking his last shot in anger, Sprewell's basketball future, and perhaps his life, rested with the four men sitting on his living room sofa in the dead of winter.

Dave Checketts, Ernie Grunfeld, Jeff Van Gundy, and Ed Tap-scott flew 1,200 miles to Milwaukee on January 17, 1999. Like the reviled Sprewell, they were on a mission; the four men represented the New York Knicks, one of the NBA's cornerstone franchises, and now they were in the home of the player who had choked his coach.

"Anybody want anything to drink?"

"You got any Diet Coke?" Van Gundy asked.

Their host retreated to his kitchen. He was unshaven and wearing gym clothes. His ultracasual appearance aside, Sprewell seemed personable and polite—unlike the man portrayed as a menace to sport and society in all the hysterical media accounts of the past year.

They sat down on three sofas in front of a large-screen television tuned to *The NFL Today,* and began talking about the possibility of Sprewell coming to the Knicks. Everyone tried to treat the occasion like a social call, a bunch of guys getting together to watch the AFC Championship Game between the Jets and the Broncos. But eventually the time came to get beyond pleasantries.

"Latrell, you mind turning the volume down on the television so we can talk?" Checketts asked.

"No problem," Sprewell said.

The purpose of the visit became clear. This was Sprewell's parole board hearing. Checketts, the Madison Square Garden president, was the warden. Image-conscious to a fault, the forty-four-year-old Mormon had no patience for outlaws. Nonetheless, he was desperate for a winner; he was willing to soften his hard-line rules of the past if Sprewell said the right things over the next one and a half hours.

Grunfeld, the team president and general manager, had his own agenda: He needed to impress his boss, the press, and the fans with a blockbuster deal.

Tapscott, the assistant general manager, had done extensive background checks on Sprewell. He had spoken with Sprewell's high school coach, James Gordon; his former teammates at Golden State; NBA security officials—basically anyone

with whom the player had come in contact during his basketball career.

Van Gundy, the head coach and the only member of the
Knick management team not wearing a sports coat, understood
the risk involved in acquiring the volatile shooting guard. He
did not see a coach-killer sitting three feet in front of him; Van
Gundy saw a job-saver, a slashing, scoring force of a type un-
seen at Madison Square Garden for the past decade.

On the two-hour flight to Bradley County Airport, Checketts
had decided how the interview would be conducted. It was
vital that Sprewell not feel as if he were on trial, and that Van
Gundy spend considerable time speaking with him, so that the
player would feel comfortable with his prospective new coach.

The conversation was going smoothly. But inevitably, it pro-
gressed to that morning when Sprewell attacked Carlesimo.
Speaking calmly, Sprewell told them of the background behind
his desperate act. Listening closely, the four executives could
appreciate the motivating power of frustration; their coming to
Milwaukee was a fairly desperate act of their own.

The Knicks had been eliminated four straight years in the
second round of the playoffs and were searching for new blood.
Sprewell, twenty-eight years old and in his athletic prime, was
the best available player out there. He was still under contract
with Golden State for two more seasons, but the club had decided he would never play for the Warriors again after he had
put his hands around Carlesimo's throat. They would hold an
open competition for his talents, and New York was among the
highest bidders.

In order to conduct this face-to-face interview with Sprewell
without risking tampering charges, the Knicks sought and were
granted a special dispensation from NBA commissioner David
Stern for the visit.

Just ten days earlier, the longest and most contentious labor
struggle in the fifty-two-year history of the NBA had ended
with a new agreement between players and owners—and a
shortened season that would begin February 5. The NBA would
try to cram fifty games into ninety days, and would have to do it

without its greatest star: Michael Jordan had retired on January 13. Again.

The chase for Sprewell was on.

For all his baggage, Sprewell's talent was mesmerizing. At Golden State, where he made the All-Star team three times in his first five seasons, the explosiveness and production masked his liabilities. Sprewell's 6-foot-5-inch sinewy frame could dart through mounds of muscle on offense. He played with passion and fire on defense. This was the kind of player the Knicks had long hoped to place alongside All-Star center Patrick Ewing, the scoring threat who could lighten the burden that Ewing had shouldered for so many years.

In his first six seasons, Sprewell averaged more than 20 points per game four times, but his teams appeared in the play-offs only once, getting swept in three games by the Phoenix Suns in 1994. That was also Sprewell's breakout year: He averaged 21 points, made the All-Star team for the first time, and became the unquestioned centerpiece of the Warriors. Even Jordan took notice after his first retirement, calling Sprewell one of the top two shooting guards in the game.

Yet even with such early success, disturbing signs developed. After that one playoff season the Warriors began to implode; trades and losses mounted, and so did Sprewell's frustration. He feuded and fought with teammates and never accepted a leadership role. During his rookie season in 1992–1993, Sprewell had gotten into a wild, free-swinging brawl with teammate Byron Houston. In 1995, after a fight in practice with Jerome Kersey, he tried to go at Kersey with a 2x4 before two other teammates restrained him.

But even these incidents did not prepare anyone for what was to come.

If ever a coach and player were likely to clash, it was the freewheeling Sprewell and the hard-nosed Carlesimo. Carlesimo was a taskmaster from the old school, nearing fifty. He had spent twelve seasons at Seton Hall University, taking a program from the bottom of the Big East to within seconds of winning the 1989 national championship before falling to Michigan in overtime. He also gained a reputation as a screamer, doling out constant criticism that some of his former players construed as verbal abuse. In college, Bob Knight and others can get away with this behavior, but in the NBA, where the majority of the players earn more than the coach and where some have more say in personnel matters, Carlesimo's style was seen as abrasive rather than productive.

He became coach of the Portland Trail Blazers in 1993, lasting three years before he was fired. He feuded with the team's star point guard Rod Strickland. Just two months into his new job with the Warriors, Carlesimo and Sprewell were at constant odds.

Three weeks before the incident, Sprewell openly laughed during a blowout loss to the Lakers after teammate Bimbo Coles said, "I'm going to foul out of this motherfucker." Carlesimo was incensed. He benched Sprewell, who called Carlesimo "a fucking joke" as he walked off the floor.

In his eventual arbitration hearing before John D. Feerick, the dean of Fordham Law School, Sprewell testified that he had lashed out at the coach because he thought it was disrespectful to take him out of a game like that and that Carlesimo did not shake his hand after the game.

Through training camp and the first month of the regular season, Sprewell testified, he and Carlesimo "got into it almost on a daily basis."

When Sprewell, the team captain, missed a flight to Utah on November 27 because he had overslept, Carlesimo could not take it anymore. Repeated fines and verbal scoldings were not working. Bad blood brewed, and three days later it came to a boil.

During a practice at the Warriors' fifth-floor facility in the Oakland Convention Center on December 1, Sprewell and teammate Muggsy Bogues and Warriors strength coach Mark Grabow were involved in a three-man, two-ball shooting drill.

"Come on, Spree, give him a better pass," Carlesimo said. The coach repeated himself, this time raising his voice. "Come on, Spree, give him a sharper, crisper pass."

Sprewell turned and slammed the ball down. "What the fuck do you want me to do?"

"You're the fuck out of here!" Carlesimo said, telling Sprewell to leave the premises.

"When he threw me out of practice, I just lost it," Sprewell said later.

In a moment of fury, Sprewell grabbed Carlesimo around the throat, changing his career forever.

"I'll kill you!" Sprewell said as he grabbed Carlesimo's neck with both hands and started choking him for seven to ten seconds.

"Don't do it!" Grabow yelled at least twice.

Carlesimo testified that by the end of the attack, he was having trouble breathing comfortably. "It was difficult to breathe and getting more difficult," he said.

After Sprewell was pulled away by coaches and teammates, he stormed off to the locker room, kicking over a water cooler and saying, "I'm going to kill your ass. I hate you."

He showered and dressed, and then returned fifteen minutes later, still in a rage.

He contended later that he wanted to talk to Carlesimo about being traded, and wound up flailing his arms as teammates converged again. Sprewell claims he may have hit Carlesimo while trying to break free, but that he did not deliberately punch the coach.

Carlesimo said Sprewell closed his fist, and that Sprewell caught him on the right side of the cheek with a malicious overhand right.

Players began pushing him toward the exit, and a defiant Sprewell still could not let it go, shouting, "Get me the fuck out of here! I'm gonna kill you."

The Knicks were preparing for a game in San Antonio the day the news broke about the incident. Sprewell instantly became a demonic figure across the country. It was one thing for players to get busted for marijuana, or to father children out of wedlock, to carouse in NBA cities late at night, or to tell autograph hounds to get lost. But this went beyond the realm of bad-boy behavior.

"Wow," Van Gundy said when asked about the attack. "It's bad. It's bad for the league, too. I feel badly for P.J. because he's a very good coach, and to have to deal with that goes beyond coaching. It's unfortunate. That's exactly the type of image you don't want to have in this league. Coaches have to make some tough decisions, and not everyone is going to like them."

The Warriors terminated Sprewell's contract and the NBA suspended him for a year—the longest nondrug-related suspension in modern sports history.

But three months later the arbitrator Feerick reinstated the contract and also reduced his league suspension to 64 games—the remainder of the 1997–98 season. Even so, the damage to Sprewell's image, it seemed, was irreparable.

He became a symbol for all that's wrong with sports, and in New York he was denounced by media and fans alike. All-sports radio was in a frenzy, vilifying him with the same venom or more as they did when Roberto Alomar spit in an umpire's face. "This is worse than [the Alomar incident]," wrote Mike Lupica, the nationally syndicated columnist of the New York *Daily News*. "This was a physical attack on what authority we have left in sports. . . . If that authority no longer holds, even in a practice gym, then no one is in charge." Nobody wanted anything to do with Sprewell after the incident, least of all Dave Checketts, who was holding the moral compass for the league.

Checketts believed in a utopian team, in which most of his players were model citizens who played for others, believing in teamwork. Whether this came from his upbringing in Bountiful, Utah, or something he had once read in a Chip Hilton novel, Checketts was firm in his beliefs.

But he was also a realist. Running the Knicks was like running any other Fortune 500 company. If Madison Square Garden was dark and empty in late May and June, the Knicks had had a bad season.

Just meeting and speaking with Sprewell represented a

change in Checketts's philosophy of how the Knicks would do
business. Maybe it was time to see if Generation Xers could coexist with mature veterans and all vie for the same thing. After
all, not everyone could be Tim Duncan, the brilliant and digni-
fied young center for the San Antonio Spurs. Sometimes, an
Allen Iverson, Isaiah Rider, Chris Webber, or even Sprewell
would have to do.

"We're not all Good Samaritans," Charles Oakley, the longtime Knick forward once said. "If you want to win a championship, you need some thugs on your team. Thugs keep you
loose. Everyone can't eat together, hang together. Everyone goes
different ways."

Still, the thought of acquiring Sprewell was blasphemous.

Were the Knicks risking a public relations nightmare for the
franchise? Or, worse, if they didn't, would that just allow
Miami, Indiana, or San Antonio to pluck Sprewell from his
professional exile?

And what of Sprewell's game? No one had seen him play in
thirteen months, except for the lunchtime crowd at the Milwaukee YMCA, where Sprewell ended up playing center against an
assortment of truck drivers, insurance salesmen, and lost souls
who had once played high school ball.

And had Sprewell really changed?

Arnulfo Perlas didn't see much remorse.

Perlas, a mechanic from the East Bay Area suburb of Anti-
och, California, and a friend, Irma Feliciano, were heading to
church on the morning of March 1, three months after Sprewell
attacked Carlesimo. Sprewell, pushing ninety miles per hour
in his customized $126,000 Mercedes, began weaving in and
out of traffic on the freeway. He eventually hit Perlas's Toyota
Corolla, causing that vehicle to flip over. Concerned motorists
pulled the couple from the overturned car. Waiting for the
police to arrive, Sprewell sat on a curb, oblivious to their
plight.

"He didn't come over to help, to even say he was sorry," Perlas said. "I have no idea if he cared about what he'd done."
Sprewell pleaded no contest to reckless driving and was sen-

tenced to ninety days in jail, which he served under electronic home detention in Milwaukee. (In a subsequent civil trial, Perlas was awarded $104,940 in damages.)

This and several other occasions would have to be addressed if Sprewell wanted to put his New York inquisitors' fears to rest.

Sprewell talked about the many incidents and problems he'd been involved in, describing the constant verbal abuse from Carlesimo that had driven him nearly insane. But even after that was put aside, there was one story that particularly troubled Checketts, one he could not easily ignore.

Back in 1994, one of Sprewell's three pit bulls had attacked his infant daughter, biting off her ear. Despite some public revulsion, Sprewell had not given immediate approval to have the dog put to sleep, and when asked about the attack several days later, he had blithely replied, "Shit happens." This bothered Checketts to no end.

"I have six kids, and I know how I feel about them," Checketts said to Sprewell as he sat across from him. "And I don't expect everyone to feel for their kids the way I feel for mine. But I have to get something off my chest and ask, Why would you say that?"

Sprewell answered the question in two parts, first picking up a picture frame of his daughter on the coffee table and handing it to Checketts.

"I love my daughter dearly," he said. "I took care of her plastic surgery, it didn't affect her hearing, and I've never had anything hurt me more in my life." The second part: "I was tired of the press crawling all over me. I didn't want them to go to the hospital."

"He was not indignant," Checketts would later say. "He was not defensive. I believed what he was telling me."

Sprewell had refused to put the pit bull to sleep until the tenth and final day of its quarantine (a process whose purpose is to keep people from destroying animals in anger). Checketts felt he had cleared that hurdle with Sprewell, but still he wanted to hear more. If Checketts was going to bring in the kind of player he'd long considered a cancer running amok in the NBA, giving Sprewell an opportunity to resume his career after his thirteen-month layoff, it would take a very strong and persuasive impression in their brief ninety minutes together to alter his perception.

Asked later what won him over, Checketts paused and said, "I'd have to say, 'Footprints in the Sand.' "

The familiar poem was etched in a mirror inside the doorway of Sprewell's home. The poem describes a man about to make his heavenly journey, looking back on his life and remembering that there were always two sets of footprints in the sand.

"The man confronts the Lord about the fact that there was only one set of footprints during his deepest, darkest moments," Checketts said. " 'My son,' the Lord replies, 'it was during those times I carried you.' It was deeply personal for me at different points in my life."

Staying behind for a few minutes as the rest of the Knicks brain trust shuffled back toward their limousine, Checketts said to Sprewell, "That's an appropriate verse for you, don't you think?"

Sprewell nodded.

"Do you ever think about it?" Checketts asked.

"Oh, many, many times," Sprewell said.

"Does it mean anything to you?" he asked.

"Yeah," Sprewell replied. "I know I've been carried."

Confident he had asked the most difficult questions, Checketts joined the group outside Sprewell's split-level, taupe-brick home in suburban Milwaukee. The four men got back into the stretch limo and motored toward the airport, discussing what to do with Sprewell. Sitting across from each other in the limo, they were holding the most important quorum of the season.

Acquiring Sprewell altered everything. Would the fans embrace him? Would his teammates accept him? Could he be coached? And the eternal question that went unanswered during his six seasons with the Warriors: Could Sprewell play *winning* basketball?

If Checketts, Grunfeld, Tapscott, and Van Gundy believed he had redeemable qualities, he could ultimately become the player to rejuvenate New York's basketball team. Conversely, his unsavory past could also end up costing the Knicks another shot at a title, and some of those same men their careers.

Returning to his home in New Canaan, Connecticut, that night, Checketts asked his family for advice.

"You know what kind of stuff I would take at school if we got him, Dad?" said one of his four sons. "Are we really going after him?"

His two youngest sons thought Sprewell deserved a second chance, which got the other one to thinking again. "You think he could help us win, Dad?"

His father nodded.

"Look, I did not lead the family in prayer to ask God whether we should take Latrell Sprewell," Checketts said. "And it wasn't like a light turned on in my head. But I felt I understood the man a lot better. The visit we had with him convinced me it would work."

Another thought had occurred to Checketts earlier that day when the four men were leaving Sprewell's home. As they approached the airport, discussing the interview, Checketts said, "I thought he was honest and forthcoming."

"He knows he has to be on his best behavior," Grunfeld said as Tapscott nodded in agreement.

Asked for his assessment before they boarded the Cablevision corporate jet back to New York, Van Gundy said he liked Sprewell, drawing an affectionate parallel to John Starks, another hand grenade in high tops for whom Sprewell would be traded. But the coach was also honest enough to acknowledge that the Knicks were taking a monstrous gamble.

"Let's not kid ourselves," Van Gundy said. "This guy's a madman. And that's what I like about him. We can't pass up a chance like this."

Two months before the sitdown in Milwaukee, Checketts and the others said goodbye to an important part of the team's past. On November 15, nearly 250 people filled Parkside Memorial Chapel on Queens Boulevard in Forest Hills, New York, to pay homage to the franchise patriarch, Red Holzman, who had lost his battle with leukemia at age seventy-eight.

Holzman, who led the Knicks to their only two titles in the early 1970s, had been mourning the loss of Selma, his wife of fifty-five years who had died four months earlier. His quiet dignity would not allow him to draw attention to himself or to the illness ravaging his body in his last days. In addition to the Knick contingent from New York, his former players flew in from all over to pay their respects.

Checketts, his voice quivering, gave an emotional and eloquent eulogy that left many in the chapel weeping. He called Holzman "a great coach who forced his will on a group of players." Everyone who attended dusted off their favorite Red stories.

The Hall of Fame coach had won 613 games, 50 or more games five times, and three Eastern Conference championships. More than any other year, he was looking forward to the start of the 1999 NBA season; with the love of his life gone and his body failing, his keen interest in the game—and the Knicks—was among the few things that truly mattered to him.

In the funeral parlor that day, Van Gundy sat in the back row with the Knicks' coaching staff. Patrick Ewing served as a pallbearer. They listened to Checketts talk about Holzman, how he came to embody the organization, how the Knicks had lost their guiding light. He was the calming force when calamity struck, the white-haired sage who chose his words carefully and was always thoughtful in his observations.

When Checketts was hired, he brought back Holzman as a special consultant. In the changing world of the NBA, where players had become commodities and assets and little else, Checketts said Holzman reminded the organization that they were still dealing with people.

"He might be a putz, but he's our putz," Holzman would tell Checketts and Grunfeld about a troublesome player. "You've got to have some tolerance. You've got to have some patience. You're talking about a person here."

Holzman had taken gambles, too. In 1980, during his second stint as the team's coach, he exited training camp with the first all-black team in franchise history. Butch Beard, the socially conscious veteran guard who became Holzman's assistant coach, spoke with Holzman about the move. After all, in the mid-1970s the league was often perceived as too black and too drug-ridden to attract sponsorship dollars for the networks. It was an era when the league's championship series was being shown on a tape-delay basis because of such alleged shortcomings, and now Holzman was fielding an all-black team. Though no one publicly admitted it, the franchise's image was partially at stake.

"Red, do you know what you're doing here?" Beard asked Holzman the last day of training camp that season.

"I don't care if they're red, black, or green," Holzman replied. "They're the best we have."

(As a cheap, throwaway line, the *New York Post* columnist Peter Vecsey said Holzman's move would give fodder to racists to call them the "Niggerbockers." Vecsey was not trying to make the situation flammable, but by introducing the name he made it a part of that era's lore.)

Red knew about talent. From 1969 to 1973, a cast that at various times included Willis Reed, Walt Frazier, Earl Monroe, Bill Bradley, Dave DeBusschere, Jerry Lucas, Dick Barnett, and Phil Jackson spun the city on their fingertips, taking New York on a dizzying ride while winning two titles in four years.

The Knicks of Holzman played selflessly, moving the basketball around, sharing and winning. Former *Post* columnist Larry Merchant wrote of Holzman's team the night they won their second title, "Some people say basketball has been described as a game of five egos and one ball. The Knicks play as though they have one ego and five balls. The Knicks' way is, again, the championship way."

How far the game and the Knicks had come: No one was will-

ing to bet five balls would be enough for Latrell Sprewell's ego.
What would Red have thought of that meeting in Milwaukee?

Less than five days after he met with
Knicks management in his living room, Sprewell faced another
inquisition, this time from the New York media. His first press
conference as a Knick was held at the Stouffer's Hotel in
Westchester, New York, less than three miles from the team's
training facility.

Already there was division in the press corps. From a basketball standpoint, the move made perfect sense; the Knicks
had acquired a three-time All-Star for three reserves—John
Starks, Chris Mills, and Terry Cummings. Mills had only been
in New York for one season, and Cummings was in the twilight
of his career—but moving Starks demonstrated the Knicks' desire to move beyond their past.

Sprewell was a younger, more explosive version of Starks,
the player who had embodied the spirit of the Knicks for nearly
a decade. He would inject more points and excitement into
their offense. But some could not forgive Sprewell for his actions at Golden State. *Coach-choker* would be the brand he
would bear forever, they decided. Others looked past the moral
question to focus on a practical one: How would Sprewell's
playing style mesh with the pound-it-down-low-to-Patrick offense of the 1990s Knicks?

Mike Lupica was among those having second thoughts about
second chances. "The people who run the Knicks have talked
to him face-to-face, [and] believe he is genuine about showing
people that he isn't a thug. . . . Professional sports is never the
CYO [Catholic Youth Organization]."

Two days before the press conference, Van Gundy flew to
Milwaukee on the Knicks' private jet to accompany Sprewell
for the two-hour flight back to New York. Ever the hoops junkie,
Van Gundy gave Sprewell a crash course in Knicks 101, talking
about the team, the city, and life in the petri dish of New York's
sports media.

Sprewell had not made a public appearance in more than a year. The Knicks' plan was simple: They would prop Sprewell up on a stage and let him confess his sins to the world, and then everybody could go about their business and begin training camp.

"I'm going up there with him," Van Gundy told Grunfeld and director of communications Chris Weiller. "I don't want him sitting up there alone."

With Checketts back in Manhattan, a safe distance from a potentially risky photo op, and Grunfeld watching the proceedings from the back of the hotel's banquet room, Van Gundy emerged from behind a black curtain with the league's top-rated troublemaker.

Sprewell was clad in a white turtleneck. The corn rows he wore the day he assaulted Carlesimo had grown longer. He was not changing for anyone. He was unshaven, and his upper torso looked as if he had been pressing weights during his exile. His posture, his mannerisms, everything about the way he carried himself suggested he was in tremendous physical shape.

"I want to be able to get on the court and feel the ball in my hands," he said. "I haven't played against NBA-caliber players since December of 1997. I don't think you rate how much I missed it. I wish I could have practiced yesterday."

The coach lightened the mood by saying the only problem he had with Sprewell is that when he wanted something to drink last week in Sprewell's living room, Sprewell didn't have any Diet Coke in his refrigerator.

But Sprewell needed no help on this day. He had been extensively briefed by the public relations staff as to what questions would most likely be asked, and he had had the last thirteen months to think about his answers. Contrite, humble, he again apologized to Carlesimo as he had eight days after the attack, and he repeatedly asked the fans for forgiveness. "I'm sorry," he said. "We all make mistakes. I made one. I said I'm sorry about that. And I'm asking for a second chance. I'm not the person I've been portrayed to be."

Even saying of the choking incident, "I just had a bad day," brought him little criticism the next morning.

Van Gundy's show of support for his newest star did not go unnoticed. Sprewell's talents excited a coach who was more used to deploying Greco-Roman wrestlers than lithe, dynamic basketball players. But Sprewell's pedigree also concerned him. On one hand, he could be the missing piece to catapult the franchise back to prominence. On the other hand, his style and personality could ruin the cohesion of a team that had made the playoffs every year since 1987.

"I have something to prove to the organization more than anyone else," Sprewell said. "To have an opportunity to come here and display my talent and show everybody the real me, you can't ask for anything more than that."

2
THE MAKEOVER

Ernie Grunfeld clicked off his cellular phone inside the Knicks' draft war room at Madison Square Garden on the night of June 24, 1998. To no one in particular, he shook his head and said, "We can't find him."

The team president was more frustrated than angry that he could not reach Charles Oakley by telephone to inform the player he was no longer a Knick.

The reconstruction of the Knicks actually began seven months before their meeting with Sprewell and the trade of Starks. Recurrent playoff failures had convinced Grunfeld and management to stop waxing nostalgic and start making hard decisions about the team's future.

Ewing, Oakley, and Starks had played together for ten seasons, sharing every heartbreaking loss and thrilling victory. But on draft day 1998, their run would officially end. Grunfeld wanted the team to get younger and more athletic and had no qualms about sacrificing experience and toughness, sending the old workhorse Oakley to Toronto for the young and unproven forward Marcus Camby.

Call it passive aggression or deep denial, but by not responding to Grunfeld's repeated attempts to contact him, Oakley forced the team to wait an extra day before finalizing the trade. He dreaded picking up the phone and hearing those awful words: "You're not needed anymore."

Of course, Grunfeld would phrase it differently. He would say how hard management debated trading their most rugged player and how much they appreciated his ten years, 7,291 rebounds, and innumerable floor burns. Grunfeld respected Oakley and knew he was taking a risk in trading him, but he was also tired of Oakley's constant needling of him in the news media, his frequent complaints that Grunfeld was not doing enough to improve the team.

Beyond the personal issues, Grunfeld believed Oakley was shopworn at thirty-four years old. He felt he was outplayed by Indiana power forward Antonio Davis in the 1998 Eastern Conference semifinals, won by the Pacers in five games. With the lockout looming July 1, Oakley entering the final year of his contract and due a $10 million balloon payment from the club, ticket prices about to be raised again, and Grunfeld's job performance up for closer inspection, the time had come to pull the trigger.

"It was difficult to do because of what he has meant to the franchise," Grunfeld said. "We grew up together and we've been through a lot of battles together. It's never easy to part with someone of his character."

Not everyone in the organization agreed with the move. Van Gundy and his assistants knew what Oakley meant to the team and felt that disrupting the chemistry would prove to be fatal in a truncated season. But if Van Gundy was upset, he wasn't letting on the day after the deal was made official.

"We could never give up a guy who has given so much to this team for someone we didn't feel could help us win now," Van Gundy said. "I think Charles will go down as one of the great Knicks. That tells you how highly we feel about Marcus Camby."

Oakley had come to represent the plodding, slow-motion Knicks; his vertical leap could be measured by sliding a subway token under his sneakers. Camby, the former college player of the year at UMass in 1996, had gained a reputation as an injury-prone underachiever in his first two NBA seasons, but he was twenty-four years old, 6-foot-11, and could run, jump and reject shots into the fourth row. He hovered along the baseline, waiting to dunk in a missed rebound.

Had he not been involved in the deal, Oakley would certainly have agreed with its intent: to make the Knicks better, more athletic. He had long since accepted his role on the court, as the ultimate workhorse in a league built for thoroughbreds.

Oakley's whereabouts when Grunfeld finally tracked him down should have surprised no one. As in every off-season, he was driving around America like a nomad. And everywhere he went, whether visiting his mother in Cleveland or his sister in Alabama, he always made sure to find a weight room and a basketball court.

To teammates and fans alike, Oakley had become something of a cult hero. His social calendar was always full; before coming to New York for a farewell press conference, Oakley rode on a private jet to the Hamptons for a party thrown by Tommy Mottola, the head of Sony Records and Mariah Carey's exhusband. Everyone wanted him around. Knicks coaches and the Garden faithful admired his work ethic and hustle. Players loved his stylish wardrobe, the orange sherbet suits and the lime green fedoras. He once walked into the locker room dressed in full lavender to the disturbed gazes of teammates.

Said Chris Childs, the point guard, "What up, Barney?"

For all his bravado, style, and cocksure ways, Oakley was self-conscious about his appearance. He would ask any reporter who happened by his locker cubicle after a game whether his latest fashion statement was working or was a faux pas.

"Does this tie go with these shoes?" he would ask. "Does it match?"

Imagine, the NBA millionaire with closets full of designer suits asking those slaves to fashion, sportswriters, about how to dress; these were the same people still trying to update their wardrobes from the late 1980s, most of whom believed that the invention of the steam iron was a sign that technology had gone too far.

But Oakley was including the media, and that means something in the sanctuary of the locker room, where there are essentially two kinds of people: players and outsiders. While some professional athletes could make you feel inferior and unwanted, Oakley could disarm you with his biting humor and feigned interest in your personal life.

What Yogi Berra was to baseball, Charles Oakley was to the Knicks' locker room. The reporters loved chatting up the man who invented Oak-Speak, a wonderful world of mixed metaphors, malapropisms, and one-liners that were as much a part of his ten seasons with the Knicks as his alligator loafers.

On the Knicks possibly making major trades: "If it ain't broke, don't break it."

On the team's early-season struggles: "When the milk is spilled, you have to wipe it up and get some more."

Oakley's preseason prediction: "It's hard to tell what you have right now. You can't throw a hook on the side of the road and expect to catch a fish in the grass."

On it went, butchered metaphor after butchered metaphor.

On being whistled for more flagrant fouls than anyone in the league: "It's just like driving on a highway. The speed limit is fifty-five or sixty-five and you do seventy they'll pull you over. It's one of those things. I'll just have to keep my eye on the speed limit, keep my eyes on the road, and keep my eyes looking out for the cops. In my case, I have to keep my eyes looking out for the NBA."

He once described his own role on the Knicks as "a butler in a mansion. I'm happy to clean up and make sure everything is all right."

He was like the rare family member you actually wanted to see on Thanksgiving.

Oakley could be extremely sensitive, too. On Easter Sunday in Orlando in 1997, he walked into the hotel lobby and noticed that Childs was wearing an identical pastel peach suit. Shaking his head in disbelief, he stormed back to his room and emerged from the elevator in an all-black ensemble—a remarkable choice for the joyous holiday. He was in an ornery mood the rest of the day.

In February of that '97 season, with the All-Star Game in his hometown of Cleveland, someone joked that Oakley should take the beat writers out and show them the town. Oakley remembered, and two days before the game, he told them to show up in the front of the Marriott City Centre hotel in downtown Cleveland at 8:00 P.M.

At the appointed time, a white stretch limousine pulled up in front of the hotel and out stepped Oakley, his 6-foot-9 strapping frame dressed in a pin-striped suit, fedora, and fur coat. The Oak Man had kept his promise. As he escorted five reporters into his company-owned limo, he was told, "Charles, you're like the Godfather of Cleveland."

Rolling his shoulders, he nonchalantly replied, "You're down with the King, ain't ya?"

The first stop was Club Togo, a supper place/nightclub he had purchased in his old East Cleveland neighborhood. Oakley paraded around the bar as if he were Sinatra at the Sands in Las Vegas. His friends talked about Oakley's Jheri-curl days, when he blew kisses to the crowd after dunks at John Jay High School.

By 9:30 P.M., it was on to his mother, Corine's, modest ranch-style house, where the walls were devoted entirely to pictures of her children. A renowned cook, Corine had Jordan and Pippen over routinely during the season—even after Oakley was traded from the Bulls. On this night, a spread of ham hocks, sweet potato pie, and collard greens (with smoked turkey and without) awaited.

Oakley retreated to his bedroom, decorated with posters of himself, and engaged in a small-wager card game with his childhood friends. With nearly half the NBA in Cleveland, he easily could have been out carousing with other players; instead, he was spending time at home with family and friends. No one ever felt Oakley was just trying to ingratiate himself or curry favor with the press; no one wrote about that night until after he was traded.

He came to be viewed as a regular guy who connected with his public. He became a small-time entrepreneur, opening car washes all over the New York metropolitan area and Cleveland. His one brother and four sisters all worked, and Charles had helped set up two of their businesses—including Nails, Etc., a manicure and beauty salon right next to the car wash in Cleveland. While the rest of the NBA was either playing above the rim or spotting up from twenty-five feet, Oakley took his lunch pail to the construction site and put in an honest day's work every day.

Oakley was surely responsible for more spilled beer at the Garden than any inebriated stockbroker. If there was a loose ball to pursue, he never hesitated to swan-dive for it, even if it meant taking out a family of four. He should have come equipped with a roll bar. The experienced fan knew to be ready to jump from his seat at a moment's notice. There were many innocent bystanders injured by friendly fire, including the wife of Patrick Ewing, Rita, who once spent the rest of the night following one collision being cared for in the back room of the Garden for a sore neck. Oakley's grit and perseverance made it easier to tolerate his inevitable, crazy behind-the-back passes.

Still, his name had always come up in trade rumors. But Toronto? This felt like the ultimate indignity. He was the kind of complementary player who made good teams better, and he was being shipped off to a young franchise that had known nothing but losing. Just as Oakley was about to finally receive the big lump sum he'd been dreaming of his entire career, he was now going to be paid in Canadian dollars. And the trade seemed more difficult to accept because of the player the Knicks were getting in return.

In his first two NBA seasons, Marcus Camby seemed to be the opposite of Oakley. Though he led the league with 3.65 blocks per game his second season in Toronto, he missed 19 games in each of his first two seasons with a variety of ailments: sore back, knee, ankle, and the flu. As far as anyone could remember, Oakley never sat out a game with the sniffles. The Knicks thought so little of Camby when they played the Raptors that undersized players such as Allan Houston and Chris Mills were regularly used to guard him.

And how shot was Oakley really? Grunfeld and Checketts

kept alluding to the Indiana series in May of '98, in which they believed Oakley was badly outplayed by Davis. It was as if the series was the defining moment of Oakley's tenure as a Knick. Yet just one round earlier, he had turned in one of the signature performances of his career in the decisive fifth game against the Miami Heat, playing all 48 minutes, scoring 18 points, and hauling down 13 rebounds. He also put his own exclamation point on the blowout win in the final five minutes by throwing down a rare dunk, to the delight of his teammates. "That was probably his first playoff dunk ever," said Childs. Oakley shrugged his shoulders and cracked a smile in the locker room as he kept getting ribbed about the dunk. "You like that?" he said. "Older guys make this league go. They keep hollering about the older guys, but all the older guys are in the playoffs. And the younger guys are at home having a good time."

So it was no surprise that on the day he was traded, Oakley would not give the Knicks the satisfaction of knowing how badly it hurt. Stubborn and proud as always, he mused, "Who do they have now that's going to do the things I do? I didn't think our problem was power forward."

Grunfeld finally reached Oakley at 12:30 P.M. on the night of June 24.

"I was like, 'What?' Ernie said, 'We wanted to get younger,' and I said, 'You ain't gotta say nothing to me. Bye.'" Grunfeld tried to further explain the trade, but Oakley cut him off. "If I'm traded, I'm traded. I'm no longer your commodity."

Oakley's dismissal notwithstanding, the Knicks knew they had grown gray around the temples. Ewing, Oakley, and Starks had given New York ten years of service and surreal playoff memories, but the general feeling among fans and management was that the triumvirate—however loyal, successful, and beloved—had gone as far as they could, and had been unable to deliver that elusive title.

Still, they came awfully close.

Pat Riley's arrival as coach in 1991 sparked the Knicks' return to prominence for the first time since the early 1970s. Over the next four seasons, they won 223 regular season games and lost only 105, won three straight Atlantic Division titles, and advanced to the championship series in 1994.

The winning brought the celebrities back to Madison Square Garden, which began a sellout run of 298 straight games through 1999. You not only got to see longtime fans Spike Lee and Woody Allen, but on any given night John F. Kennedy Jr. might show. Or Tyra Banks. Alec Baldwin and Kim Basinger. Billy Crystal, Jerry Seinfeld, Elle MacPherson, and Michael Douglas all stopped in from time to time.

The Knicks were doing great box office, as hot a ticket as any Broadway opening. More than any other Knicks, Ewing, Oakley, and Starks were Riley's guys, the trio of warriors most responsible for the franchise's success. Along with Anthony Mason and Derek Harper, they had more heart than talent, and endeared themselves to Knick fans by simply trying as hard as they possibly could. They were all flawed characters in the script, but somehow Riley siphoned everything he could out of them.

Ewing was the All-Star, the number one pick in the first draft lottery. Oakley was the enforcer, with the forearms and temperament of a modern-day gladiator. Starks was the gunner, a live wire who declared himself open from the moment he entered the arena. He was a virtual creation of Riley's, and the players often joked that he was actually Riley's son.

They came to symbolize the Knicks of the 1990s, the core players whose only real misfortune was to play in the same era—and the same damn conference—as Michael Jeffrey Jordan.

"He could embarrass you on any given night," Starks said. "When he gets on a roll, he just can't be stopped. Lord knows we tried."

You can blame Ewing's selfishness, Oakley's stubbornness, or Starks's erratic shot selection, but it was Michael Jordan, the world's most accomplished player, who did more to prevent the Knicks from winning a championship—with sufficient help from Hakeem Olajuwon in 1994—than any of the team's own shortcomings. Between 1989 and 1996, the Knicks met Jordan's

Bulls five times in the playoffs. And while the theater was incredible, New York always ended up playing the role of runner-up. In twenty-seven playoff games against New York, Jordan averaged 33.1 points per game. He scored more than 40 points seven times.

"We may have won some battles, but Michael always won the war," Ewing said of his 0-5 showing against Jordan in the postseason.

The 1993 Knick team was probably Riley's strongest, and all New York needed was two wins in five games to vanquish the two-time defending champion Bulls after winning the first two games of the conference finals at home. But when the series shifted back to Chicago, the Bulls' greatness resurfaced. Scottie Pippen scored 29 as the Bulls blew out the Knicks in Game 3, and then Jordan obliterated the Knicks for 54 points two days later. Still, the Knicks had two of the next three games at home, where they had won 27 straight. All they needed to do was hold serve at home in Game 5 to regain their confidence.

Ewing was dominant that night, using every post move he had to pour in 33 points. He even hit an improbable 3-point goal with the Knicks down by eight points, a shot that led to a 16-7 run to give New York a 93–92 lead with less than 90 seconds left. They were closing in on a 3–2 series lead.

But Bulls point guard B.J. Armstrong knocked down a 3-pointer from the corner with one minute, 16 seconds left. Charles Smith then missed one of two free throws—one of 15 the Knicks would miss that night.

Down 95–94, the Knicks regained possession after forcing Chicago into a 24-second violation. With the Garden percolating and the series swinging like a pendulum, Ewing found the 6-foot-10 Smith under the basket in the closing seconds. In what became the defining moment of the Knicks' never-ending climb to scale Jordan and his team, Smith was denied four straight times from point-blank range, never getting the ball to the rim as the shot clock kept ticking down. A cluster of Bulls, including Jordan and the power forward Horace Grant, either rejected or altered each attempt under the basket. The Knicks cried foul as Jordan sprinted into the locker room with both arms raised and his fists clenched.

"You just say, 'Game 5' and everybody has the same thought," Van Gundy said. " 'Put it in the basket.' I don't think anyone will ever forget that."

Four months later, Jordan retired to try to make it as a baseball player in the bushes of the minor leagues. The Knicks had a right to feel good about their chances to win it all.

In 1994, they finally made it to the Finals but lost to Olajuwon and the Rockets in seven games, the first of Houston's two straight titles, and the Riley era was nearing an end. He had taken them as far as he could. The next season saw the first of four second-round exits, and was the last year of Riley's reign.

Their role as a contender kept fading, especially after Ewing went down with a devastating, freak wrist injury on December 20, 1997. Without their franchise center, they managed to secure the seventh seed and gain a measure of redemption by stunning Riley's Miami Heat in the first round in five games. But their run of good fortune ended swiftly in the next round. Although Ewing returned for Game 2 of the semifinal series against Indiana, the Knicks were overmatched in five games against a determined Pacer team coached by Larry Bird.

It was not just the frustrated fans calling into WFAN radio in New York who implored the organization to make immediate changes; the Garden's top management had also grown weary of lost playoff dates. Given the effect of Ewing's injury, completely reinventing the team may have seemed premature and unnecessary to some, but neither Grunfeld nor Checketts felt they could wait any longer. In the summer of 1998, Ewing, Oakley, and Starks had played their last game together.

Less than a week after the Oakley trade, the question was not who would play together in 1998–99, but whether there would be a season at all. On July 1, the players were locked out by Commissioner David Stern; the league placed a moratorium on free agent signings and trades, and the Knicks, like the other twenty-eight NBA franchises, were closed for business.

Teams were not allowed to have any contact with their own players, and even workout facilities were off-limits. To the control-freak coaches around the NBA, this was the worst kind of torture. Van Gundy wanted to keep tabs on Ewing, who was entering what was surely the most important off-season of his career.

He still had not fully recovered from wrist surgery. And with no Oakley to watch his back on defense, Ewing would be asked to be more of a rebounder and less of a scorer. The Knicks needed him to be in the best shape of his life, but his schedule would not allow it.

The NBA labor dispute was in full swing and nowhere near a resolution when Ewing, the president of the players association, found himself in an unfamiliar position: in front of the cameras, trying to come across as a sympathetic labor leader instead of a millionaire basketball player who had everything he wanted in life and, to most observers, still wanted more. He had spent much of his career shunning the spotlight; now, some of the same media people he had alienated through the years were the people he was dependent on to get the union's message out.

Beyond the question of how to divide the league's annual revenues of $2 billion, the owners wanted to install ceilings on how much any one player could earn. The players wanted to protect their right to make as much as possible, a system that they believed had worked well for the past two decades as indicated by those staggering revenues. In the last negotiation, in the fall of 1995, the players had helped the owners stem the meteoric rise in rookie salaries by agreeing to a pay scale for a player's first three years. But this merely shifted the skyrockets a bit further into the future; the contract that shook the basketball world came when Kevin Garnett, about to enter his third year in the league, turned down a $100 million offer from the Minnesota Timberwolves. Garnett eventually agreed to a seven-year, $126 million deal—at the ripe old age of twenty.

This madness had to stop, Stern warned. Backed by his

owners, he was dug in for the long haul and used every ounce of public relations savvy he had to sway the media and the public toward his side.

Even Jordan's charisma might have been ground to dust by the league's spin cycle. Ewing, with far less PR talent, was doomed from the start, and he did nothing to help himself by sticking his size fifteens repeatedly into his mouth.

"We're fighting for our survival," he said. "I don't see us being any different than any other union, except for the pay scale being a little different."

Somehow, the Teamsters and the plumbers union did not feel a kinship—and neither did the public, given the magnitude of that "little" difference in pay. The average NBA salary was $2.6 million, not exactly sweatshop wages. Ewing, the point man, was scheduled to earn $18.5 million for the 1998–99 season—the highest annual salary in the league. Were fans, already being hit with soaring ticket prices, supposed to pass around a collection plate?

It was hard to take the players' cause seriously, and their own actions did nothing to make converts. They held their first general meeting at Caesars Palace in Las Vegas. Some of the players went directly from the conference room to the crap tables; Jordan was being put up at a brand-new suite at the swank Bellagio.

Two weeks later, Boston Celtic Kenny Anderson joked in the *New York Times* that life had gotten so tough, "I might have to sell my Mercedes"—leaving him with seven automobiles, a mortgage in Queens, and rent in Beverly Hills. The quote was repeated as if Anderson were serious. Distorted and misused by columnists for the next several weeks, it became the symbol of the disconnected, out-of-touch athlete.

As the union's figurehead, Ewing became a human dart board. Even a little-known agent by the name of Steven Woods blasted his leadership, saying, "I wouldn't let Patrick Ewing and [the Miami Heat's] Alonzo Mourning organize my picnic, much less a labor negotiation."

In a weekly column written for *The State* newspaper in Columbia, South Carolina, Woods compared Ewing and Billy Hunter, the players association executive director, to Thelma and Louise: "I could see the car carrying 400 players in the trunk going over the cliff as Billy and Patrick were singing their mantra over and over, 'We are unified. We are unified.' "

In December, with two months of the season already lost, Pistons great Isiah Thomas and Celtics Hall of Famer Bob Cousy lashed out against the current players. The two were also former heads of the union.

"I'm ashamed I ever started the players association," Cousy, seventy, said. "The owners created this Frankenstein, and now the monster is ready to turn around and eat its maker. For the first time in my life, I regret starting the players association."

Of Ewing and the negotiating committee, he added, "They've done so much damage to the game we love for the sake of unbridled greed, ego, and control."

"They can take a tough deal or they can get some new blood at the table," Thomas said. "This is no knock on anyone, but the way I always ran the union was if we brought in talent—and that talent wasn't performing—we had the opportunity to bring in someone else who would perform."

Hall of Famer Bob Lanier, another former union leader, showed up at a bargaining session in November—on the owners' side of the table. He had been hired as a special assistant to Stern.

Ewing interpreted the remarks as more hard-line tactics by Stern. After all, Cousy, Thomas, and Lanier, through their various broadcast and league office jobs, were all employed by the NBA. "It's very obvious to me which side they're on now, and that's the side that pays them," Ewing said. "They're all talking out of the other sides of their mouths now. But that's after they reaped the benefits of being here."

Ewing was especially ticked off by the comment made by Thomas, an NBC studio analyst. "Isiah never negotiated a [union] contract," Ewing said. "I can't worry about what Isiah, Bob Lanier, Bob Cousy, or whoever else thinks or feels. When they were here in our shoes it was different. Now they're getting checks from the other side and they're not going to say anything bad about their bosses."

Stern publicly praised Ewing for his involvement, but privately made it clear that he thought Ewing was doing the dirty work of his agent, David Falk, who had stacked the negotiating committee with his clients. The idea that Ewing was a puppet, manipulated by a man he was paying to work for him, bothered Patrick to no end. The introverted superstar was portrayed as being incapable of understanding the nuances and complexities of the issues. No matter what he did, he couldn't win.

During Red Holzman's funeral in November, Harvey Araton of the *New York Times* began a column by describing Ewing with a cell phone pressed up against his ear on the steps of the chapel just moments after the legendary Knicks coach was eulogized. On the surface, Ewing seemed to be one of those athletes who did not get it.

Van Gundy, for one, was incensed at Araton's use of the image. He remembered Ewing rising from his pew when the call went up for pallbearers, how the franchise center felt it was his duty to carry Holzman's casket even though he had never played for him. Walt Frazier was in St. Croix, the Virgin Islands, too far away to be able to attend; Phil Jackson did not make the service, either.

Ewing may have been losing badly in the court of public opinion, but he was winning the respect of the vast majority of players. They saw that Ewing had nothing to gain from his position as president. Financially secure, he had three years remaining on his contract, so any new deal would not affect him. He was losing more salary than anyone during the lockout. Jordan might have been more effective leading the charge, but he, Tim Duncan, and Grant Hill (to name a few) didn't want to sully their images, so they kept their distance from the labor dispute for the obvious monetary and marketing reasons.

"Patrick held the ship together during some stormy times," said Mitch Richmond, the veteran guard of the Washington Wizards. "People always criticize him for not standing for anything outside of basketball, and here he is, trying to make sure the players that come after him don't have to take a bad deal."

As much as Ewing was supposedly carrying out orders from Falk, he was in many ways competing with the specter of Michael Jordan once again.

Playing second fiddle was nothing new to Ewing. He had lost to Jordan's North Carolina Tar Heels in the 1982 NCAA championship game, and he never beat Jordan in a playoff series. Then, when Ewing was putting all his energy and focus in the off-season into getting his constituency a better deal, Jordan suddenly swept in and received praise for holding the 420 members of the players association together.

During an early October meeting in Manhattan, Jordan sparred with Wizards owner Abe Pollin in front of Stern, other owners, and more than 100 players. After an impassioned Pollin, the league's senior owner, talked of his struggle to keep the team, Jordan interrupted. "If you can't make it work economically, you should sell the team."

Pollin became enraged. The seventy-five-year-old owner had purchased the team in 1964. In an act of modest but authentic civic propriety, he changed the franchise nickname from Bullets to Wizards in May of 1997—mostly because Washington, D.C., had been recently dubbed the Murder Capital of the United States. He spent $200 million on a modern arena, choosing not to build in the suburbs but rather downtown in the hopes of triggering a broader commercial revival. He served as chairman of the Advisory Council for UNICEF, and he was the honorary chairman for the Salvation Army's leadership committee for Centers of Hope. And here was Jordan, bullying the old man. Imagine if Ewing had the temerity to go after Pollin, how much he would have been vilified for disrespecting a civic-minded philanthropist.

Instead, incredibly, Stern credited Jordan with bringing a sense of urgency and savvy to the proceedings. The general perception was that Michael was there to save the season in spite of Patrick.

It was Stern at his best, using classic divide-and-conquer techniques. He knew that anything Jordan said would resonate with the public, while anything Ewing said would backfire. They may not have been on a basketball court, but in many ways Jordan was beating Ewing once again, for the final time.

A month later, Jordan would appear at another bargaining meeting. Only this time, he left midway through, citing family obligations. As it turned out, that obligation was an appearance at the Tourneau Time Machine store several blocks away in Manhattan. While Ewing was trying to save the season and negotiate a deal, Jordan was off peddling watches and collecting $50,000 he hardly needed.

Jordan also shrewdly avoided being part of an ill-conceived charity game put on by the agents Falk and Arn Tellem, who represents Kobe Bryant among other players. With a sense of genuine concern growing about whether there was going to be a season, the idea was to put as many Dream Teamers on the floor for a game as possible. They picked Atlantic City as the site, and to add insult to absurdity, the initial announcement said the proceeds would go to "needy players." What was next, a mink coat drive?

The game was televised as part of a free weekend on the Showtime pay-cable service. It was an abject disaster. The crowd was sparse and the play was a disturbing harbinger of things to come. Shawn Kemp, who had been recently pilloried in *Sports Illustrated* for fathering seven children out of wedlock, looked rotund enough to have cleaned out a casino buffet by himself. Ewing clearly had spent a lot of late nights at the bargaining table chewing on numbers and pizza.

Going into the game, Falk and Tellem had boasted they could start up a new league in case the season was lost. The Game, its actual title, suggested they could hardly start a car, much less a league. Basketball fans everywhere were fed up with players and owners bickering over $2 billion and had grown apathetic. They didn't care anymore if the season was lost.

Somehow, Ewing, Hunter, and the negotiating committee managed to hold the players together. But their leverage was slipping as the new year approached. With the threat of a drop-dead date looming and the players fearful of losing a full season's salary, the cracks began to show.

In the final hours of January 7, the day a vote was to be held to either accept or reject the owners' last offer, Ewing became even more of a polarizing force. Some felt his stubbornness had contributed to the standoff. When Billy Hunter and Stern prepared to hash out a deal at the last minute to save the season, the president of the union was not asked to participate.

The deal was struck six months after the lockout began. Ewing had lost approximately $8 million in salary and had gained twenty pounds. The day after the deal was signed, Ewing was on a StairMaster at Manhattanville College in Westchester trying to negotiate his body back into playing shape. It was another losing battle.

"I'm ready to go back to my real job," he said. "I need a break, but I'm not going to get one."

Said Danny Schayes, the journeyman center for the Orlando Magic who was a member of the negotiating committee, "He's a fighter. It was pretty stressful for him. Patrick could use a mental health vacation right now."

But Ewing would have no time to unwind. Training camp was two weeks away, and there were more losses to absorb. His best friend on the team, Starks, would soon be packing his bags for the West Coast.

John Starks Jr. wiped his eyes and rose from his bed on one of those 30 degree, mid-January mornings in Stamford, Connecticut. The night before, he had heard someone on the radio say his dad was about to be traded for the guy who choked his coach. With snow on the ground and the season still two weeks away, the ten-year-old decided to confront his father that morning.

"My son asked me today, 'Dad, I got to leave school?' I said: 'Yeah, maybe. I'm not sure.' He said, 'But, Dad, we've already been out to Golden State.' "

In 1989, John Jr.'s father had a job in Northern California. But then the Warriors cut him after just 36 games, and he had to scramble for a spot in the moribund Continental Basketball Association for a year. He kept himself motivated by remembering the time he'd spent bagging milk and eggs in a grocery store in Tulsa, Oklahoma, after which he'd punch out, go work on his game, and dream about the NBA.

Two years later, he was playing in New York for Pat Riley.

All or nothing: That was how the John Starks story began, and it rarely strayed from the plot. He would either become an NBA All-Star or remain a Tulsa grocery clerk. He would either throw down the most monumental dunk in team history, over Michael Jordan in 1993—or he would shoot 2-for-18 against the Houston Rockets in Game 7 of the '94 NBA finals.

It was easy to get charged emotionally when the subject was Starks, who never met a shot he wanted to pass up, and let Reggie Miller get too far under his skin for rational thought. Even on the road, kids screamed and teenage girls cooed; no player resonated more with Knick fans than Starks, whose failures and successes were bigger than life and whose own emotions were always on display.

He was a player whose love of the game was so great that he left his own wedding reception to get to a junior-college game. "I drove from the reception in Tulsa to a small town about an hour and a half away," Starks recalled. "Picked up a speeding ticket, scored about 30 points in that half. Some people wrote that I ripped off my tuxedo when I got there. But that part isn't true. I changed before I got to the gym."

The Dunk in which he posterized Jordan came in the 1993 conference semifinals, a lean-in, left-handed slam that shook the Garden and the Bulls in Game 2. Starks went around Scottie Pippen and then over Jordan and Horace Grant. "I knew John could go upstairs, but the thing about it is, he brought the ball back to the defense with his left hand," said Herb Williams on the day Starks was traded. "And as high as Michael and Scottie jump, you figured they would have got it. But they couldn't do nothing with it." Then Williams reenacted the dunk, rubbed his chin, folded his arms, and smiled. "He got both of them that day," he said.

Starks reminisced that day, too, calling his 2-for-18 performance against Houston in 1994 his lone regret with the franchise.

"When I wasn't able to perform the way I'm capable of performing and bring a championship to this city, which is so deserving of one—that's the only thing I'll regret about being here," Starks said. "That one game."

To this day, Riley is taken to task for staying with Starks too long in that game and not tapping the resources of the veteran Rolando Blackman. Starks had held the Knicks' championship hopes in his hands in Game 6, too, but his last-second, 3-point attempt was blocked by Hakeem Olajuwon. Ewing was open, a few steps left of the free throw line, but Starks wanted the ball with the season on the line. And after Game 7 at the Summit in Houston, he stayed in the shower for an hour, head down, crying. He admitted to having nightmares about that game the following season.

But Starks refused to let that one game define his career. Nothing could keep him down, not even a personal feud with Don Nelson, who took over for Riley to start the 1995–96 season. Nelson tried to move him for Vinny Del Negro at the trading deadline in February of '96, a move shot down by Grunfeld. Nelson started Hubert Davis in front of Starks, and made a point of saying he believed Davis was a better player. He was toying with Starks's emotions as much as he was with his playing time.

Nelson was ruthless in his efforts to get rid of Starks, whether talking trade with other teams or talking behind Starks's back to the media. In a bar one night at the Ritz-Carlton Hotel in Marina Del Rey, California, Nelson told two reporters a mean-spirited story about the erratic shooting guard.

"We were getting onto the team bus," Nelson said, "and a guy ran up to Starks and said, 'John, I'm a big fan. Will you please sign this?' Starks said, 'Sure.' And as he begins to sign the fan's program, the guy says, 'Can you make it out to my brother, Marc. It's Marc with a C.'"

Starks obliged and signed. The fan looked bewildered at his program: "To Cark," it read. "Regards, John Starks #3."

Nelson nearly tipped over his beer telling the story. Trying to portray Starks as an unsophisticated Tulsa kid merely lucky to be in the league, Nelson left you thinking the same about him that night.

Starks attended four colleges in four years and was a shy kid with a speech impediment when he arrived in New York. By the time he had been traded, he was one of the team's most beloved players. But he had his downside, too.

Van Gundy, among others in the organization, felt he had lost some of his passion for the game by the end of the 1997–98 season. He became obsessed with golf, playing whenever he could. He lent his name to a cell phone business. Suddenly, he was no longer the hungry CBA player who would bust his ass and yours to keep a job in the league; he was kibitzing with the corporate set on the links, taking his clubs to Miami and Indiana during the playoffs.

Larry Johnson, for one, was furious that Starks had brought his clubs to Indianapolis the day before the Knicks would be eliminated by the Pacers in five games in May of '98. Van Gundy, who felt too many players on his team were practicing their chipping more than their free throws, was pissed off enough to plan to tell Starks how he felt. Inside the Knicks' coaching office at Purchase College, poster-sized action pictures of current players adorn the walls. Instead of a basketball photo of Starks, Van Gundy commissioned a shot of Starks playing golf. He was ready for the moment when Starks would spot it on the wall and ask about it; Van Gundy would tell him, "This is the sport you love so much. So I thought I'd put it up as a reminder."

But that day never came. On a cold January day four days after the Sprewell meeting, with snowfall fresh from the night before buffeting the area around the Knicks' practice facility, a numb Starks was officially traded to the Warriors. Unlike Oakley, he handled it well. The player who once said someone would have to tear the No. 3 jersey from his chest before he was traded to another team did not express regret that he was headed back to Golden State; instead, he remembered how far he had come.

"Later on down the line, I'll probably shed a tear or something," Starks said as he stood outside the Knicks' practice facility.

"Funny, huh? Not in my wildest dreams did I ever think I would have this much effect on people. But I think when you grow as a person and people get to see you grow—the way you mature—well, that's insight for people to help them grow and mature."

He did not seem angry at Grunfeld, but he did believe the trade was a mistake. "I thought we had another run left in us," Starks said. "When you trade away two of your core guys—guys that go on out there who are committed to winning and being vocal when things are going bad so that they push each other—then you lose something.

"I think they lost a little bit of that when they got rid of myself and Oak. You look at the teams that are making runs for the championship, and they're normally a veteran team that gets in there over youth. But they have to live with those decisions. I wish them the best."

Starks walked out of the practice facility, shook the hand of the Knicks' equipment manager, Wayman Manning, walked down two flights of stairs, and tossed his duffel bag into his jet-black Mercedes. He would get his money, he still had his health, and this was only the business side of sports. But another piece of the Knicks' soul drove away that day, headed to some new town where he just didn't seem to belong. John Starks, the boom-or-bust player, was gone—and nothing felt the same about this team anymore.

Allan Houston sobbed. Patrick Ewing, forever the stoic, stone-faced veteran who shunned the media, turned around and said somberly, "I'm going to miss him. It's a business, but we did everything together and it just won't be the same without him around."

They were not just longtime teammates; they were longtime

friends. The players were confused and emotionally torn. And, within days, Latrell Sprewell would be joining the team.

All the ties had been severed. Other than Ewing, Charlie Ward and Herb Williams were the last remnants from the Riley era.

The old Knicks were dead. And Jeff Van Gundy had very little time to make the new parts fit; in two weeks, the season would begin in Orlando.

3

SON OF A COACH

Jeff Van Gundy pulled into the driveway of his Chappaqua, New York, home, fifty miles north of Madison Square Garden up the Saw Mill River Parkway. With millions of thoughts racing through his head, all having to do with his 0-2 team, he kept on driving—until he rammed his 1995 Honda Civic smack into the garage door. He had forgotten to hit the remote control button to raise it.

The damage to the car and the garage was reparable. His team was another story. The Knicks had just dropped their home opener to the reviled Miami Heat 83–79, their second loss in forty-eight hours. Against the Orlando Magic, the Knicks played as if it were a pickup game at the Y instead of the season opener, losing 93–85.

Van Gundy, the eternal pessimist described in *The New Yorker* magazine as looking like "an umbrellaless man standing in the rain having just missed the six-fifteen to Babylon," was convinced that the Knicks would go 0-50.

They had entered the Garden earlier that afternoon with huge expectations. Latrell Sprewell had not played a regular season home game in 435 days. And his was not the only comeback from professional exile: Because of an assault case, Marv Albert had not broadcast a game at the Garden that mattered in 632 days. He had a much better return than Sprewell and the Knicks. In NBC's first televised game since

Michael Jordan's going-away present to the Utah Jazz, Sprewell missed his first eight shots and finished an abysmal 2-for-12 from the field. Worse, with Miami holding a three-point lead in the final seconds, Sprewell launched an off-balance 3-pointer that never had a chance. The nearly 20,000 fans who had anticipated wondrous things from Sprewell were left with an empty feeling.

"I can't remember the last time we were 0-2," a morose Patrick Ewing said in the despondent locker room. Sprewell had just been exposed defensively by Jamal Mashburn, the whole team was moving as if they were playing underwater, and Van Gundy knew that his undersized lineup featuring the 6-7 Larry Johnson at power forward and the 6-5 Sprewell at small forward was not working.

Van Gundy had foreseen these problems before the season began. In late November, he complimented the Indiana Pacers players for holding their own private workouts during the labor dispute—sending a less-than-subtle message to his own team that they should get their out-of-shape carcasses into the gym.

"I hope they're working out," Van Gundy said. "The thing I've read about Indiana is that they're a team ready to go. They've got eleven, twelve guys each and every day working together, and I think they'll definitely have another jump on all the other teams because they're just more committed. I think they showed their commitment last year. And I think they're showing their commitment right now. It's a great indicator of where they're at. Our team? I haven't heard those reports."

During the lockout, the Knicks' unofficial workout site was Manhattanville College in Westchester. Attendance was as sporadic as it would be for an 8:00 A.M. calculus class. Many players lived in different parts of the country and were waiting for the lockout to end before returning to the New York area. Ewing, Herb Williams, Allan Houston, and Charlie Ward were semiregulars, but some days it was just the creaking bones of the Big Fella and Herb trying to match up against guys who would soon have to pay to see the Knicks play. Camby showed up once; he was given the cold shoulder by Ewing and decided not to return.

The Oakley trade had done immeasurable damage to team camaraderie. When Charlie Ward held a charity golf tournament in September, Camby was a no-show; Oakley came, though, doling out one-liners and playful insults to his former teammates.

Once the lockout ended, the gymnasiums were open a week before training camp officially began. Workouts were optional, and the turnout was just as disappointing. At Purchase College, where the gym was open for the first time to Knick players since July 1, an assortment of borderline NBA players outnumbered actual Knicks. Houston, Starks, Ward, and Camby showed, as did Oakley, who still owned a house five miles away in White Plains. But Ewing was nowhere to be found.

He had taken the advice of Danny Schayes to take a vacation after spending the last six months in labor negotiations, and flew to Miami to hang with Alonzo Mourning and the enemy. Riley was not too crazy about this and neither was Van Gundy; Checketts was upset, too, and was privately wondering whether Van Gundy had enough respect among his players to persuade them to work out together. And as for Ewing, the franchise, practicing in Riley's backyard, if his intention was to strike fear into the Heat he was whiffing badly.

"You could tell he was out of shape; he looked terrible," said Rex Walters, the Heat's reserve guard. "When it was game point, we couldn't even pass the ball to him. We didn't think he'd make it through the season."

Van Gundy had his doubts as well. Ewing was struggling, and with the sudden acquisition of Sprewell, Van Gundy had to incorporate six new players into the fourteen-man roster. With only fifteen days of training camp before the season began and just two exhibition games, against the Nets, a crash course in chemistry and continuity was in order.

Further change was afoot, though; three hours before tip-off of the first exhibition game, seventeen-year veteran Buck

Williams retired. Another blow to continuity, as one more aging warrior made room for the young and the restless.

The son of a North Carolina sharecropper, Williams was proud that his work ethic had sent his son to the same Connecticut private school that George Bush's children attended. A gentleman before a competitor, the NBA had been good to him—and, in turn, he was good for it.

"Players have an obligation to the public to carry themselves in a certain way and be held accountable," he said at his farewell press conference. "I never wanted to do anything to embarrass myself, the organization, and my family.

"Those things really weighed a lot heavier than some of the other issues I was confronted with through my career. It made me want to be a role model and do the right thing."

On Buck's last night at the Garden, a very different kind of player took center stage. Latrell Sprewell's Garden debut was an unmitigated success, complete with standing ovations and chants of "Spree! Spree! Spree!" in the third quarter. In those surreal 12 minutes, he nearly took off the Garden roof by scoring 17 points, including a barrage of 3-pointers that left him raising his arms and asking for more adulation from the crowd.

He had accomplished in one preseason game what Ewing failed to accomplish in 14 years: winning the heart of a basketball-consumed city in a New York minute.

Ewing was all thumbs and love handles that night. He moved like a slug and elicited these heartwarming words from the crowd: "What's going on, Pat? Too many jelly donuts during the meetings?"

Their next exhibition game was even more discouraging. Camby didn't play because he had a blister on his foot, a malady that raised eyebrows in the locker room and questions about his durability. Ewing suffered a sprained right knee in the second quarter and did not return.

Breaking down, poorly conditioned, and an on-court flop . . . Your 1999 New York Knicks.

Grunfeld and Van Gundy envisioned a backcourt in which Houston and Sprewell complemented each other's styles—the sweet-shooting, disciplined son of a coach and the slashing scorer who had no use for a playbook, running, gunning, and taking over where Jordan and Scottie Pippen left off. Ewing could still be Ewing, taking fallaway jumpers and getting superstar treatment from referees in the fourth quarter. Johnson would blend into the background, deferring to his high-maintenance teammates when they were going well and employing his low-post game against overmatched defenders. Kurt Thomas and Chris Dudley could do the grunt work with Oakley gone, Camby would give them energy and hopefully rebounds off the bench, and Ward and Childs would orchestrate the whole show within their limitations. It was a nice little dream.

But after two exhibitions and two games in the regular season, it had nothing to do with reality. And Van Gundy had another serious concern other than his team: He needed to watch his back at the Garden.

Grunfeld was already meddling with the team. He was upset that his prized acquisition, Camby, had played just 19 seconds in the season opener at Orlando, and he was angry that Van Gundy had criticized Camby's work habits in the first week of training camp. Other Knicks upset over the Oakley trade— Larry Johnson, Ewing, and Herb Williams—were also disappointed with Camby's lethargic first-week performance, but Van Gundy's public complaints were viewed as disobedient and destructive. Grunfeld felt the coach was trying to make him look bad, and by making it open season on Camby's character he was indirectly encouraging a backlash.

Moreover, after Camby played only five minutes against Miami, Van Gundy conveniently let it slip that his new forward had asked out of the game after his brief cameo. "I was going to keep him in there longer but he asked out because he was tired," Van Gundy said. He threw Camby a bone, explaining that, "The guy playing ahead of him [Kurt Thomas] is doing a good job. [But] I'm encouraged by Marcus's play. It's very hard for a guy who has played his whole life, been a big star, and now has to take a back seat. He's done it with class."

Camby said he asked out of the game because he was hyperventilating. Before the third game of the season, Van Gundy met with him; although the coach had called his work habits "unacceptable" the first three days of camp, "since then he's done everything we've asked for," Van Gundy said.

"I really appreciated the things he told me," Camby said. "He told me if I keep working hard, I'll get a chance."

Grunfeld had his doubts, though. He also did not appreciate how Van Gundy was using Dennis Scott, the portly 6-7 swingman who was noted for his equal facility at knocking down 3-pointers and Double Quarter Pounders with Cheese. A self-styled comedian, he was listed at 229 pounds, but on the first day of camp he was easily pushing 250.

Grunfeld envisioned Scott as a savvy veteran who could come off the bench and open up the floor with his outside shooting. Scott had made a name for himself with the Orlando Magic, but then his career began a slow decline; the Knicks were his fourth team in three years. He was out of shape, working too much on his stand-up routine and not enough on his physique or his shot.

Van Gundy saw him as a detriment to the team, a class clown who didn't take the game or winning seriously. He figured trouble might be on the horizon when Camby, Sprewell, and Kurt Thomas—the new Knicks who had all come from losing franchises—quickly accepted Scott into their club.

The day after the loss at Orlando, Grunfeld paid a surprise visit to the Knicks' practice. Grunfeld rarely made the trek to Purchase, New York, from either his office at Madison Square Garden or his Franklin Lakes, New Jersey, home. But since training camp began, Grunfeld had been a frequent observer at practice. The last time Grunfeld made himself this visible at Purchase, Don Nelson soon disappeared.

The Knicks' practice facility at Purchase College and the team's corporate offices at Two Penn Plaza adjacent to Madison Square Garden are roughly an hour's drive apart, assuming traffic on the West Side Highway is moving well. But in truth, those buildings are ideologically much further away from each other.

Purchase was the home base for the players and coaches. That was their territory. They did not exactly embrace management types when the suits deigned to show their faces on the gym floor. Likewise, Van Gundy and the players rarely ventured into Manhattan to visit the fourteenth-floor office suites in Midtown. The basketball operation was in one county, the business operation in another. Grunfeld had an office at Purchase and would sometimes work from there if he needed to talk to Van Gundy about personnel decisions, but mostly he handled the day-to-day operations from New York City.

His increased attendance at the start of the '99 season piqued Van Gundy's interest.

Although Van Gundy and Grunfeld had worked together for ten years, they had a mutual understanding: *I don't trust you, you don't trust me.* Van Gundy always respected Grunfeld as a family man, but believed he was too enraptured by Garden politics and too worried about surviving to excel as a general manager.

Their strained relationship began when both men were assistant coaches on Stu Jackson's staff in the 1989–90 season. The following year, Grunfeld was promoted to the front office and Jackson was fired; Van Gundy, who was convinced Grunfeld was trying to undermine Jackson from the start, held him partly responsible for Jackson's dismissal.

If they'd had problems before, the Camby issue added to the rift. In Van Gundy's mind, his relationship with Camby was just another example of his needing time to build trust in a new player. He knew how Camby was coddled in Toronto, how the number two pick in the 1996 draft had driven the Raptors mad with his inconsistency. He felt Camby had come into the league like many young players today, with a sense of entitlement.

No matter what a player's reputation was, Van Gundy believed that it was that player's responsibility to adapt to the

Knicks, not the other way around. The coach had watched too many teams hand over the keys to Generation X stars, only to crash and end up in the lottery again a year later. For better or worse, he wanted Camby to earn his minutes, to break him down and then build him back up.

It was old-school stubbornness. But it had worked for him before. Van Gundy had gone through similar adjustment periods with Chris Childs and Allan Houston in the 1996–97 season. He often heard the words, "I guess I'm not one of Jeff's guys" from both of them. By 1999, they were trusted veterans and Van Gundy loyalists.

But Grunfeld could not wait that long.

If Van Gundy's mission was to take a team with a $68 million payroll—the highest among the league's twenty-nine teams—past the second round or else, Grunfeld needed to show immediate dividends on his substantial investments. Neither Grunfeld nor Van Gundy had job security, and Grunfeld's status was especially tenuous. He had spent $24 million on Childs, who after one season in the starting lineup became a high-paid reserve. For $56 million, Houston was streaky—and Johnson, owed the balance of $84 million on the contract he'd signed with Charlotte, was on the downside of his career and a medical liability. Throw in the Nelson debacle that cost the team $5 million for 59 games of coaching and Grunfeld's inability to land a quality point guard in the off-season, and it was safe to say that Grunfeld's spending habits were up for review. He needed to win. And if Grunfeld was going down, he was taking Van Gundy with him. In almost all franchise power struggles, the coach gets whacked first.

Van Gundy understood his job was on the line. No one would remember that he had lost Ewing in late December the year before to a freak wrist injury, revamped the offense, finished seventh overall in the Eastern Conference, and somehow coaxed the Knicks past Miami in a free-swinging, first-round series. Knick management didn't care what the circumstances were; all it saw was three consecutive second-round eliminations under Van Gundy, and that wasn't good enough. When the season began, Van Gundy was seventh among NBA coaches in tenure, behind people with true job security: Riley. Lenny Wilkens. Jerry Sloan. Rudy Tomjanovich.

Big deal. He knew he could vanish off that list at any moment.

"You know what that tells me?" he said. "Rent, don't buy."

Jeff Van Gundy grew up in a household that revolved around family and basketball. His father, Bill, and older brother, Stan, shared the passion, as did his mother, Cindy, who made many road trips and was notorious for baiting referees from the stands. Among other stops on the circuit, Bill Van Gundy coached at SUNY-Brockport and Genesee Community College in upstate Batavia, New York. Stan, now an assistant with the Miami Heat, had a stint as a head coach at Wisconsin. Every coaching member of the family knew what it felt like to be fired; Jeff was part of a Providence staff that was dismissed in 1988.

Dating back to Bill's days as a high school coach in Visalia, California, the Van Gundys had been in the business for forty-one years. Coaching was only part of the job; counselor, tutor, psychologist, and father figure were also part of the job description, not to mention chauffeur.

Jeff was frequently described as a Riley protégé, but he was really more an extension of his father, a basketball lifer. When Bill was ill one day while coaching high school ball in California, he sent his sons across town to scout a high school game for him. Jeff was ten years old at the time.

An outstanding high school student, Jeff was accepted to Yale University. One of his classmates was Jodie Foster, who lived in the dorm across the street. In the spring of 1981, the twelve students who lived on Van Gundy's floor anted up $100 each for a pool, with the money to go to the first one with the gumption to ask and go out with Foster on a date. Anything would suffice. A movie. A game. Dinner. Lunch. A walk on campus.

One evening as Van Gundy walked back to the dorm, a convoy of fire engines screamed past him as bystanders stood and watched. He was standing in front of a store that made popcorn when a voice behind him said, "Jeez, that popcorn smells really good." Van Gundy turned around, and it was Jodie Foster.

"Yeah, it does," he said.

Van Gundy froze. He didn't know what else to say. Moments later, Foster and $1,200 walked away.

"Finally one guy had the guts to ask her out, and she went with him to a hockey game," he said. "He got the twelve hundred dollars. But I vowed that I would never be that flustered, or that unprepared, again."

That same semester Van Gundy had another unusual encounter. One afternoon there were federal agents in his English class to speak with Foster. That day there had been an assassination attempt on President Ronald Reagan by John W. Hinckley, who said he was doing it to impress Foster.

While Yale was clearly a stimulating environment, from an athletic standpoint it was a disappointment. He was cut from varsity basketball, and so that summer he told his mother he was headed to California's Bay Area and leaving the Ivy League institution. Such transfers are not unusual, but Jeff was not heading to Stanford; he was going to Menlo Junior College, a two-year school, to play basketball for a family friend.

"From Yale to Menlo Junior College?" his mother asked. "Are you sure?"

"I'll have a better chance to play ball," Van Gundy replied.

Said Kim Van Gundy, his wife of ten years and his girlfriend back then, "I thought he was nuts. But I did know that he needed to play."

He would go on to attend four colleges in five years, including a stint at SUNY-Brockport playing for his father until economic cutbacks led to Bill's dismissal. He finished as a scrawny point guard at Nazareth College in Rochester, New York, where, with wristbands and wavy black hair flying to and fro, he averaged 10.3 points and 5.1 assists while shooting 56 percent from the field. His other key stat: Van Gundy graduated magna cum laude with a degree in history.

After graduation, he came back home to start his career. He took his first coaching job at McQuaid Jesuit High School in Rochester, making $1,600 as a part-time head coach for the boys varsity. To eat and pay rent on his one-bedroom tenement, he worked as a teacher's aid for a behavioral management class at a local elementary school—the perfect training for the NBA.

He may have been happy to spend his life there, but a great job opportunity opened up courtesy of a sweet-shooting, left-handed tenth grader named Greg Woodard who was already attracting college recruiters. Several Big East schools, including Providence College, were interested in the McQuaid star.

Stu Jackson, then Rick Pitino's assistant at Providence, made several recruiting trips to western New York. He liked Woodard, who ended up playing at Villanova. But in Van Gundy, he felt he had uncovered a true gem. Impressed with how Van Gundy ran his practices—and with a graduate assistant position available on the Friars' staff—Jackson asked the twenty-four-year-old coach if he was ready for big-time college basketball.

Jackson was in charge of the interview process, so Van Gundy already had the job by the time he met with Pitino for the first time in Pitino's office. But there was still the formality of meeting his immediate boss.

"So, you want to be a college basketball coach," Pitino asked.

"Yes, I think so," Van Gundy replied.

"Well, congratulations, Jim," Pitino said. "You've got the job."

It was that kind of anonymity that came to characterize his early coaching years. Three years later, Van Gundy had moved up to a full-time assistant job at Rutgers when Jackson came calling again to offer him an unlikely spot as an assistant coach in the NBA. Jackson, who had succeeded Pitino as Knick coach, lasted only 15 games into his second season; his successor, John MacLeod, came aboard for the final 67 games.

MacLeod, too, was fired after Michael Jordan and the Bulls swept the Knicks in the first round of the 1991 playoffs, and Van Gundy figured that was the end of his pro coaching tenure.

Van Gundy was prepared to return to Rochester when the Knicks' front office lured Pat Riley out of the NBC studio. Riley gave Van Gundy an interview with no promises or contracts attached. Management viewed Van Gundy as a possible head scout, but Riley had bigger plans for him: Two hours after they spoke, Van Gundy was retained to be part of Riley's staff.

Almost immediately, Van Gundy impressed his new boss with his work ethic and attention to detail. Riley, a workaholic himself, liked seeing the extra hours Van Gundy would spend working individually with players after practice, watching film and doing whatever Riley asked of him.

Van Gundy viewed Riley as the perfect mentor. He was working for the game's greatest coach, learning from the master by osmosis. He considered it a privilege and an honor to be part of his staff. He was an anonymous assistant, and he was loving every minute of it.

True to his character, Riley never got too close to his assistants. On road trips, he would eat separately and go his own way. But professionally, there was a respect that was almost more important than any personal relationship.

When Kim Van Gundy suffered a miscarriage at a crucial juncture of the 1994 season, Riley gave his loyal assistant all the time he needed before he returned to the team. What seemed like the right thing to do for any boss was magnified because of Riley's maniacal approach to the game.

After the 1994–95 season, Riley abruptly resigned amid a firestorm of controversy. Frustrated by Checketts's refusal to give him final approval in personnel matters and recognizing that he had taken the Knicks as far as he could, Riley simply faxed his resignation to Checketts. The subsequent revelation that he had negotiated a king's ransom from the Miami Heat while he was still coaching the Knicks—a five-year, $40 million deal that included part ownership of the club—transformed

Riley from Knick savior to Pat the Rat. For his part, Riley claimed Checketts misled him, and that the Garden's revolving corporate infrastructure prevented him from luring the players he wanted to New York.

Either way, his timing, like his wardrobe, was impeccable. It was the perfect moment to get out. Michael Jordan's return to basketball meant that the good times were about to take a hiatus at the Garden.

Van Gundy was ready to follow Riley to Miami; Riley had verbally agreed to give him a raise that would make Van Gundy one of the league's highest paid assistants. But there was one major snag: the Knicks were so outraged by Riley's stunning departure that they refused to allow Van Gundy to get out of the final year of his contract. He would have to stick around for another year in some capacity.

"I really wanted to go, and I was told I'd either be an assistant or work in the front office for a year," said Van Gundy. "Then Don Nelson came in and I explained the situation to him. He picked up the phone and called Ernie and said, 'I need Jeff on the bench with me and he needs to get paid what Riley was going to give him.' "

To this day, Van Gundy owes a debt of gratitude to Nelson and will never say anything against the former Knicks coach, whom he considered a brilliant basketball mind. No one in New York during Nelson's disastrous five months would agree. To most observers of the team, Nelson came to the Knicks looking for a big score at the end of his Hall of Fame career, and his heart was never truly in it. Nelson, a longtime friend of Grunfeld's (he was the team president's first pro coach in Milwaukee), quickly decided that the Knicks of Ewing, John Starks, and Derek Harper had run their course. The only problem was, management was not ready to break up its core players no matter how hard Nelson pushed to have Ewing and Starks traded. Soon, the players carried out a mutiny, led by Ewing. In Nelson's offense, Ewing had become the second option behind point-forward Anthony Mason. The Knicks quit on Nelson, and on March 8, 1996, Grunfeld took an early morning train ride to Philadelphia, where the Knicks, imploding by the day, were to face the 76ers that night.

Grunfeld first knocked on Nelson's door at the Ritz-Carlton Hotel in downtown Philadelphia. He told him matter-of-factly he was making a coaching change. Then he walked down the corridor and paid a visit to Van Gundy, whose obscure days on the Knick bench had come to an end.

The 5-foot-9, former Division III point guard, whose only previous head coaching job was ten years earlier at a Catholic high school, had just become the eighteenth coach in Knickerbocker history. His world was spinning. A few hours after he was named interim coach, reporters from the *New York Times,* New York *Daily News,* and *New York Post* were brought into a public relations assistant's hotel room for Van Gundy's first interview. He looked as if he had just been to a funeral, and tried to balance the feelings of getting his greatest professional break at the expense of Nelson losing his job.

Sitting five feet away was Thomas Hill, then of the *Post,* who had helped provide a test of Van Gundy's character weeks before Van Gundy took over the team. Hill had written a story in which John Starks's grandmother and sister blasted Nelson for misusing and mistreating their beloved John. As reporters entered the gymnasium at the end of practice, Van Gundy, who had learned from Riley to keep a safe distance from the media, shouted, "Hey Tom, I can get you an interview with John's four-year-old daughter, Chelsea, if you want."

Starks was unaware of the article, but his interest was piqued when Van Gundy opened his mouth. Starks left the gym to read the newspaper clipping, and within five minutes came storming back and headed straight for Hill, bounding like a kangaroo on a caffeine binge.

"Don't you ever call my family again!" Starks warned as a local television crew filmed the entire incident. After several seconds of Hill trying to explain himself and Starks shouting expletives and waving his finger in Hill's face, Van Gundy stepped in and pulled Starks away, saying, "Forget it, John. He's an asshole. He's not worth it."

Although it was clear that Van Gundy was sticking up for one of "his guys," his treatment of Hill was indefensible and he later apologized for it. *Post* columnist Wallace Matthews ripped into Van Gundy and labeled him nothing more than a "Riley gofer." But the fiery young assistant coach had scored points with the person who mattered most. Sort of. When privately asked if Van Gundy's behavior could hurt his career in New York, Dave Checketts shook his head. "Just the opposite," he said. "We didn't know Jeff had that in him. If he plays his cards right, he might be able to someday land a good college coaching job somewhere."

Two days after he was named interim coach of the Knicks, Van Gundy made his Garden debut against Jordan's Bulls, who were on their way to winning a record 72 games. Van Gundy looked uncomfortable and out of place sitting in the coach's office, a space occupied by his four previous bosses in New York. Nervous and worried about facing such a superior team, Van Gundy did not want to start his new job 0-2. The Knicks had been beaten by the 76ers on Friday, the day of the Nelson firing; Van Gundy wanted to remain coach at least until Monday.

"I know we're going to win this game," Derek Harper said two hours before tip-off. "We had our best practice of the season on Saturday. Jeff ran us for three hours. We hadn't done that all year."

The Knicks rewarded Van Gundy by blowing out the greatest regular-season team in league history, in a 104–72 victory that ended with Van Gundy pumping his fist as he walked off the Garden court. He returned to his office to call his father and mother and began crying.

The spring of 1996, Van Gundy coached his way into a full-time job when the Knicks, seeded fifth, swept Cleveland in the first round before losing to the Bulls in five. He would soon have the interim tag removed, and the guy who once nearly incited a player to physically assault a reporter was learning that the media could be his best friend. The writers who covered the team admired his honesty and wit. After Riley's brainwashing attempts and Nelson's suffocating clichés and condescending looks that seemed to say, "You couldn't possibly know anything I don't about this game," Van Gundy was a refreshing change.

Van Gundy would fill up notebooks and tape recorders. He told stories that took you into Riley's locker room, or talked about some obscure high school player who taught him a lesson about the game. No subject was off-limits, but there was a tradeoff: He could also use the media to wage his battles, and his first target was Phil Jackson.

In his first week on the job, he lashed out at the Bulls coach for campaigning for the Knicks job during a postgame interview on NBC following Van Gundy's first NBA victory. Van Gundy's credo was that coaches support one another, not solicit already-filled jobs. Jackson broke the code, and in Van Gundy's world that was treason. He would go on to poke fun at Jackson's unconventional coaching philosophy, which was loosely comprised of Zen teachings, Native American beliefs, and the triangle offense. Van Gundy pegged most of the Bulls' success on Jordan, and was amused that Jackson thought ancient Indian artifacts or spirituality had anything to do with Chicago's winning six titles in the 1990s.

He coined the name "Big Chief Triangle," a label that annoyed Jackson to the point where he began referring to the Knicks' coach as "Gumby." But Van Gundy saved his most pointed remarks for Jordan, the Teflon icon whom no one in the league dared lay a finger on, much less utter a bad word about.

It all came to a head in January of 1997, the day the Knicks were to face the Bulls in Chicago for the first time since their playoff elimination. Van Gundy was on a Chicago sports talk show and gave his analysis of Jordan's greatness, saying that players are more concerned about being liked by Jordan than beating him. He believed Jordan knew this and used it to his advantage.

"His way is to befriend them, soften them up, try to make

them feel that he cares about them—and then he goes out there and tries to destroy them," Van Gundy said. "For some reason, league-wide, it's important to be liked by him and I don't know why. There's such a mystique about him that everybody wants to be like him, play like him, make as much money as he does, and be able to do all the off-the-court things he does. You see him every game, he smiles at guys, pats them on the ass, then goes out and kicks their ass. Then they hug him after the game like it was some great thing that he scored 45 points against them.

"I admire him for it," he went on. "He uses everything he has to his advantage, whether psychological or physical. He cons them by inviting them to his movies. He cons them with the commercials. He pretends to enjoy guys, like them and befriend them, and all he wants to do is win.

"The brighter players in this league and all the coaches realize what he does. I don't think what I'm saying is so outlandish. Everyone knows that it's true. I don't have a problem saying it."

Van Gundy was also taking a less-than-subtle shot at Ewing, who shares the same agent, David Falk, as Jordan. Ewing also had a cameo role in Jordan's movie, *Space Jam.* However harsh his characterization of Jordan, Van Gundy claimed he was also paying homage to Jordan; Jordan, however, did not see it that way. He was particularly furious at the implication that he was a con man.

That night Jordan scored a season-high 51 points, glaring at Van Gundy after he hit a jumper in the fourth quarter. As the two teams crossed paths following Chicago's 88–87 victory, Jordan sneered, "You little fuck," at Van Gundy. In the corridor of the United Center, Jordan shook hands with the filmmaker and lifelong Knick fan Spike Lee, saying, "You better tell your coach to shut up."

Jordan later said, "He's playing a con game with his own team, trying to get them motivated. Come on. When you step on the basketball court, it's all about the game of basketball."

The exchange was indicative of how far Van Gundy would go to get at Jordan. He became obsessed with beating the best team and the greatest player. On a wall outside the Knicks' locker room at their Purchase training site, Van Gundy had an annual list of goals for the season posted up on plexiglass. They included things as simple as, "Be the best defensive field goal team in the league" to "Win 15 playoff games." At the very bottom, there was also a puzzling acronym that simply read "FJ." Translation? Fuck Jordan.

One of the most rewarding parts of being the Knicks coach for Van Gundy was the opportunity to involve his father in his life and vice versa.

In the fall of 1998, Bill Van Gundy was suffering from a stomach ailment that alarmed doctors, who advised Bill to resign from Genesee. At age sixty-three, he was determined to make it to the end of the semester and the Christmas break before handing over the team to one of his assistants. In one of his final games, he drove the team van through a snowstorm, down Interstate 90 toward Cleveland for a game against Cuyahoga Community College. As he left the locker room for the start of that game, he saw a familiar figure standing in a doorway across the gymnasium: Jeff had flown in to watch his dad.

"There's this ratty-looking bum out there, not shaved, just like he looks now," Bill said. "His mother and me didn't know he was coming. It was unbelievable. To fly into Cleveland to just watch a game—and it wasn't like he was flying in to see the world's best basketball."

Bill repaid the favor several weeks later, surprising his son at Purchase College one day during training camp. Bill arrived late, and opened the gymnasium door just in time to be screamed at by his son.

"You know how secretive we are," said Jeff, whose Knick practices are closed to the public and media. "I saw someone's head peek in, and I yelled, 'Close the door!' Then I noticed it was my father. The players thought I was kicking my own father out. I had to stop practice and apologize to him."

Bill did not have a team to call his own for the first time since 1958 when he left the Army. After watching his son conduct a Knicks practice for the first time, he came back the next few days to watch more.

"I have problems, but I also have resources," Jeff said. "His only resource is himself. He has to take on every problem by himself. It's all interesting, this talk of second chances with La-trell. My dad has been giving second chances at Genesee for the past fifteen years. I've seen some of the guys as they've come into his program—and again as they've come out—and I've seen changed people."

Jeff cherished the time he could spend with his father.

Two days after the loss to Miami, the problems grew worse for Van Gundy and the Knicks. Spre-well's return had been preempted; a magnetic resonance imaging test on February 9 revealed a hairline fracture in his right heel. His foot had been bothering him for a week.

Although surgery would not be required, Sprewell could be out from three to six weeks. Wearing a walking boot and unable to put pressure on the foot, he would have to watch the Knicks adjust without him and rehabilitate the injury in a swimming pool and on an exercise bike.

The Knicks were catching an early break in the schedule. They would face the lowly Bulls, Detroit, and Cleveland twice each over the next twelve games, and also play such mediocre squads as Washington, Toronto, New Jersey, Minnesota, and Boston.

In some ways the injury was a blessing for the Knicks. Van Gundy was able to use a more conventional lineup that fea-tured Kurt Thomas at his natural power forward position. Thomas had been practically out of basketball for two years, playing in just twenty-three games the last two seasons because of ankle injuries. But he was impressive during training camp, and Van Gundy felt his physical presence could provide muscle and rebounding in the low post—the qualities he had been searching for since Oakley had been traded.

That meant Larry Johnson could return to small forward,

and the offense could again revolve around Ewing. The Knicks were now only integrating one new player into the starting lineup. But it made you wonder what would happen when Sprewell returned.

In their first game without Sprewell, five players scored in double figures and they won for the first time, beating Washington 101–88. Johnson, back at his familiar position, scored 18 points and grabbed 7 rebounds. The following night, the Knicks beat the watered-down Bulls and the pieces were starting to mesh a little. With Thomas in early foul trouble, Van Gundy used Camby for 28 minutes—quite a change for the guy who played just six minutes in the first two games. He responded, rejecting eight shots, holding the lone Bull survivor Toni Kukoc to 4-of-22 shooting and displaying the kind of energy Grunfeld had promised.

"He's putting out the effort and playing hard," Van Gundy said. "A player with his talent, if he puts out that much effort, he will get results."

Camby's big date against his former team was only five days away. He and the Knicks would face Toronto at the Garden. Oakley's homecoming would be the featured subplot, but at least Camby was playing and the Knicks were winning. A victory over Detroit gave the Knicks a 3-2 record heading into the much-anticipated reunion with Oakley.

For a week leading up to the game, the organization debated how to honor Oakley properly for his ten years. The issue was complicated by the fact that he was bad-mouthing the Knicks daily, with Grunfeld taking the most abuse.

Grunfeld was not going to make Oakley feel like the conquering hero returning home. The Knicks created a video montage, but could not decide whether to play it before the game or during halftime. Dave Checketts remembered that when the beloved Rangers captain Mark Messier came back to the Garden after signing with the Vancouver Canucks a year earlier, the New York players were so awestruck by the pregame ceremony that they went on to lose the game.

They decided to play the tribute at halftime, a decision that

Oakley felt was just another slap in the face. "Why do something at halftime? I'll be in the locker room," Oakley said before the game. When Oakley was introduced, he was given a standing ovation and seemed to be moved by the crowd's response. But by the time the halfhearted halftime tribute began, half the crowd had filed out to the concession stands. The Garden never looked so petty.

Oakley looked strange in a pin-striped purple jersey with a dinosaur on the front. In the most telling moment of his return, Oakley looked instinctively toward the Knick bench after the ball rolled out of bounds with six seconds left on the shot clock. He looked to his former coach for a play, a scene that had the bench laughing.

"Did you see him?" Van Gundy said. "He wanted to know what play we were going to run."

Four minutes into the game, he dove into the crowd for a loose ball. Moments later, he drove against Ewing and had his shot rejected. Later in the first half, he found himself isolated against Camby to the left of the foul line; putting the ball on the floor, Oakley drove around Camby, converted a sweeping layup, and was fouled. At one point, Camby inbounded the ball in front of the Raptors' bench and Oakley, from a sitting position, began tugging at his shorts. It was a good show, but the night belonged more to the Knicks, who won handily 95–85, and Camby, who outplayed Oakley by scoring 11 points and grabbing 12 rebounds. Camby was also named player of the game.

"It was weird," Ewing said of the reunion with his former teammate. "But that's the nature of this business. Here today and gone tomorrow. We chitchatted for a minute and then he tried to take my head off."

For the moment, though, the heat was finally off the general manager and the coach.

The Knicks appeared to be in a groove. They were 4-0 without Sprewell and 4-2 overall, and already speculation was beginning about whether Van Gundy would bring the team's main off-season acquisition off the bench. From a chemistry standpoint, it seemed to make sense; Sprewell could fill the role of Starks, providing instant offense to the second unit and giving the Knicks a bona fide scoring threat.

But how would it play with Sprewell's psyche, changing the role of a player who had started for most of his career? When reporters first broached the subject to him on February 18 before a game against Cleveland, he sounded less than enthused about a sixth-man role. But he kept away from controversy. "I'll do whatever," he said. "At this point, I just want to win and fit in however I can."

The Knicks were blown out by the Cavaliers 98–74. The next day in Philadelphia, Van Gundy met with Sprewell to reassure him that he had not yet made up his mind about what role the injured player would fill once he returned. Sprewell seemed to already know which way Van Gundy was leaning when reporters pressed him about his conversation with the coach. In regard to coming off the bench, Sprewell smiled and said, "I might be forced to. I can deal with it. I'm not going to mope around. I see what the coach has in store for me."

New York won its next four games, beating the 76ers, Bulls, and Nets before pulling out a wild overtime victory over Minnesota. Houston scored 26 points, including a 3-pointer with 4.6 seconds left in the extra period.

Stephon Marbury, the Timberwolves point guard who was a New York schoolboy legend at Lincoln High School in Brooklyn, was rumored to be on the trading block. His Garden homecoming was ruined by Charlie Ward, who scored 18 points and distributed 13 assists.

"He played great tonight," said Marbury. "But if he played like that every night, they wouldn't need a point guard. But what are the chances of that happening?"

Sprewell's absence began hurting the Knicks the next game, when they could have used his energy and scoring. Instead, they fell flat against Boston and Detroit in consecutive double-digit road losses. Then they returned home and beat Cleveland, moving to 9-5 overall and 9-3 without Sprewell.

Heading into Miami on March 2, talk abounded whether

Sprewell would be activated off the injured list. But with the Knicks playing their third game in three nights, Van Gundy wanted Sprewell to practice once with the team before he played again. Sprewell saw no reason to push up his return date; after all, he could return in his hometown of Milwaukee three nights later.

It was New York's first game in Miami since the Knicks stunned the Heat in last year's first round, and Van Gundy knew it was going to be physical. The Knicks pounded the ball inside to Ewing, and he responded with a dominant performance: 31 points and 16 rebounds in 43 minutes. Johnson contributed 19 points.

Mourning erupted for 28 points and Tim Hardaway had 17. The lead changed hands 17 times. They were going at it just like old times. Ewing had a chance to give New York the victory, but he missed the potential game-winning shot over Mourning. In overtime, with the Knicks trailing by two and only 5.1 seconds remaining, Ewing missed again. His off-balance, pull-up jump shot from the foul came off the rim.

Camby watched all this from the bench. He registered his first DNP (Did Not Play, Coach's Decision) as a Knick. In the twelve games since his five-minute stint against Miami on February 7, Camby was averaging 21 minutes of playing time—but in a playoff-charged environment, Van Gundy decided not to use Camby once during a 53-minute game.

"Certain matchups aren't good for him," said Van Gundy, defending his decision. It was a remark that resonated loud and clear with Grunfeld back in New York.

With two days off before the Knicks headed to Milwaukee, Van Gundy threw his weary team a bone by deciding to remain in the balmy South Florida weather for another day. They practiced in Miami before flying to the Midwest.

The next day, Van Gundy's pregame lineup card would make it official: Sprewell was New York's new sixth man.

Sprewell bought fifty tickets for family and friends in Milwaukee. Happy that he was home for the first time in two months, he publicly grasped his new role. "Of course I want to make an impact," he said. "It's not like this team hasn't played well. I just want to be the player that pushes us over the edge."

Van Gundy was looking for a spark, with the Knicks having lost three of their previous five games and the shortened season nearly one-third completed. Milwaukee, a much more respectable team under new coach George Karl, gave the Knicks problems. Sprewell returned with a bang, scoring his first points on an electrifying tomahawk dunk. He finished with 18 points, but the final seconds took on a familiar pattern. Ewing relived his Miami nightmare, missing another potential game-winning shot at the buzzer, and the Bucks had an 88–87 squeaker. Sprewell was back, but the Knicks were only two games over .500 and they were hard-pressed to win a road game.

Four days later, their season was downgraded from promising to questionable. Twenty-nine seconds into a rematch against the Bucks at the Garden, Ewing took himself out due to severe pain in his left Achilles tendon. It began bothering him nine days earlier in a win over Cleveland. The pain was worsening.

Just as concerned as the Knicks were over the first few seconds of that game, the last 40 seconds were equally cruel. They had possession of the ball and a four-point lead, and somehow managed to self-destruct.

The fatal blow came with 3.4 seconds left when the 3-point marksman Dell Curry buried a shot from behind the arc in front of the Knicks bench to give Milwaukee a one-point lead in front of a shell-shocked crowd. Sprewell played the goat to the hilt, leaving the dangerous Curry open to double-team Glenn Robinson when it was imperative that the Knicks not give up a 3-pointer. Sprewell had a chance to redeem himself, but badly missed a wide-open 25-footer at the buzzer.

"That was totally my fault," Sprewell said after the 87–86 loss dropped the Knicks to 10-8. "I know how good a shooter he is. I should have stayed home."

"To lose Patrick and play as hard as we did . . ." began Chris Childs, "this one was a tough one to swallow."

Van Gundy was beside himself. His franchise center was lost indefinitely and the guy he campaigned to acquire had just blown the game. What's more, their record with Sprewell had dipped to 1-4.

There were new problems for Van Gundy, and he still hadn't fixed his garage door yet.

4

THE BIG FELLA

For the second straight season, an injury to Patrick Ewing had cast a pall over New York's hopes. Eighteen games into the season, he was diagnosed with tendinitis of the left Achilles. Doctors were leaving the decision up to Ewing, but they made it clear: The injury would take at least six weeks to heal properly.

"I don't have six weeks," was Ewing's response. Instead, he hoped to stay out of the lineup for just two weeks while his teammates were attempting to keep their heads above .500. As he limped slowly toward his ivory Mercedes, dragging his left foot in the parking lot of Purchase College, his stride reminded you not of a professional athlete filled with élan and grace, but of an old man looking for a park bench under a shady tree. Ewing was resigned to playing in pain and at his own risk; a ruptured Achilles tendon could mean the end of his career.

Either the curse of the lockout had struck or Ewing was simply breaking down. A year earlier, Ewing had severely damaged his right wrist when he crashed to the floor on December 20, 1997, in a game at Milwaukee.

The play began with Charlie Ward throwing a lob pass to Ewing behind the Bucks' defense. As Ewing leaped, Milwaukee reserve center Andrew Lang shoved him from behind, enough to knock the Knicks center off balance. Ewing tried to brace his fall, but all his weight landed on his shooting hand. He screamed in pain, as Jeff Van Gundy and Knicks trainers Mike

Saunders and Said Hamdan ran to his aid. In those fleeting seconds, the Knicks' season was essentially over. Ewing tried to ignore the pain and went to the foul line to shoot free throws. But
he could not even hold the ball in his right hand. He attempted
two left-handed shots, missing them both with 24.9 seconds left
in the half. He retreated to the locker room, never to return in
the regular season.

Within the hour, team physicians back in New York were
preparing to perform surgery once the team charter arrived
from Milwaukee. The injury was much worse than anyone
imagined: He had torn ligaments and dislocated his lunate
bone, one of eight bones in the wrist. Two hours of surgery
at 4:30 A.M. at Beth Israel Hospital North Division in Manhattan followed. Dr. Norman Scott, the team physician, compared Ewing's condition to a high-speed, high-force injury
usually associated with car accident victims and football
players.

"I was glad we got to him within six hours of the injury because the bone was truly out of place and pressing against the
nerve," said Scott, who added that he had never seen such an
injury to a basketball player in his twenty years of treating professional athletes. Ewing missed the final 56 games of the regular season, and real concern lingered over whether his shooting
hand would ever heal properly.

From 1987 to 1996, he had played at least 76 games a season.
Now he could not remain injury-free through the first two
months of the last two seasons. The time away from basketball
had caught up with his thirty-six-year-old bones. Too many late
nights at the union's Manhattan offices and not enough early
morning wind sprints on the court made him susceptible to injury and the Knicks vulnerable.

For fourteen seasons, Ewing showed
himself to be one of the best jump-shooting centers in the history of the game. An eleven-time All-Star and the reason the

Knicks kept advancing in the postseason, Ewing was named one of the NBA's top fifty players of all time in 1997, a legend in a city that worships its sports heroes.

Yet Ewing, while respected in New York, is not loved, and that feeling goes much deeper than his play on the court. He never revealed himself to the people he played for, never endeared himself to the fans. Whether he was walking right past a young child asking for his autograph or was rushing out of a charity event after barely making an appearance, Ewing could be aloof, stubborn, and downright selfish.

He never had a great relationship with the fans. Unlike Hakeem Olajuwon in Houston, Larry Bird in Boston, or Reggie Miller in Indiana, Ewing could not find a way to connect with the public anywhere but on the floor. He only wanted to be admired for his work ethic and his consistency. He did not have the personality to do stand-up like Charles Barkley or to captivate Madison Avenue with his smile like Jordan. He was plain old Patrick.

Some blame John Thompson, his overbearing college coach at Georgetown who first instilled the Us-against-the-World mentality in the young center. The Ewing years at Georgetown were known for Hoya paranoia, in which Thompson would shield players from the media and their critics. During the NCAA tournament, when everyone else was being housed in hotels in the host city, Thompson would reserve rooms thirty minutes from downtown. Hoya players never had their majors included in their media biographies. It was in this environment that young Ewing learned to deal with the public. Georgetown was an all-black team with a black coach playing for the pride of a predominantly white Jesuit college in Washington, D.C. Actually, they were playing for themselves.

The issue of race was a recurring theme for Thompson's teams during the Ewing era and beyond. No matter how hard they worked or how much they won, they were viewed by a part of America as menacing, angry black men. Standing at the forefront was Ewing, playing with a perpetual scowl, swatting shots, dunking maliciously on tall, white guys from Villanova and Seton Hall in the formative days of the Big East. The Hoya Destroya. This was his persona.

In reality, he was an insecure, shy, Jamaican-born kid who happened to grow 7-feet tall. He never understood how some-one could be mean enough to hold up a sign at a Georgetown game that read, "Ewing Can't Read This." If this was how fans were going to treat him, then the hell with all of them.

Coming to New York as the Knicks' savior in 1985, Ewing felt immense pressure to produce for a cynical and often fickle crowd. Regardless of the talent around him or the revolving door of coaches that kept spinning, Ewing became the scape-goat for every playoff failure.

Patrick Can't Win the Big One and The Knicks Will Never Win a Championship with Ewing became familiar laments. Ewing had a loyal fan base, but the boos always seemed to drown out the cheers. For most of his career, he shrugged off the criticism. But as he got older and felt entitled to speak his mind, he let it be known that the doomsayers were wearing thin on him.

During a game against the Los Angeles Clippers in 1996, Ewing lashed out at Garden fans who loudly booed the Knicks despite an 89–80 victory. "Yeah, they're annoying me," Ewing said. "If they're going to act the way they're acting, they might as well stay home. If they're going to support us, support us. You go to other places, and even when the team is playing bad, the fans still support the team. Here, they support you one minute and then something goes wrong and they jump off the bandwagon. I'm just tired of it. It's been like that for twelve years and I'm fed up with it."

The next day's tabloids essentially read, "Ewing Rips Knick Fans." Great. Beautiful. Another public relations disaster. Just what he needed. Management wanted him to issue an apology, but he refused and was booed even more loudly at the next home game.

"I said what I said and I meant what I said," Ewing said.

Neither was Ewing afraid to take on management from time

to time. He gave loyalty and he expected it in return. He opted out of his contract in 1991 because he was upset over the direction of the team; he had played for five coaches over the previous five seasons and never gotten further than the second round of the playoffs.

Ewing came within hours of being traded to Golden State that summer as David Falk tried to leverage a deal. That fell through, and then he paved the way for Riley to take over the team by agreeing to an extension; Riley had told Checketts he would want no part of coaching a Knicks team without Ewing.

The next time Ewing came up for a contract renewal was the summer of 1997, and there were rumors that he would give the Knicks two days to make him an acceptable offer or he was gone. Taking no chances, Checketts contacted Falk at 12:01 A.M. on July 1, the first day teams could negotiate contracts with free agents. Within forty-eight hours, Ewing signed a four-year, $68 million contract.

"I've said it all along, we'd like Patrick to finish his career in New York," Checketts said.

But even the incredible amount of money he would earn in the final years of his career could not make up for some of the hard feelings he had toward management. Following his wrist surgery in December '97, Ewing spent three days convalescing at the hospital. Van Gundy and several teammates visited, but Ewing never forgot that neither Checketts nor Grunfeld came to visit. This showed two facets of Ewing's personality: He was sensitive, and he could hold a grudge. He was also immensely private. If those perceived slights bothered him, he was flat-out embarrassed when the New York gossip pages began talking about marital problems between him and his wife, Rita, and rumors of an alleged affair with a Knicks City Dancer.

"I can't believe you guys would write that crap," he said to a group of reporters covering the team, who tried in vain to explain that they had nothing to do with that section of their newspapers.

"Well, it was in your paper. So the hell with all of you," he said, smiling.

Soon after, Rita filed for divorce. The only dynasty Ewing was part of seemed like a production of Aaron Spelling's.

He was even less thrilled when his wife co-authored a fictional book with Crystal McCrary, the wife of former Knick Greg Anthony, entitled *Homecourt Advantage.* The book chronicled the private lives of the New York Flyers. The maniacal coach was modeled after Riley, and the unpredictable shooting guard seemed like a dead ringer for John Starks. Only the names were changed to protect the guilty. It was Ewing's worst fear: Rita had become one of *them.* Suddenly, Ewing's pillow talk was available at Barnes & Noble for $20.95.

Rita contracted famed divorce lawyer Raoul Felder to represent her, but the couple never divorced. Feeding speculation that they had attempted a reconciliation, Ewing was always seen wearing his wedding band. Even reporting that innocuous fact, Ewing believed, was tantamount to crossing the line of ethics.

"That's why I don't talk to you guys," he said.

Ewing would never allow the media into his private world. You could have a pleasant enough relationship with him, but don't ask for his home number or request an interview the day of a game. He would talk about anything but basketball, engaging reporters in casual conversations. The longer he knew you, the friendlier he became. But never fool yourself into thinking you're one of his boys. Unless you played with him, coached him, or went into business with him, that wall is impenetrable.

Some in the media resented him for not being more accommodating. They expected more from Ewing than just being a great player, especially since he came along at a time when the league was enjoying unprecedented success, when Magic Johnson and Charles Barkley would hold court in front of their lockers before games. From the moment Ewing was drafted, he was expected to be someone he never was, a media-friendly player trying to sell his image by cultivating relationships with people he had nothing in common with. He did not want to play that game.

But in many ways Ewing was a 7-foot contradiction. While

he said he never cared about what was said or written about him, if you wrote a critical article, he would often approach you at some point in the next week, flash a wide grin and say, "I heard you killed me in the papers. But I don't care what you guys write."

He always believed the media was out to get him. Sometimes he went out of his way to make life difficult for them. He never speaks before games and rarely grants interviews after practices; if you want to talk to Ewing, you have to be in the locker room ten minutes after the game and elbow your way into his three-minute, nonexpansive Q&A. Sitting there in his royal blue terry cloth robe, a bucket of ice covering his shins and ankles and a water bottle in his hand, Ewing always talks. In defeat or victory, he never hides.

Not that he has much to say. Some of his patented responses: "I still think we're the better team . . . That's my shot, I'm going to keep taking it . . . We just didn't execute . . . Please, don't step on my toes . . ." and his signature closing line, "I'm done, fellas."

The Knicks were less formidable but also less predictable without Ewing. The latter was something that infuriated Ewing and bothered Van Gundy, who was always clear about why he had kept his job in New York: If Ewing was the Garden's meal ticket for nearly fifteen years, he was also a major reason why Van Gundy had survived in the post-Nelson era.

Whenever the expression "He's a players coach" is thrown around, it means the best player on the team is tight with the coach. Magic Johnson and Pat Riley. Michael Jordan and Phil Jackson. Patrick Ewing and Jeff Van Gundy. You could even take Jimmy Chitwood and the Gene Hackman character from the basketball movie *Hoosiers*. Their common denominator: Great players with influence over personnel decisions. Translation: The coach stays.

In 1998, Van Gundy saw how the fans and the New York media had fallen in love with the underdog Knicks after

Ewing's wrist injury, how they became a more free-flowing, guard-oriented offensive team, and, in turn, how the Garden responded to the new-look Knicks. In print and on the airwaves, the anti-Ewing faction began speaking out, suggesting simply, "Maybe the Knicks are better off without Patrick." Many New Yorkers had grown weary of Ewing monopolizing the ball in the low post while failing to lead the team to a title.

They had their evidence in the first round of the '98 playoffs against Miami, when the Knicks stunned the Heat in the first round by blowing out Riley's team on Miami's home floor in Game 5. In the next series, Ewing became their scapegoat for the Knicks' loss in five games to Indiana. Lacking rhythm and clearly still finding his bearings, Ewing returned in Game 2 to contribute to a loss. The team would go 1-3 upon his return.

To his harshest critics, Ewing rushed back because he could not accept the Knicks winning a playoff series without him. As absurd as that premise was, there were others who blamed Van Gundy for toying with the chemistry so late in the season. But the coach realized that the Knicks had finished the regular season 26-26 without Ewing, didn't clinch a playoff spot until the 81st game, and barely avoided certain first-round elimination at the hands of the Bulls by gaining the seventh seed by just a 1-game margin.

The coach dug up numbers to support his arguments, taking every knock against Ewing as a personal affront to what the game was supposed to be about. But many fans didn't want to hear about stats; based solely on aesthetics, they believed the Knicks were more fun to watch when Ewing was out. Van Gundy viewed it as another example of Ewing being underappreciated.

"To me, winning is fun," Van Gundy said. "If our best player isn't playing and we're having trouble winning, how can that be fun?"

Now, with Ewing's left Achilles tendon keeping him out indefinitely at the start of the '99 season, it was time to see what kind of dividends Grunfeld's great investments would pay.

In January, he gave the backup center Chris Dudley a four-year contract worth $28 million. But everyone in the organization understood the Knicks could only go so far with Dudley playing major minutes.

The day after Ewing was injured, Grunfeld opened the Garden coffers again, this time for Marcus Camby, extending Camby's contract for $30 million guaranteed over six years and $48 million if he met all the incentives.

Camby would not be a free agent until August, when he could command as much as $71 million for a player of his experience. Several players drafted after Camby was taken number two overall in the 1996 draft had secured the maximum deals, including Vancouver's Shareef Abdur-Rahim, Boston's Antoine Walker, Milwaukee's Ray Allen, and the Lakers' Kobe Bryant.

"I can't worry about what the other guys got," Camby said. "The way I look at it, I'm financially secure for the rest of my life."

Grunfeld had promised Camby they would work something out before the summer. The team president's reasons for signing him in March were twofold: He could secure Camby's rights at a bargain-basement price, given his recent playing time; and with Ewing not getting any younger or healthier, Grunfeld could make an investment in the player he believed could become the Knicks' center in the millennium.

But the other message Grunfeld was sending spoke volumes: Maybe Van Gundy was not sold on Camby, but Grunfeld was letting the coach know that his prized acquisition was here for the long haul—and Van Gundy had better learn to deal with it.

On the night he was signed, March 11, Camby responded with 19 points and 12 rebounds against a bad Washington Wizards team. Yet to New York fans, it did not overshadow Grunfeld's otherwise unproductive day. The trading deadline came and went, and the Knicks suffered a devastating loss earlier that afternoon.

Stephon Marbury was available. For two years, the one item on every fan's wish list was an All-Star-caliber point guard to complement the backcourt. A month earlier, Marbury told the

New York *Daily News* he would do everything in his power to try and orchestrate a deal between the Knicks and the Minnesota Timberwolves, who were fearful of losing him for nothing if he became a free agent that summer.

Instead, Grunfeld and Checketts were caught napping as Marbury was scooped up by the New Jersey Nets. David Falk had leveraged the future contract extensions of clients Keith Van Horn and Kerry Kittles to lure Marbury to the Meadowlands, across the Hudson River just ten miles from Madison Square Garden. The indignity—Grunfeld had been outfoxed by the Nets, once a bumbling organization that now seemed to be putting the parts together much more quickly than the Knicks.

"We had conversations," said Grunfeld, "but they were going nowhere." But all was not lost; Grunfeld announced he had a last-minute deal. The Knicks had acquired the rights to Mirsad Turkcan, a Turkish forward who had been with the Philadelphia 76ers.

Fifty feet away from where Grunfeld was explaining himself, Van Gundy was sending his own clear message. He marveled at the Nets' ingenuity in pulling off the deal, saying, "They're geniuses"—a double-edged compliment if ever there was one.

Grunfeld was seething. In his mind, Van Gundy had taken another cheap shot.

5

THE DYSFUNCTIONAL FAMILY

The laughter came from the back of the plane, an annoying cackle that resonated loud and clear with Van Gundy. The Knicks were returning from Chicago, where hours earlier they had set franchise records for offensive futility.

Van Gundy had cautioned his players before the Bulls game about learning to accept mediocrity, that reaching the playoffs was no sure thing. The Knicks came into the game 11-8, Ewing was out indefinitely, it seemed like the new players were never going to find their niches.

"If we think that we're just waiting for the playoffs, there'll be no playoffs," Van Gundy said. "And I mean that sincerely."

What happened against the Bulls on March 12 was not only unexplainable but downright embarrassing, the kind of performance that makes coaches lose their jobs and their lunches. Against a low-rent, post-Jordan team whose starters included Dickey Simpkins at power forward, Bill Wennington at center, and Randy Brown at point guard, the Knicks never led and were run off the United Center floor by a 76–63 score—though the game was not nearly that close.

They scored five points in the second quarter and had just 22 points at halftime. They came out after that humiliating first half and scored a paltry 11 points in the third quarter. Thirty in the fourth quarter rescued them from tying the franchise low by two points; their 19 field goals for the game tied an all-time NBA record.

It was not just the worst performance by a Knickerbocker team since the inception of the shot clock; it was arguably the worst display of Knick basketball since the inception of the peach basket.

The Bulls had not conjured up their old magic against the Knicks, and the debacle was not just the result of New York being unable to put the ball in the hole. The Knicks appeared lifeless, as if it was a midsummer pickup game at the park in which the only goal is to avoid injury.

"I'm embarrassed by it and I know this team is," said Sprewell, whose 2-for-12 shooting mirrored the team's accuracy. He was one of the few players who bothered to talk about the loss.

Larry Johnson made one of five shots. That two-headed point guard monster of Charlie Ward and Chris Childs was truly horrifying, combining for three points, two assists, and six of the most hideous turnovers imaginable. Everyone knew that the quality of play in the league had been awful at times in this shortened season, but this was a standout even by the year's gruesome standards.

The lockout forced many teams to play games on three consecutive nights for the first time in ten years, and the Knicks were playing in Chicago the night after hosting the Wizards at home. Bad basketball wasn't endemic to the Knicks; Utah and the Lakers had been blown out by inferior teams, too. But this Chicago team, soft in the middle and led by Toni Kukoc, was worse than merely inferior.

When you're in the middle of a feud with the general manager, a loss like this is hardly recommended in the coaching manual.

"You have to do everything wrong to be as bad as we were," Van Gundy said. "I don't know if it can get worse than this."

They walked off the floor at the United Center hanging their heads, but you never got the sense the Knicks were truly demoralized by the loss. They put on a good show, however, leaving the locker room door closed to the media for thirty minutes, twenty minutes longer than allowed by NBA rules.

Inside the spacious room, Ewing, Johnson, and forty-one-year-old Herb Williams, the oldest player in the league, were trying to drive home Van Gundy's point to their unfazed teammates. Sprewell and Camby and Kurt Thomas had been a part of a lot of nights like this in their careers. Another shellacking on a visiting floor—what was the big deal? At least the team's tri-captains were trying to inject a sense of urgency into a season on the brink of already being lost. While their intentions were noble, not even Van Gundy was putting much stock in the impromptu group therapy session.

"Those player meetings . . . that's all bullshit," he said. "Meetings accomplish nothing. Actions do. Tangible results are on the floor."

And now he was hearing laughter from the back of the team's charter, from Sprewell and that rascally cutup Dennis Scott, who had played 10 minutes against the Bulls and didn't put up a single shot. It made the loss even more infuriating and confirmed his worst fears about the nouveau Knicks: Some of them just did not give a damn.

The arrival of Sprewell, Camby, Thomas, Scott, and the second-year point guard Rick Brunson changed the dynamics of the locker room. The Knicks were suddenly younger, more single, more hip-hop, and more Generation X.

On the surface, it was a natural progression from the old guard. But if they gave the Knicks unbelievable athletic feats on the floor, they also did not treat the game like a life-and-death struggle.

Those five players quickly formed a bond as newcomers who didn't subscribe to the tired old Knick ways. Their attitude seemed to be brash and straightforward: *Why should we conform to you? We've got just as many rings as you do.*

Sprewell was their leader, doing his own thing and never adhering to convention. During his days at Golden State, he often befriended the younger players on the team and was accused of corrupting number one pick Joe Smith. Larry Johnson made an attempt to forge a relationship with the controversial star, telling Knicks officials to place Sprewell's locker cubicle next to Johnson's. It was a nice try, but Sprewell showed no interest in hanging out with L.J.

It's not that he didn't like or respect Johnson; he just felt more comfortable around the young Turks. Some of his teammates admitted they could not figure him out. But Camby and especially Brunson gravitated toward the carefree guard; they loved Sprewell's game, his I-don't-care-what-you-think attitude. Sometimes they holed up in Sprewell's hotel room and played Sony PlayStation for hours. Other times, they hung out on the road together. They especially liked to tease him when he was interviewed by female television reporters, making faces at him and trying to force him to laugh with a microphone in his face.

They were all under twenty-eight years old. Camby was born in 1974; he was seven when Herb Williams played his first NBA game. They bordered on immature, and in some way they all carried a major chip on their shoulders.

Part of what bonded them was their belief that Van Gundy was doing them wrong. They were outsiders, expected to follow the lead of the veterans, and largely uninterested in doing so.

Brunson, who played for John Chaney at Temple University, was the third-string point guard on a team that did not have a bona fide starter at the position. He had a long history with Van Gundy, having attended a youth camp where Van Gundy served as his camp counselor. "I remember him yelling at me to play defense," Brunson said. He, like most Knick fans, probably wondered to himself on occasion, Why can't I get some more time? I can run an offense just as well as those other two guys.

Brunson had a bad piece of real estate in the locker room, the cubicle a few inches left of Patrick Ewing's in the far corner. Players like Chris Jent and Brooks Thompson—guys happy to be on an NBA roster—were usually assigned to the same locale. They graciously put up with the endless foot traffic of cameramen, reporters, and assorted hangers-on pressing forward during Ewing's postgame briefings.

Without fail, Brunson was always returning from the shower as the masses stormed into his personal space. It made for some uneasy encounters, in which Brunson would either stare down someone who had gotten too close or offer up some surly comment like, "Mind getting away from my locker?"

For a guy who could use as many allies as possible to remain a twelfth man, he wasn't making friends. Nor did he seem to care. The irony was, his best friend on the team, Sprewell, was charming the press with his candor and his ability to break down a game. You almost felt sorry for Brunson; instead of feeling fortunate to be part of an environment he might never get to revisit, he acted like he was a put-upon five-time All-Star.

Ben Davis was in a similar position. He had the cubicle to the right of Ewing's and his situation was even more tenuous than Brunson's; the third-year forward from Arizona had spent much of the season on the injured list while trying to hang on with an NBA team. Quiet, unassuming, he never made waves and understood the consequences of occupying space next to the Big Fella.

Camby was extremely pleasant and easygoing, too. He handled himself well considering that he was the lightning rod for most of the ill will between Grunfeld and Van Gundy. He was being vilified in the newspapers, and he knew the names of the reporters who were taking him to task. When one reporter approached him before the first game of the season and said, "I'm the guy who's been killing you since the Oakley trade," he calmly looked up from his locker and replied, "You too, huh?"

If there was one Knick who may have had a legitimate beef, it was Camby. But he always treaded lightly when it came to questions about how Van Gundy was using him and whether he was happy with his minutes. And no matter how many people asked him about Oakley, he always paid homage to the for-

mer Knick and never was baited into some wild, back-page
headline along the lines of "M.C. Hammers Van Gundy."

Camby did, however, have a very visible business entourage.
His agent, Alex Johnson, was tabbed "Jerry Maguire" by reporters. Johnson was likable and young for his profession, and
Camby was his only big-name client. He seemed to be at every
game, home and away, selling Camby harder than even Grunfeld. Camby had also hired a personal public relations assistant, former Raptors media director Rick Kaplan. While Camby
said nothing publicly, Kaplan and Johnson privately waged
their own campaign to free Marcus from the bench.

Also working behind the scenes was NBC analyst Isiah
Thomas, who drafted Camby while in Toronto and was essentially serving as his pro bono senior adviser. He often chastised
Van Gundy for his use of Camby. The head coach was concerned that Camby's representatives, while well-meaning, were
acting as divisive forces, and in late March Van Gundy finally
addressed the issue with Camby: "Don't let your people drive a
wedge between us," he said. "I don't have a problem with you. I
want you here."

Going back to his college days at UMass, Camby had a history of listening to people around him and taking their advice.
And discerning who was offering good advice and who wasn't
was often a problem for him.

When Camby was on his way to the Chicago predraft camp
in June 1996, the *Hartford Courant* reported that Camby and
friends had for months allegedly been accepting cash and gifts
from a Hartford trial attorney and another man who wanted to
become Camby's agent. Further reports of the would-be agent
providing prostitutes to Camby and his friends soon surfaced.

Within a year, the program he helped put on the map with
coach John Calipari was under investigation by the NCAA.
After the penalties were doled out, Camby reimbursed the
school for the $150,000 in forfeited NCAA tournament revenue
UMass had been forced to return. The ordeal tarnished
Camby's image, but he did seem to learn a valuable lesson
about surrounding himself with the wrong people.

Kurt Thomas did not have a business team and did not need one. His bravado spoke louder than any agent. He had been out of the game for most of two seasons due to ankle injuries, and was having trouble taking pounds off in training camp. Van Gundy thought Thomas was a great find, a former first-round pick of the Miami Heat out of Texas Christian who, along with Xavier McDaniel, is one of only two players to lead the nation in scoring and rebounding in the same season.

In Dallas, Maverick coach and general manager Don Nelson gave Thomas a job as an assistant during the 1997–98 season while he was injured. He was set to re-sign Thomas for $1 million before the power forward bolted for New York and a two-year, $3.6 million contract.

It was impossible not to like the self-assured Thomas. He had big, round, brown eyes and a pudgy body that belied his intensity and his skill. He had stronger opinions about his game than perhaps even his mother. He ran like he was wearing clown shoes. Clump. Clump. Clump. When Van Gundy removed him from games, he took it as a personal insult, rolling his eyes to the rafters—even after he had just picked up his second foul in the first two minutes.

He balanced his playful, fun-loving personality with the crazed look in his eye that always surfaced when the Knicks were headed for disaster. Once, during a team meeting, Thomas asked if he could address his teammates for a moment. When he was given the floor, Thomas went into a diatribe on how he could better serve the team.

"I'm the only stone-cold motherfucker in here!" he said. "I'm the only one who wants the motherfuckin' ball. I need to get more shots."

Asked later about the outburst, Thomas laughed.

"They were lookin' at me like I was crazy. But I figured, what the hell? I'll give it a try."

Ewing's jaw nearly hit the floor that night, and many of the other Knicks wondered where the outburst came from. Along with grandfather Herb, Ewing was from the old school. Everyone on the team was supposed to know his place, when to shut up and listen and when to speak. But now all the rules were changing. Ewing's influence in the locker room was diminishing. His best friend, John Starks, was on the West Coast, and his on-court protector, Oakley, was in Toronto.

As far as aging warriors went, it was down to him, Williams, and Larry Johnson.

Herb Williams was the most respected voice on the Knicks, an old sage who doled out advice to anyone at any time. He came in with the Pacers in 1981, and saw the rejuvenation of the league up close. At the 1998 All-Star Game in New York, he popped his head into the West locker room after the game to get a Kobe Bryant autograph for his young son. "Ask him about Jellybean," he told one reporter, referring to Bryant's father, the former journeyman Joe Bryant. The young Bryant smiled and shook the veteran's hand. Eighteen seasons after his rookie year, Herb had been around long enough to have played against a father and son.

But his days as a contributing player were long gone. In his two previous seasons combined, he had appeared in just 48 games, averaging less than eight minutes a game when he did get to play. His ability to maintain a roster spot said more about his character than his on-court talent. Van Gundy, four years his junior, needed him to be a counselor in the locker room. Williams was also gravitating toward a role as an assistant coach, but every year there he was at the end of the bench, working the officials and giving the young fellas, as he liked to call them, the benefit of his years in the game.

"He has a lot of knowledge," Thomas said. "When I go out on the floor, I look to him and ask him what I should do and what I should expect from the other players."

It was not an uncommon sight to see Williams running a mini-clinic on the end of the bench during a timeout, showing a player like Camby how to better keep his man off the offensive boards.

Knicks coach Jeff Van Gundy's peacekeeping efforts in the 1998 Knicks-Heat playoff series left him in an undignified and futile position with Alonzo Mourning.

A dejected Patrick Ewing can only roll his eyes after an 83–79 home loss to Miami dealt the Knicks their first 0-2 regular-season start in eight years.

A longtime Knicks fan favorite, Charles Oakley (34) was traded to Toronto before the 1999 season. Getting the worst of this collision, Knicks guard Chris Childs receives a painful reminder of his former teammate's toughness.

3

Ernie Grunfeld (left) was all smiles after signing Van Gundy to a multiyear contract extension on July 7, 1997. But their relationship cooled and Grunfeld, who wanted to fire Van Gundy, found himself reassigned instead.

4

5

With Ewing slowed by injuries, Kurt Thomas picked up some of the defensive slack against Mourning during the Knicks' first-round play-off series against Miami.

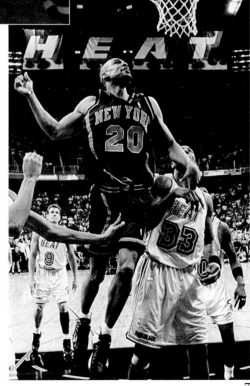

6

7

Left: With the Knicks trailing Miami 77–76, guard Allan Houston releases the fateful shot that would determine the fifth and deciding game of their wild first-round series. *Right:* The ball tells it all. Falling through the basket with 0.8 seconds left, Houston's shot puts a smile on his face and New York into the second round.

Erratic during the regular season but fantastic in the playoffs, Marcus Camby screams with delight after dunking against Atlanta in the Eastern Conference semifinals.

Ewing briefs the press while wearing a walking cast for the partially torn left Achilles tendon that would sideline him for the rest of the year.

8

9

At a press conference before Game 4 against Atlanta, Garden president Dave Checketts admits to having met with Phil Jackson about Jackson's becoming New York's next coach.

10

To the horror of Antonio Davis and Pacers coach Larry Bird, Larry Johnson gets off his game-tying 3-pointer in the waning seconds of Game 3. Fouled by Davis on a controversial call, Johnson finished the 4-point play for a stunning 92–91 victory.

After beating Indiana in Game 6 to advance to the NBA Finals against San Antonio, Latrell Sprewell enjoys the sight of frenzied Knicks fans as he drives away from Madison Square Garden.

11

Never one to shy away from controversy, Johnson begins a profanity-laced interview session during the Finals. The NBA fined Johnson and the Knicks $25,000 each for his comments.

13

14

Van Gundy confers with Sprewell at practice the day before Game 3 against the Spurs.

Sprewell shakes free for a monster dunk in Game 3 of the Finals. He scored 24 points in an 89–81 victory that cut San Antonio's lead to 2–1.

With Ewing unable to play, Spurs center Tim Duncan towers above the Knicks' frontline defenders. The talented 7-footer was named most valuable player of the Finals.

Guards Charlie Ward and Chris Childs applaud the Madison Square Garden crowd after losing the championship to San Antonio.

"Herb's universally respected by all players and coaches, and that's hard to achieve in this league," Van Gundy said.

Incredibly, the Knicks traded him twice in four years only to reacquire him within two weeks each time. No matter how much the Knicks thought they wanted him gone, they couldn't do without good old Herb.

Larry Johnson was one of the few who could bridge the gap between factions and generations in the locker room. In his three seasons in New York, he had emerged as a leader. Acquired from Charlotte for Anthony Mason and Brad Lohaus in 1996, he immediately endeared himself to Van Gundy, something most newcomers don't achieve until their second and sometimes third season, if at all. What separated Johnson from the pack was his unselfishness and his willingness to do whatever the coach wanted.

"Larry Johnson, to me, is the perfect example of a guy who is able to focus in on what's important," Van Gundy said. "He's ready to work, comes early, and has his routine down."

He would play small forward, power forward, with his back to the basket or out on the perimeter. No matter how much quicker or taller the opponent he was assigned to guard, he never whined about his role or complained about his shots.

"At Vegas, at Charlotte, and in New York, people always tell me I'm too unselfish," Johnson said. "Sometimes, I just can't help it."

"It's kind of overwhelming to me just how unselfish he's been," Allan Houston said. "I'd love to be able to say I've been an All-Star at this point in my career. He's been there, and he can say that."

Once, in his junior season at UNLV, Johnson felt responsible for a last-second loss against New Mexico. The following morning, he knocked on head coach Jerry Tarkanian's front door. He was in tears. "I said, 'Larry, what's the matter?' " Tarkanian said. "He was so upset by what had happened. He told me he felt he could do more. He wanted to score more, but he didn't want to come across as being selfish to his team-mates."

No matter the adjustment, Johnson made it. The top overall pick in the 1991 draft, a two-time All-Star with the Hornets and a member of the second Dream Team, he came into the NBA with great expectations. In no time, Converse had produced a catchy advertising campaign with Johnson playing the role of Grandmama. He dressed up as an old lady dunking the basket-ball, showing off his gold-tooth smile. With the Hornets rou-tinely making the playoffs, he lived a charmed NBA life those first few years.

Yet by the time he was traded to New York, Johnson had al-ready accrued some baggage—most notably a bad back that cheated him out of his explosiveness. He had also developed a reputation as a moody enigma.

If he wasn't grabbing his crotch during the World Champi-onships in Toronto, he was cursing reporters he viewed as divi-sive and meddling. Van Gundy had heard the stories about how difficult Johnson could be, but found out firsthand that he could be reformed in the proper environment.

Johnson had no problem deferring to Ewing, to Allan Hous-ton, and eventually to Sprewell. He also warmed quickly to Van Gundy, who reminded him of Tarkanian. Like Tarkanian, the Knicks coach stressed defense, loyalty, and the feeling that the outside world did not matter.

That included the media, with whom Johnson had a con-tentious relationship in his first season in New York. He was warned they would go after him, and he went on the offensive quickly.

An early-season debate in 1996 centered on whether the Knicks erred in trading Mason, who was coming into his prime, for a player who no longer resembled an All-Star. Scot-tie Pippen, who took immense pleasure in verbally tweaking the Knicks, came out in March of 1997 and said Mason was flat-out the better.

"He's garbage," Pippen said of Johnson. "He's been doing nothing but making money since he's been in the league."

Johnson replied, "He's a bum. His only move is, pass it to No. 23 [Jordan]."

He seemed to be winning friends everywhere. Ornery, non-communicative, and just rude, Johnson did not embrace the reporters covering the team until his second year. But by the third season, his extroverted side started showing more often.

He was the loudest man in the locker room, and if you could wait him out during his twenty-minute showers and the extra fifteen minutes it took for him to groom, Johnson was the most engaging interview among the Knicks. He would turn on his South Dallas charm, raising his baritone voice a few octaves and bellowing, "You're crazy, man."

The more you spent time around him, the more he grew on you. He was the consummate pro. If he wasn't stretching with the conditioning coach Greg Brittenham before the game, he was working on his low-post moves with assistant coach Tom Thibodeau.

There was also a sensitive side to Johnson, who did not deal with criticism or rejection well. When he was not invited to play in the Atlantic City charity game—as a member of Dream Team II, he thought he was a shoo-in—it hurt him that Ewing would not insist that his Knick teammate should be included. Johnson was snubbed by Ewing's agent, Falk, whom Johnson felt still harbored a grudge left over from Charlotte; Falk represented Alonzo Mourning, the player Johnson hated more than any other in the league. The feeling was mutual.

They were teammates in Charlotte, both franchise players whose relationship soured when Johnson signed an $84 million, twelve-year deal in 1993—the most exorbitant, outlandish deal of the time, and a harbinger of more inflated deals to come.

"You know, there was probably some ego there between me and him," Johnson said.

Mourning was said to be jealous of the contract, which eventually forced the Hornets to ship him to Miami. Two gargantuan egos and contracts were too big for a small-market town. Their rivalry was born out of a genuine hatred; they had no use for one another, which was rather refreshing given the current climate of NBA fraternization.

Since the Celtics and Lakers rivalry died in the late 1980s, and Detroit's Bad Boys grew old and crotchety, everyone in the league worshipped Michael Jordan's team and got along blissfully. They were all making money, hanging out together after games, and conceding championships.

There was no such love between Mourning and Johnson, who finally came to blows with 1.4 seconds left in Game 4 of the 1998 first-round playoffs. Something deeper than a physical box-out play led the former teammates to risk suspension.

"There were these two cats on the radio saying, 'We know there's a woman involved,' " Johnson recalled in a *New York Times* interview. "I don't know these dudes. And they're like, 'Well, we know this is over a woman.' At one point, I wanted to talk to Zo and say let's cut this stuff out; we're opening ourselves up to this crazy speculation. But you know, I don't have nothing to say to him. What I tell you today is, there was no woman involved."

When Johnson played with Charlotte, he and Charles Oakley nearly traded punches several times. Upon hearing he would be joining the Knicks, even Johnson's mother, Dortha, asked him, "Are you and Charles going to be able to get along?"

Oakley and Johnson eventually became good friends, both adhering to their own beliefs about how the NBA should work: *If you're on my team, we're cool. If not, I'm going to beat you down.*

But Johnson did not hold a grudge toward Ewing, one of Mourning's best friends. On the contrary, Johnson made it a point to keep the locker room as harmonious and unified as possible given the circumstances.

He could move freely between cliques, just as easily sharing a conversation with the religious Charlie Ward as he could with the rebellious Sprewell. His best friend on the team was David Wingate, Ewing's former college teammate at Georgetown who spent three seasons in Charlotte with Johnson and whose enthusiasm on the bench kept him on the roster.

The players all liked Johnson because he had a presence about him. Even in a galaxy of free-spending multimillionaires, he stood out as knowing what living large meant. He hired a full-time driver, who doubled as his personal assistant, when he came to New York. He spared no expense on his clothing and took pride in picking up the tab whenever he took his teammates out. Everywhere the Knicks went, it seemed, the drinks were on Larry.

He was going to enjoy every penny of his $84 million contract. When he visited his favorite Manhattan restaurants, the waiters would argue over who would get to serve Johnson. He was known to tip generously, from the parking attendant to the chef.

It was not just his personality, either. Though it went largely unspoken, players were in awe of Johnson's physique. He was listed at 6-foot-7-inches tall and 235 pounds, but really Johnson stands about 6-5. His body seemed chiseled from cobalt, a rock of a man who could have won a pose-off with Adonis. A tremendous athlete, he had boxed as a youth and was a highly recruited quarterback at Dallas's Skyline High School, the same school that produced Olympic gold medalist Michael Johnson.

Time and injury may have stolen much of his vertical leap, but Johnson reinvented his game. He relied on his quick post moves around the basket, pirouetting either way until he beat his man, and his ability to hit the 3-point shot made him at least two-dimensional. And no one seemed to take the losses harder than Johnson, who never had a problem pointing the finger at himself when things were going bad.

It was hard to reconcile that Johnson, the selfless teammate, with another Johnson. During the same week he traded blows with Mourning, he showed up in a *Sports Illustrated* article that focused on pro athletes and their trail of paternity suits. Johnson was prominently mentioned. According to the article, he was supporting five children by four women and he was involved in two paternity suits at the time.

"It hurt," Johnson said of the story. "But you know what? The majority of it, I did to myself."

Johnson grew up in the Dixon Circle housing projects in South Dallas. Though he did not drink or use drugs, young Larry became a regular at the police station. His mother would routinely pluck him out of the holding room and take her son away by the ear.

One day, as seventh grade came to a close, a white bus with chicken wire in its windows and a police emblem on the side pulled up in front of the projects.

"I'm thinking, I'm gone, going to jail for good," Johnson said in the *Times* story. "The bus comes, picks me up, and there are about forty of us on there. I'm boo-hooing. Just know I'm gone. But thirty minutes later, I realized my mom had enrolled me in this program with the Police Athletic League."

The bus dropped the children off at a gym, where Johnson learned to box and discovered basketball. He became a folk hero for once dunking the ball and ripping a rim off a playground backboard.

Dortha Johnson's son had found a way out of Dixon Circle.

"She was getting on me pretty good," Johnson said of his mother's words regarding the paternity suits. "But I'm like, wait, you've raised children, and I've never seen a man around the house."

Having never met his father, Johnson had no male role model growing up at home. By the beginning of the '99 season, he was approaching thirty years old. A child of the projects, he still had no road map for his journey through the mainstream world of the NBA.

If Johnson was the unquestioned leader, Chris Childs was the Knicks' resident wise guy. On the court, he was the well-known architect of many doomed fast breaks, his no-look turnovers sending Knick fans straight into therapy.

A trash-talking, self-proclaimed tough guy, Childs was also one of the more remarkable stories in New York sports.

He nearly drank himself out of basketball seven years ago. He admitted to once binging on a case of beer and a bottle of

Jack Daniel's in one night. But he went into recovery while playing in the Continental Basketball Association and began to routinely attend Alcoholics Anonymous meetings on the road and at home.

He put his game back together, too.

From playing for a pittance in Quad Cities, Childs began backing up Kenny Anderson in New Jersey for a pro-rated salary of $60,000 in 1994. He parlayed that into a six-year, $24 million contract in New York.

Grunfeld saw him as the answer to the team's point guard woes in 1996. But the worse Childs performed over his first season, the more his contract became an albatross. By his second season, he accepted a backup role and flourished coming off the bench with a more up-tempo unit.

He was not afraid to take a big shot at the end of a tight game, but his habitual inability to make good decisions infuriated Van Gundy and some of his teammates. He was a spot-up shooter more than a playmaker who could beat his man off the dribble and create easy shots for his teammates. He would often end up underneath the basket with nowhere to go and surrounded by defenders.

Adding to the difficulties was the fact that Childs sometimes could not make up his mind when to pass or shoot, which is only the most fundamental decision for a point guard. Still, beyond clutch shots, he had his strengths.

Childs established himself as one of the top defensive point guards in the league, which earned him minutes despite his offensive transgressions. He was a little tough guy with a quick temper. He constantly nagged the officials. Childs never believed he committed a foul and he never backed down from anyone on the court.

In a game against the Bulls in December of 1997, Jordan grew agitated at Childs's aggressive defense. He spun around and struck Childs with an elbow to the side of the head. Childs retaliated by firing the ball at Jordan. Childs, who had been whistled for a technical after a heated exchange with Randy Brown earlier in the game, was ejected.

"I play physical, and if he is offended by that, it's his problem," Childs said. "I got hit. I don't care who he is, it's not part of the game. When you get elbows to the head, you cannot let it go. I have to defend myself."

Depending on his mood, Childs could take a tough question and either be combative or give you the best quote of the night. His humor was brutal and merciless. Cracking on teammates, reporters, ball boys, Childs spared no corner of your personal life. If he found a weakness, he kept needling away like a sixth-grade bully. Starks was his favorite target.

"Last time I went out to eat with John, this knucklehead kept sending his lobster back," Childs said. "He told the waiter, 'It's not cooked enough. I want to eat it off the bone.' "

He once commented on a poorly dressed reporter's outfit by saying, "Yo, you get a bowl of soup with that shirt?"

Childs was a long shot to begin with, an obscure college star at Boise State who overcame his demons to play in the NBA. He was going to make up for lost time.

"I've been carrying a big chip on my shoulder ever since I was in the CBA," he said. "It has to do with being there for five years and not having been drafted by the NBA. Maybe that's just the way I am."

Charlie Ward was the polar opposite of Childs. The two point guards' only common denominator was that they were among the most maligned floor leaders to ever play in New York.

Sprewell was the Pied Piper of the Gen-X faction; Ward led the Christian soldiers onward. Since accepting Christ as his personal savior before he came to the team, Ward has been the Knicks' religious conscience. He would encourage players to attend pregame chapel, organize Bible study classes in his hotel room on the road, and wonder why the coach and some of his teammates felt the need to swear up a storm every time they got angry about something.

He had won a Heisman Trophy at Florida State in 1993, guiding the Seminoles to college football's national title. But his star never gleamed that brightly again, and as he kept being called the Best Quarterback in New York, his distaste for the secular media gained steam.

He mentioned "God" or "Jesus Christ" in most interviews, whether the question was about a particular play or the mood of the team. In his own quiet way, he would challenge the merits of a journalist's question, even something as innocuous as, "You guys think you're a better team when you run?" To Ward, that meant controversy was around the corner. The person in front of him was obviously trying to divide the team and not simply desperate for any semblance of an off-day story.

Ward was soft-spoken and sometimes barely audible, but he was a powerful influence in the locker room. He converted Starks, and it was not too long before Houston was wearing a cloth bracelet around his wrist given to him by Ward and bearing the letters "W.W.J.D.," which stood for What Would Jesus Do? The bracelet soon began cropping up all over the league. Houston and Chris Dudley, a veteran whose career was based on the fact that he played heavenly defense and hellish offense, had the best attendance at Bible study. Many of the Knicks attended the pregame chapel, and it wasn't beyond Ward to go into the visiting locker room and drag a few sinning souls out.

Oakley once joked that Ward "had a little Waco in him" in reference to the cult leader David Koresh, but he and every other former and current Knick truly respected Ward for his beliefs. The reason was simple: With so many poseurs and frauds running around the league, Ward did not just talk about clean and spiritual living, he lived that way. He went so far as to counsel married teammates against being seen with other women on the road, no matter if those teammates were having a platonic lunch with a female companion. He handed out prayer leaflets to teammates and the media, and gave Van Gundy tailor-made scripture verses for his game preparation.

Ward was a ferocious competitor. His football background was obvious. Flying around like a roving linebacker, he could take a hit and give one. He often went down in a heap under the basket, only to get up quickly and walk down the floor. Ward sometimes played like an annoying gnat.

P.J. Brown, Glen Rice, and Kevin Willis all had accused Ward of dirty play over the past three years. In February of 1997, Rice accused Ward of punching him in the stomach as he went to shoot a jump shot. Ward gained national infamy for his all-out style later that season, when he was boxing out the 6-foot-10 Brown in Game 5 of the conference semifinals against Miami.

Brown felt Ward got too low and leaned into his left knee at the free throw line. He flipped Ward into a row of photographers, setting off a bench-clearing melee that led to multiple suspensions for the Knicks. "Charlie isn't the choir boy everybody thinks he is," Brown said. "They don't do that in church."

The fallout from the incident tarnished his career. "I don't go out there and try to play dirty against anyone," Rice said after his run-in with Ward. "I won't forget that."

On February 16, during Oakley's return game at the Garden, Willis was ejected for throwing an elbow in Ward's face after he felt Ward was trying to take out his knees.

"I don't like a guy that goes at my knees like that, especially from the side," said the 7-foot Willis. "You hit a guy like that from that position, you can seriously damage a player, especially a guy my height."

Ward wasn't thrilled that his peers labeled him a cheap-shot artist, but he took it in stride. "John Stockton gets the same type of treatment, so I'm very honored to be part of that company," he said. "We just play the game and play it hard and people try to say that we're dirty. You can check the tape out. I was just doing my job. I didn't do anything—once again."

Chris Dudley was the butt of more NBA jokes than he cared to remember. Most of them reflected his status as the worst free throw shooter in league history, 46 percent for his career. The 6-foot-11, thirty-three-year-old backup center once missed 124 of an attempted 182 foul shots during a single season. A brick mason of great renown, his thirteen seasons in the league were the result of his desire and his defense rather than anything skill-related.

He was the only white player on the team, though his color was never an issue. He often attended Bible study with Ward, Williams, and Allan Houston, and blended in as well as anyone with a vastly different background from some of his teammates could.

Dudley's grandfather, Guilford Dudley, served as ambassador to Denmark under Presidents Richard Nixon and Gerald Ford. Chris was a Yale graduate who debated economics with Dave Checketts during the labor standoff, and infuriated the league's lawyers by winning two arbitration cases in which he was able to retain free agent rights while moving to another team in the 1990s.

He was acquired prior to the 1997–98 season as insurance for Ewing. Dudley was a banger who could mix it up with anyone. On the surface, he came from a well-to-do home and had advantages many of his teammates did not while growing up. But Dudley overcame his own obstacles to play in the NBA.

Sometimes in the middle of games—and always during halftime—Dudley opened a small black box about the size of a sewing kit. He would pull out a small needle, prick his finger, and transfer the blood to a test strip, which is placed on a blood sugar level reader inside the kit. If the reading is normal, he can go back in the game. That crucial adjustment was the difference between the Knicks' veteran center coping with diabetes and controlling the disease completely.

"You have to know your own body, you have to be your own doctor," said Dudley, who found out he was diabetic when he was sixteen years old. "The biggest difference from other diseases is that it's twenty-four seven. You can't take a break. You always have it. It's not like you can work out hard for a week and then take a week off. You have to deal with diabetes constantly."

Beyond testing his blood sugar, he administered four insulin injections a day into his right or left thigh—one before each meal and another before he goes to sleep.

"It's kind of scary to be told you're diabetic," he said. "The thing that helped me was that my uncle has it, so I knew something of it and knew it could be dealt with. The first question I asked was, 'Will I still be able to play basketball?'

"They said, 'Yes, but you have to take care of yourself.' "

For the past eighteen years, that has been his mantra. It also inspired him to help other children living with diabetes.

Since 1995, sixty-four children have trekked to Vernonia, Oregon, a hamlet thirty miles northwest of Portland, where Dudley used to play. They not only learn to dribble, shoot, and rebound better, but they also learn to live with diabetes—just as Dudley had to as a teenager.

The fraternity of athletes living with diabetes is infinitesimal; Dudley is the only player in the NBA known to have the disease. Dudley has type 1 diabetes, which is usually hereditary and characterized by its juvenile onset. It is more severe than type 2 diabetes.

It begins when the pancreas no longer produces insulin, the chemical that breaks down sugars. Once a person is diagnosed, a constant balancing act takes place between the insulin and the food you take in.

Dudley's discipline has helped him avoid any dangerous episodes during his career. He remembers feeling dazed his rookie year in Cleveland, and the trainer having to run and find him some juice to raise his blood sugar level. But that was an isolated incident.

"There's just times when you know you have it," he said. "You just have a reaction. You might start having a cold sweat. You're kind of out of it. Dazed. I don't know how else to describe it. You're not all there.

"I'm just fortunate I was able to control it and play this long in the league."

Amid the noise and commotion surrounding him each night in the Garden, Allan Houston's voice was a calming influence. Just as Houston blended seamlessly

into the background on the court, he did the same in the locker
room.

Whether it was his easygoing demeanor, his smooth approach to the game, or his handsome profile—perhaps all of
the above—Houston became a PR project at the Garden. The
organization wanted his face everywhere.

He showed up in NBA community-service commercials,
cleaning up a Harlem neighborhood with schoolchildren.
Houston and his beautiful wife, Tami, were photographed for
the *Sports Illustrated* swimsuit issue in 1999. Though Houston
was slowly emerging as one of the league's top shooting guards,
he was curiously picked ahead of several more prominent players to represent the United States in international competition
the summer of 1998. The fact that he played in the nation's
largest media market may have had something to do with this.

With Ewing nearing retirement, the Knicks simply needed a
wholesome new star—even if that star was not yet ready to
glow.

Not that Houston did not deserve the accolades or the attention. He was not only one of the most genuine people in the organization; Houston was one of the best people in professional
sports. As he became more newsworthy, Houston was even
more accommodating with fans and the media. He would ask
you about your new baby or what you thought about a certain
movie—and mean it. He made you root for him. Maybe his was
not the most controversial voice or even the most candid in the
locker room. But he had this rambunctious, kidlike quality to
him that always kept you off-guard—"a little Eddie Haskell in
him" was how his former coach in Detroit, Doug Collins, described his personality.

Mature and self-assured at age twenty-eight, he was one of
the few young players in the league to successfully balance his
celebrity with the pressures of marriage.

Born and raised in Louisville, Houston, like Jeff Van Gundy,
grew up the son of a coach. Houston actually verbally committed to play for Denny Crum at the University of Louisville,
where his father, Wade, was an assistant coach. But when

Wade Houston was given the head coaching job at Tennessee, Allan decided to play for his father.

Wade coached at Tennessee from 1988 to 1993, compiling a 65-90 record over five seasons. Going into his senior season for the Volunteers, Allan was under the impression that his father would keep his job. But once Allan graduated, Wade was fired. He felt betrayed by the school, as if they had used his father and him.

He learned then that sports and business don't always mix, a lesson that he would remember when he left Detroit to sign with the Knicks several years later. To this day, Houston refuses to wear Tennessee hats or shirts and barely acknowledges he went to the school.

"If it wasn't for my father, I would've played at Louisville," Houston said. "I had a lot of great memories at Tennessee. And I earned my degree there. But my father deserved better."

Disenchanted with the profession, Wade eventually found another line of work. Today, he and his wife, Alice, own and operate the Dallas & Mavis Trucking Company in Louisville, the nation's largest minority-owned trucking and supply company.

Allan didn't do badly after college either. In 1996, he signed a $56 million, seven-year deal with New York—a contract that financially changed his life. Soon after, he bought a palatial home in chi-chi Greenwich, Connecticut, down the block from designer Tommy Hilfiger, Mariah Carey, and talk show host Montel Williams.

The Houstons have a full-size indoor pool and a television room the size of a local multiplex. But the money hasn't changed him; while giving a visitor a tour in 1998, Houston showed he had not lost his grounded side.

Getting down on his hands and knees, he began trying to remove an accident made by his new puppy, the one yet to be paper-trained. "I can't let my wife know about this," he said.

Suddenly, Tami entered the room, smelled something funny, and gave her husband a stern look.

"Allan," Tami said, "the dog went to the bathroom on the rug, didn't she?"

The deflating Chicago loss was still fresh in Van Gundy's mind when he arrived at Purchase on Saturday at 8:00 A.M. Normally, after playing two straight games, the players are given the next day off. But when they arrived at Westchester County Airport in the wee hours of Saturday morning, Van Gundy was ready to make alterations to his slumping team.

It was not only about how bad the Knicks were playing. He was angry about the mood on the team plane afterward. He saw signs of indifference, saw some players who were not crushed by their dreadful performance. Grieving over one of fifty games was not mandatory, but there was an unspoken grace period in which players were expected to at least pretend losing mattered.

To drive the point home, Van Gundy called a practice for Saturday night, much to the dismay of the Knicks who had planned to attend the Lennox Lewis–Evander Holyfield fight that night at Madison Square Garden. They would have to rush from practice just to make the main event.

Dennis Scott, however, had plenty of time to watch the preliminaries. His Knick days were done, and he would have to find his fifth team in three years.

Scott was a nonfactor against the Bulls, his first sniff of the court in five games. Winded and flabby, he had become all that Van Gundy despised about the game. Maybe the coach could tolerate his physical condition and his silliness if Scott produced, but that wasn't happening; in 15 games, Scott was shooting 30 percent and had made only eight-of-29 3-pointers. When his jumper wasn't falling, he was even less funny.

Van Gundy needed to do something after the debacle against the Bulls, and so he took it upon himself to release Scott. It was yet another slap in the face to Grunfeld, who had signed Scott to a guaranteed one-year deal worth $750,000 and who felt his authority was being usurped daily by his coach.

In an edgy phone conversation between the two over Scott's release, Grunfeld voiced his displeasure about Van Gundy making the move without Grunfeld's approval. Grunfeld then addressed Camby's role, an issue that clearly divided the coach and team president.

The fed-up Grunfeld felt Van Gundy was on a one-man quest to undermine him. If Grunfeld needed ammunition to fire the coach, the loss to the Bulls gave him a surplus. Late that afternoon, Grunfeld spoke to Checketts and strongly expressed his dissatisfaction with Van Gundy.

Grunfeld made it clear that his complaints were not just about Camby, that he wondered if the players were not responding to the coach. Checketts was as upset with the team's performance as anyone, but he wanted to step back and evaluate the situation. After all, Sprewell and Ewing had only played together in 15 of the team's first 21 games because of injuries.

And though he never let it be known, Checketts also wondered if Grunfeld was venting out of anger instead of thinking clearly. Checketts knew Van Gundy still had the support of the majority of players, including four fifths of the starting lineup (Ewing, Johnson, Houston, and Ward). But Checketts wanted to see for himself. Before practice began that Saturday night, Van Gundy had a surprise visit from Checketts. This was not a good sign for the coach.

Checketts would preside over one of the biggest nights of his career hours later, hosting the first major heavyweight title fight at Madison Square Garden since Muhammad Ali–Joe Frazier I. What was he doing here on a Saturday night? Trying to take the pulse of the team before deciding to fire the coach? To see firsthand whether Van Gundy had really lost control?

The two men spoke briefly that night. If Checketts had indeed harbored thoughts of dismissing Van Gundy, he came away from their meeting unconvinced that any coaching change was immediately necessary. Still, if the Knicks were embarrassed by the Charlotte Hornets on Sunday night at home, that might force Checketts's hand.

This did not prove to be a good weekend at the world's most famous arena.

A scoring fiasco robbed Lewis of a clear-cut decision over Holyfield, and left thousands of fight fans feeling duped. Checketts found himself taking the heat for shaking hands and doing business with Don King.

By Sunday afternoon, Van Gundy began to fully understand the ramifications of his time spent with Checketts. Sitting at home in Chappaqua, New York, and watching the new Net Marbury scoring at will against the Miami Heat, Van Gundy heard his name mentioned during an NBA halftime report on NBC. Analyst Peter Vecsey claimed that the Knicks coach was in jeopardy of being fired if the team lost to the Hornets that night at the Garden.

Van Gundy went numb.

"Anything is possible in this town," Van Gundy told a confidant within minutes of hearing the report. "Maybe they're going to make a change and name Don Chaney [the former Pistons coach and loyal Knicks assistant] coach."

After dodging a barrage of near-firings over the past three years, he felt the end was truly near this time. His voice cracking and almost near tears, he said, "It hurts because I feel I work hard, I do a good job, and it's not appreciated."

Checketts and Grunfeld were vehemently denying the report. Grunfeld called it "ridiculous."

"I have no idea where it came from," he said.

Van Gundy knew better, and felt there had to be some shred of truth behind the report. "Until they fire you, they're never going to say, 'You know what, we're thinking about firing your ass,' " Van Gundy said. "Hey, if we play like we did in Chicago, someone is going to pay."

That night, with speculation swirling about the coach's future, the Knicks handled the Hornets, winning 94–86. If the report was correct, the win granted Van Gundy a stay of execu-

tion. Johnson and Houston, two of Van Gundy's most ardent
supporters, combined for 39 points and one great intangible: a
major vote of confidence. As the buzzer sounded and the
Knicks walked off the court, Ewing, sidelined with his Achilles
injury, massaged Van Gundy's shoulders. The coach's players
then stroked his ego.

"I'm a Jeff Van Gundy fan," Johnson said. "We're the most
prepared team in the league. Why would you get rid of him?"

"I'm not going to comment on the report, but I'll comment
on the concept," said Houston. "I have a valid answer, being a
coach's son. I don't think there's ever been a more prepared
coach than Jeff. I don't know what else he can do. We have to
look at ourselves in the mirror as players and compete."

Ewing: "If they get rid of Jeff, they can get rid of me."

Sprewell, of all people, seemed the most affected by the
rumor. He blamed himself for the Knicks' slow start. "I think
it's all on me," he said. "For whatever reason, I'm not playing
the way I like to. I think the coach has done an excellent job."

Any notion that Van Gundy had lost his players was
squashed that night. Checketts was on the side of his coach,
and the mistrust between Grunfeld and Van Gundy had
reached a new plateau.

They could never work together again. In the most unin-
tended of ways, the report, which Van Gundy believed origi-
nated from Grunfeld, had actually helped Van Gundy solidify
his position for the moment. The coach essentially reclaimed
the locker room, with the help of the man who wanted him out
of it.

Twenty-one games into the year, and the season's first crisis
had come and gone. There were still 29 games remaining,
which in New York means there were 29 potential calamities
ahead.

6

HOW THE WEST WAS LOST

The Van Gundy Watch was over for now, but after beating Charlotte, the Knicks still fluctuated: some nights decent, some nights dreadful. They did win three of their next four games, beating the Bucks, Clippers, and Celtics, losing to Orlando.

Sprewell averaged 28.6 points in those three wins. He was starting to get his legs under him and was beating everyone down the court on the break. He threw down a monstrous two-handed, tomahawk dunk against Boston, right over the top of the Celtics' defense. The irony of his situation was that while making the Knicks a better team for a change, he was playing himself right out of the starting lineup.

"I don't know if Jeff is going to keep him there or not," Larry Johnson said. "But it's definitely working out well for us, having that spark coming off the bench."

The Knicks' spirits were further lifted when Ewing returned sooner than expected on March 20 for that Celtics matinee game.

If Van Gundy was concerned about the long-term prospects of his team that day, all he had to do was look down at the other bench where his first real mentor, Rick Pitino, was presiding over an awful and disjointed Boston team. Antoine Walker, the team's star player, and point guard Kenny Anderson were feuding, and Walker was getting routinely booed at the FleetCenter in Boston. And the team president could not even threaten to fire the head coach, because they were one and the same. Pitino was responsible for and stuck with this sorry squad.

Ewing looked rusty against Boston, but he still managed 11 points and 11 rebounds in New York's 18-point win. Sprewell was awesome, scoring 18 of his 27 points during a wild second-quarter explosion.

"I just try to do the things I've always done," he said. "Attack the basket, get to the free throw line, defend, and play with heart and energy."

All these qualities befit a starter, which Sprewell was not. Van Gundy could have elected to start Sprewell in the second half, but the head coach held to his normal philosophy that the starting five always began the third quarter. After that second-quarter binge, Sprewell had to wait seven minutes into the third quarter before he returned.

"That's the most difficult part," Sprewell said. "When you're warming up before a game, and at halftime, you try to get loose. Then you have to sit and wait and you get stiff. You're just kind of anxious to get out there, to see if you still got it."

Before the Celtics game, Van Gundy addressed the fact that Sprewell was not happy about playing with the second unit. He told reporters that he wished Sprewell would be more accepting of the role.

"I wouldn't say I'm totally happy with it, but I'm not going to start crying about it," Sprewell said. "It's his decision."

Reporters tried to lighten the mood by informing Sprewell that the NBA gives out awards for the top sixth man—an honor previously bestowed upon former Knicks John Starks and Anthony Mason. "I'm not big on awards," he said. "I've never been that way." Still, he was making the coach's decision not to start him look almost prescient.

But Sprewell bombed the next day in Toronto, making just three of 11 shots as the Raptors won in overtime 85–81. It was an all-around abysmal game for the Knicks, who were making their debut in the Air Canada Centre. They committed 22 turnovers and threw away a seven-point lead in the final minutes. Oakley had a lackluster offensive game, but he hit a huge jumper with 52 seconds left to seal the win.

"A veteran team would have found a way to pull it out," he said.

Camby's first game in Toronto since the trade was an embarrassing bust, too: When he entered for the first time, the sound of a baby crying blared over the public address system. He finished with six points and four rebounds.

The Raptors were also taking shots at Sprewell, flashing the word "Choke!" on the scoreboard while Sprewell missed two crucial free throws in overtime. Showing his maturity, Camby, who fouled out in 24 minutes, shrugged his shoulders and said of his former fans, "They're just coming into their own, so you'll just have to excuse them."

The Toronto debacle had a bad effect the following night at home against the Hawks, the Knicks' third game in as many days. Ewing appeared sharp, outscoring Atlanta center Dikembe Mutombo 23 to eight, but Houston and Sprewell combined to shoot 8-for-25. The Knicks managed to score just 15 points in both the second and fourth quarters and were booed in the final seconds of Atlanta's 80–71 victory.

Suddenly, the Knicks were reverting to their old ways. They headed out to the West Coast 15-12 and no one seemed to care if they ever came back.

Five years earlier, Pat Riley had used a Western Conference swing in March to rejuvenate the Knicks. Surprising everyone, he rerouted the team's charter to Reno, Nevada, for a night of camaraderie at the craps and blackjack tables. The Knicks proceeded to win their next fifteen games—the second-longest winning streak in franchise history—en route to their first Finals appearance in twenty-one years.

"If I thought gambling was a way to fifteen straight wins, we'd be in Tahoe right now," Van Gundy said.

Reeling and running out of time, the Knicks were heading to Sacramento to begin a three-game trip out West. They were also about to get their first taste of White Chocolate. In two short months, Jason Williams had become as well known on ESPN as longtime anchors Chris Berman and Dan Patrick.

The Web site for the sports network had dedicated a page to the Kings' scintillating rookie point guard. When it was learned that Williams, who is white, and his family were not enthralled with the nickname "White Chocolate," ESPN held a contest to come up with a new moniker for Williams. The winner? The Thrilla in Vanilla.

The kid from Belle, West Virginia, was causing a commotion all over the NBA. Shoulder-faking, stutter-stepping, going behind his back in midair, Williams was dubbed the second coming of Pete Maravich. He created his own little two-on-one break against perception, especially the long-held belief that all little white guys could do well was throw two-handed chest passes and drain 3-pointers.

With America's obsession over race, Williams opened the doors for a debate: If a white player had what was perceived to be a black game, were the lines blurring? "That's almost like the black community saying, 'Oh, that white boy Larry Bird sure can play,'" Buck Williams, the former Knick, said of the nickname. "It means you're legitimate. You're not on the roster merely because of your complexion. 'White Chocolate' is just a stamp of approval, that's all."

Yet as the hype grew, you wondered how much attention from the news media and fans Jason Williams would have received if he were black.

"I think I would if I came out and did the same thing I'm doing, but maybe not," said Williams through a thick West Virginia drawl. "Who knows? I'm not going to lie: I think me being white helps me out a little bit. In my eyes, there's not too many white people that play the game like me."

Young black kids thought he was the coolest white player they had ever seen, and viewed the label "White Chocolate" as Williams's ascendence into hip-hop culture. Over and over, clips of Williams using a cross-over dribble and hesitation move to get by a stunned Gary Payton of the Seattle SuperSonics, the best defensive player in the league, were repeated on late-night highlight shows.

"Jason deserves the attention because he's one of the best ballplayers out there, regardless of color," said Chris Webber, Williams's teammate. "But when Allen [Iverson] did it his rookie year, he was viewed as a thug," Webber said, referring to the Philadelphia 76ers guard who was the NBA's leading scorer and most breathtaking player. "That's all I'll say. It's just society. I don't understand it."

Vernon Maxwell, the Kings' reserve guard, said, "I hate to say it, but he's a little white guy and that helps. They ain't seen that for a long time in the NBA. Everywhere we go on the road, you hear, 'White Chocolate! White Chocolate!' They ain't used to seeing a white guy play like that. That's what he brings to the table and he's reaping the benefits."

The public forum was indeed open. Did the nickname reinforce the stereotypes about black athleticism, or did it do away with the opposite one about white players only having the tools to play fundamental, "smart" basketball? Was the commotion over Williams and his nickname a complete capitulation to racial stereotypes and a further sign of division? Or was it a step toward putting those preconceptions aside?

The current exemplar of the black game, born on the playgrounds, was Iverson; his cross-over dribble, darting moves to the basket, and open-court scoring forays were all about creativity and improvisation. That was perceived to be God-given talent and on-the-spot invention.

The ultimate white game, which seemed to come out of a John Wooden handbook, belonged to John Stockton. Running the classic pick-and-roll with Karl Malone and directing the Utah offense cerebrally, Stockton had surely been tutored well and worked long and hard to overcome his physical limitations.

In truth, they were both gifted athletes who had maximized their talents through years of practice and perseverance, playing as much as they could and learning from their coaches and peers. Iverson could be a thinking man's player; Stockton often relied on instinct. No matter how much one was perceived as the Gen-X poster child and the other the old-school veteran, their games could not simply be defined as black or white.

"Don't matter if you're from Kuwait or South America, it's all the same," Bird once said when asked to compare styles. "It's just that the city guys play an up-tempo, wilder game. And if you're from the country, you play the way the coach tells you to play."

The writer Terry Pluto once noted that former Cavaliers guard Craig Ehlo helped sever the connection between "white" and "fundamentally sound." If that was true, Williams was flat-out cutting the cord with his showtime brand of ball.

"Race doesn't mandate your game," Commissioner Stern said. "I think it's ridiculous. There's a fair amount of racial stereotyping going on all over. You hear people describe rookies and college players, and they're always invariably likened to a person of the same race. Vince Carter has to be the next Michael Jordan. [Keith Van Horn was similarly hailed as the next Larry Bird; so was Danny Ferry.]

"Very few people, white or black, tend to permit themselves to cross over. They should cross over. They'd be more relaxed about it, and they'd be able to relax and enjoy our game more instead of being constrained by race. I just laugh. Basketball is basketball. And I think one of the best things about sports is that it does shatter stereotypes."

Stern grew tired of addressing issues of race, believing the league had moved beyond the issue long ago. After all, the NBA had recovered from its drug-tainted image of the '70s with a savvy marketing strategy that made pop-culture superstars out of its predominantly black players.

But as the specter of a lost season loomed large in December of 1998, both sides in the negotiations—the 100 percent white ownership, and the players union that is 85 percent black—believed that the combustible question of race had something to do with the impasse.

Players, including several on the union's negotiating com-

mittee, had found the league's bargaining style to be disrespectful and provocative, and they suspected that this stemmed in
part from a belief that a predominantly black union somehow
did not have to be taken completely seriously.

At the same time, members of ownership's negotiating team,
as well as several agents, acknowledged that the perception
that the negotiations were racially tinged served to solidify the
players' ranks. "We don't deny the possibility that the union
had the ability to use race as a rallying point," said one member
of the owners' negotiating team, who spoke on the condition of
anonymity. "There may be code words used to rally its members, code words that have racial connotations."

Many players believed the owners and league officials like
Stern had all too willingly allowed them to be publicly portrayed as greedy materialists interested only in their multiple
car payments, or as too unintelligent to appreciate the financial
stakes involved.

"The league cast us as dumb and stupid and uninformed,
but they'll be waiting for us to get out there and pitch comput-
ers for IBM," said Karl Malone. "In the end, you've degraded
me, called me unintelligent, but you're going to want to sell me
to the public after this. You're going to want to make money off
of me. You don't treat people that way."

In an interview with *Newsweek* magazine, Alonzo Mourning, the Miami Heat center and a member of the union's negotiating committee, said, "I think there is a perception from the
owners to even some fans that we're blacks who should be
happy with what we got, fair or not. There's a lack of respect
given us in large part because we're athletes. I'm not saying it's
all about race, because it's not. But it plays a factor."

The dispute was indeed over money. But as the vitriol was
hurled back and forth, it also became about power and respect.

"There is a sense among some of the players that race was a
subtext," said Buck Williams, the former union president. "I say
that because there are some in the American public who have
difficulty with African-Americans—some of whom don't have
college degrees—commanding the salaries that they do in the

league. I think some players may look upon that perception when dealing with the owners. In the end, it's sheer business. But I think, just like in society, race is a subtext. I don't think the NBA is excluded from that."

As for the Jason Williams story, the attention surrounding the Sacramento rookie struck most people as a positive note about race and the league rather than anything negative. Yet at its root was an acknowledgment that the basketball court is one of the few areas of American life where to be white is to be assumed to be inferior. And if that kind of racial categorizing is unfair here, then it's as unfair in other aspects of life, too.

Martin McNeal, the Kings' beat writer for the *Sacramento Bee,* who is African-American, wrote in a column the week before the NBA draft, "The only thing white about Williams is his complexion."

It was bold and provocative, but it also made you wonder if a white political reporter wrote, "The only thing black about General Colin Powell is his complexion," what kind of furor would ensue.

"If there was a stereotype to be placed, you'd say he acts black, you'd say his game is black," McNeal said. "That's only because of this ridiculous society we live in. I was having a conversation with another reporter who didn't like the name White Chocolate. I don't even think of the fact that it's about him being white. I think of the fact that his game is so sweet. I don't even think about the fact that he is white when I hear that name."

And if people were indeed embracing Williams now because of his skin color, how much did race play a part in the vilification of Sprewell after he choked Carlesimo? The Knicks were not alone in asking themselves that question, especially in light of a football incident that fall. Kevin Greene, the volatile linebacker with the Carolina Panthers, was caught on camera lunging at an assistant coach on the sidelines during a heated argument.

"I would like to choke my coach and just get a day off," Charles Barkley said of Greene's one-game suspension for his actions.

Among those willing to put aside the racial questions surrounding Williams was Kobe Bryant, the Lakers' wunderkind
guard: "My friends back home in Philadelphia have accepted
him. For all they know, he's a brother. They respect him for the
fact that he has the confidence to pull off those moves, not to be
intimidated. He's got an old-school playground game, like Earl
the Pearl or Nate Archibald. You don't see moves like that from
anybody, period. White, black, Croatian, or whatever."

Responding to a similar question about the Nets' Keith Van
Horn appealing to a cross-over audience recently, Stern said,
"It's silly. We worked too hard on this. I think that whether the
player is white or black, there's a certain level of game you have
to have. What do they call Mark Jackson?" he said, referring to
the slow-footed Indiana point guard, who is black. "What kind
of game does he play? Should we start looking for someone
playing like that? If a big, black guy plays slow, is he playing a
white man's game?"

Van Horn and his Nets teammate Jayson Williams (no rela-
tion to Jason) acted in a skit on *The Chris Rock Show* during
the lockout. After it was finished, Rock, the comedian and loyal
Knick fan, struck up a conversation with the two players.

"You know, Larry Bird had game and all, and Tom
Gugliotta's got game," Rock said. "But I think Keith is the only
white person where black people actually *want* his game.
Brothers want his game. Brothers don't usually want white
people's game. He's the only white man in America where
brothers want his game."

Now people wanted the Sacramento point guard's game.
Magic Johnson said he was impressed by Williams's flair and
fearlessness. "You probably have more blacks talking about
Jason than whites talk about him," Johnson said. "That's amazing. The NBA players talk about him. He has captured the
imagination of a lot of the black people. Pistol Pete did it. Larry
Bird. And now Jason Williams. Forget that color stuff. They can
play basketball. They've got flavor."

Jon Barry, a teammate of Williams's, is the son of Rick Barry,
the white superstar who led the Warriors to a championship in

1975 and attracted similar attention out West. "Maybe there are situations out there where they say, 'Hey, we need a white guy at the end of the bench.' Maybe that's happened, I don't know," Jon said. "You wish you could stop talking about it being an issue, but there are so few white players in this league that are marquee guys. Who's a marquee guy? John Stockton. But he's not really marketable. There's not a marketable white player in the top fifteen players in the league. I guess when they see a guy come along like this, he's so embraced because there are so few."

Suiting up on the night of March 24 to face Sacramento, the Knicks weren't buying into the White Chocolate phenomenon. For all his highlight-reel flair, they pointed out, Williams's game right now had a lot more style than substance. Chris Childs said the media had fallen in love with Williams solely because he was throwing behind-the-back passes. Williams, Childs and his teammates pointed out, was shooting only 38 percent from the field and he was often taking ill-advised jumpers at important junctures of games.

"Once you guys see those behind-the-back passes, you all go crazy," he said. "Black players do it all the time." Flashy play was fun, he was saying, but what matters is how your game contributes to winning. Sometimes it was easier to see your coach's point when you applied it to the other guy's team.

The game in Sacramento marked Sprewell's long-awaited return to Northern California. The lockout-shortened season had eliminated the usual trip to Golden State, so the ARCO Arena would have to do for at least a year.

He heard every imaginable taunt up to that point, from "Choke, Spree!" to "You should be in jail." But this crowd was different. Nastier. More personal. A middle-aged white man began screaming, *"Who's your daddy, Spree? Who's your daddy!"* from his seat a few rows behind the Knicks' bench. From the opening tip, they treated him like a convicted felon. When Sprewell's shot was rejected by Lawrence Funderburke in the second half, the deranged fan finally crawled beneath his thick skin.

During a timeout, Sprewell glared menacingly, the kind of look he may have more than once given Carlesimo. Just when he thought he was about to be accepted back into society, there was always another road game.

But they weren't going to get to him. Sprewell understood he would be pelted with every insult the fans could dream up. It began the first game of the season in Orlando, and the abuse followed him from city to city, everywhere but in the safe confines of the Garden—where Sprewell was accepted immediately by fans craving his dunks and all the things he could do that other Knicks could not.

But while he was being celebrated in New York, the rest of the league wasn't ready to forgive the reformed player. Sprewell had the perfect response for his vocal detractors: silence. No words, gestures, or, until that night in Sacramento, menacing glares. He knew he had to be on his best behavior. His every move was being scrutinized. Any slipup—a shouting match or, dare we say, a physical altercation, would confirm everyone's worst feelings about him. He would have to start all over again.

"I've heard it all before," Sprewell said of the abuse. "But it doesn't bother me. In fact, it gets me pumped up. It makes me want to go out and play even harder."

For different reasons, Sprewell and Williams were both being surrounded by notebooks and cameras on the night of March 24. Meanwhile, Sacramento center Vlade Divac was sitting quietly on his locker stool. Lost in the discussion over the merits of Williams's game and its racial implications, or even Sprewell's return to the West Coast, was a far more gripping drama, one with vastly more serious consequences than anything the NBA can offer.

Divac, the Serbian center, was watching on CNN his country being torn apart by war. That morning, NATO troops began bombing his homeland. His family was miles away from the fighting, but he was unable to get through by telephone to see if everyone was safe. Five years earlier, during the ugly civil war in Yugoslavia, his wife, Ana, had lost three cousins. "I can't believe this is happening again," he said, shaking his head in disbelief.

He used the game as an escape, almost recording a triple double with 18 points, 10 assists, and seven rebounds. Williams showed occasional flair while committing six turnovers. But he also made the night for that deranged fan riding Sprewell. He scored the final six points of the game, including the tie-breaking free throw with 11 seconds left. He went to the line because Sprewell had inexplicably lost control of a high dribble behind the top of the arc, and Williams simply scooped it up. With Van Gundy screaming, "Don't foul!" Sprewell, half out of frustration and half out of instinctive behavior, grabbed Williams and wound up giving up the crucial free throws. Williams made one of two and the Knicks, who had lost a nine-point lead in the final 6:25, went to Ewing for the win. Van Gundy got the matchup he wanted: Webber, not Divac, was guarding Ewing. But instead of driving to the basket against the defensively challenged Webber, Ewing took a fade-away jumper. His shot went off the back iron, and not even Charlie Ward's desperation heave had a prayer.

In the locker room, Sprewell's teammates were fuming at him—not for the turnover, but for that stupid foul. What was he thinking? "I really wasn't sure what I wanted to do," he said. "We're at the bottom of the barrel. I don't think it can get any worse. The one thing we have to do is stick together, not starting pointing fingers and blaming people."

Two hours' drive north from where he had sunk one franchise, Sprewell had contributed mightily to another Knick collapse. The team was 6-9 with him in the lineup. Maybe this was as good as it gets.

With a day off before another game in Phoenix, Van Gundy elected to give the players a free afternoon in the desert. He had some depressing numbers to pore over: The Knicks were 15-13 overall, 3-9 on the road, and 0-4 in one-point games. The next night, the tension in the visiting locker room of the America West Arena was palpable. If they lost to the Suns and to the Lakers in a game looming large two days later, the team with the highest payroll in the NBA would return home with a .500 record.

Touring the arena, you felt the contrast in the franchises and cities. Here were the Knicks, intently watching game film of the Suns, seeing how Jason Kidd ran the break and how they could perfect their transition defense. The players snacked on fresh orange slices, bananas, and bran muffins, a nutritious spread laid out every game by their fitness guru and conditioning coach Greg Brittenham, one of the most earthy, upbeat characters in the organization. The whole room took on the aura of a playoff game. The Knicks were businesslike, serious, and in no mood for chitchat with reporters.

Less than fifty yards down the corridor, the Suns, who entered the game a .500 team, were slowly filing in as if they were about to play eighteen holes at a Scottsdale country club. The television was tuned in to the Women's Final Four, and the players were trying to ascertain who was lesbian and who was straight. Suddenly, Danny Manning and Clifford Robinson appeared toting a bag filled with McDonald's Big Macs, french fries, and Chicken McNuggets. This was health food for the Suns. "Yeah, it's pretty laid-back here," said Chris Morris, surveying the scene. Robinson finally assessed the emotional state of the team and decided to sarcastically announce, "Hey, maybe we should be getting a little more serious. After all, we do have a game tonight." Manning and his teammates busted up laughing.

The Knicks played like the more desperate team. They beat Phoenix 94–87, with Houston scoring 29 and Sprewell adding 23 in a much-needed victory. Ewing reached a great milestone when his fourth rebound of the game made him one of only twelve players to record 20,000 points and 10,000 rebounds.

But these are the Knicks; whenever there is good news, bad

news is sure to follow. Van Gundy saw a column in the *New York Times* the next morning that did not go well with his Raisin Bran. In it, Sprewell was asked whether it bothered him that the Warriors and Knicks were a combined 7-22 with him in the lineup over the last two seasons. Sprewell's response: "That's just one of those stats," he said. "That doesn't bother me."

Before the Phoenix game, Sprewell was talking hoops at his locker, describing how it feels to dribble down the court and launch a jumper on a whim. He called it, "Just ballin'," playground vernacular for those players who move at warp speed and have no conscience about missing two, three, four shots in a row.

"To me, that's fun," Sprewell said. "And that's when basketball is fun, going up and down. I would like to be in a system that caters to that style of play. At this point in my career, I'm not going to change."

Van Gundy had convinced his bosses that Sprewell, despite his unsavory past, was worth the risk two months ago. One of the team's long-term problems was that the vortex known as Ewing and the Knicks offense had absorbed and stifled the talents of many gifted players. It was not wholly wrong to say that Ewing and his teammates needed to get their rears down the floor if they wanted to play with Sprewell.

But privately, at least two of Sprewell's teammates wished that he would wait for them to at least cross midcourt before chucking. They liked his aggressiveness, but they questioned whether he could incorporate anyone else into his offensive mind-set.

Old habits die hard, even on the court. Sprewell after all had run the floor unabated at Golden State, an All-Star who responded to every defensive challenge the only way he knew how: Shoot and shoot some more. He played for a team that was used to losing, so a part of him must have been wondering what all this New York fuss was about; in the Bay Area, 15-13 was a more-than-decent record. Remember, at the time of his suspension for choking Carlesimo, the Warriors' record was an abysmal 1-13.

But *just one of those stats?* It was a comment that sent Van Gundy through the roof, and he was determined not to let it pass without making his feelings known. He began to seriously wonder whether the club's key off-season acquisition, the player management had declared was the missing link to a title, genuinely cared about winning or if he merely wanted to get his points.

Things came to a head on March 27 during a practice at Pauley Pavilion on the UCLA campus, in the same gym where the legendary John Wooden once lectured the likes of Lew Alcindor and Bill Walton.

With their nationally televised game against the Lakers less than twenty-four hours away, the Knicks were concluding a light, ninety-minute practice when Van Gundy told Sprewell he wanted to meet with him after practice. He wanted to call the player aside to hear him explain what he meant by his "just one of those stats" comment.

The last fifteen minutes of each practice was set aside for foul shooting. As the Knicks were taking their free throws, Sprewell excused himself to use the rest room.

It became an awkward moment, because the media had already been allowed in the gym, and Van Gundy was heading straight for the reporters to conduct his daily briefing. Suddenly, the Knicks' director of public relations, Lori Hamamoto, redirected Van Gundy, reminding the coach that Sprewell was waiting for him on a vacant stairwell out of view of the players and the media.

Van Gundy walked out of sight and met with Sprewell, who was sitting down. They talked about roles, shot selection, and being a good teammate before Van Gundy brought up Sprewell's recent comments. The conversation was not heated; neither Van Gundy nor Sprewell raised their voice. They were merely on different pages.

When the meeting ended, Sprewell headed straight for the

team bus and, for the first time all season, he conspicuously dodged the beat reporters, turning down interview requests from those who had followed him back to the Ritz-Carlton Hotel in Marina Del Rey. He seemed surprised that reporters were privy to the meeting, and wondered whether Van Gundy was trying to pull a power play in front of the media.

On the surface, he was ducking out on the media for selfish reasons. But his penchant for being open and honest had gotten him into trouble before, and he felt enough controversy was already swirling around the team; fostering the perception that he could not get along with authority figures would be counterproductive.

"If I had my druthers, I would have him say, 'The Knicks brought me here, they showed a lot of faith in me, I'll do whatever they want me to do to help us win,' " Van Gundy said. "Yeah, that's what I'd rather have him not just say, but believe in his heart. But this is the NBA, so I'm not necessarily sure that's going to happen."

The whole encounter with Sprewell had brought up longheld feelings he had about the league. "I don't know if it's ungrateful or not," Van Gundy said. "We all fight, not just NBA players. But all of us fight our basic selfish nature to want everything to be the way we want it to be. Chris Dudley wants to play more. He doesn't like to sit. Marcus is the same way. They've been asked to sacrifice a lot more than other guys on this team. Sometimes, what you believe sacrifice is—and what true sacrifice is—are totally different."

Sprewell had a hard time reconciling the whole idea of sacrificing his game. His stubbornness—and selfishness on the court—was part of the reason he was rich and famous. When he put his head down and drove to the hole, nothing else in life mattered but putting that ball in the basket. At every level, his desire overcame his lack of fundamentals and experience.

Sprewell did not play organized basketball until his senior year at Milwaukee's Washington High School. Averaging 28 points per game, he took his frenetic, open-court ways to Three Rivers Junior College in Poplar Bluff, Missouri, and then to the

University of Alabama, where he starred for two seasons. In 1992, he was drafted in the first round by the Warriors, but he was not taken until the twenty-fourth pick. Then he made the All-Star team three times in his first five seasons.

His first two NBA coaches, Don Nelson and Rick Adelman, gave him the green light to shoot, create, and do what he wanted. His third coach, Carlesimo, did not.

Sprewell lived and played like a free radical, undermining structure and reason. It is no wonder that growing up he had little of either.

Latoska Fields, his father, left the family when Latrell was six years old. Latrell went to live with him in Flint, Michigan, but returned to his mother in Milwaukee after his sophomore year in high school. The reason: His father was sent to jail in 1986 on a count of possession with intent to distribute marijuana.

Pamela Sprewell, Latrell's mother, was beaten by her husband when Latrell was a child, he said. Those violent moments made him vow never to abuse his own children. He eventually reconciled with his father.

"I don't want to make it sound like my dad was a total jerk and he beat my mom and us when we came home every day," Sprewell said. "But there were occasions that I remember abuse was going on that was too excessive. Physical fighting . . . whipping kids . . . I would spank my kids, but I just think he went overboard with it."

Sprewell fathered his first child at seventeen years old, while he was still in high school. He now has five children by three different women.

"I'm family-oriented," he said. "Although that might not be the image certain people have of me. Some people are going to hate Spree, no matter what."

A week after the meeting between Sprewell and Van Gundy, the coach was asked again about Sprewell's comments.

"I think if he had to do it over again, he'd give a different answer," Van Gundy said. "It's not a valid stat? Every player has to be concerned first and foremost with winning. That is going to be their legacy in this league. He would probably like to have a do-over on that."

Sprewell: "No, I said what I said and I meant it. I didn't think what I said was that big a deal. I don't know why Jeff had to say anything to me about it. Basketball is supposed to be fun. Sometimes, I think they forget that."

Undermining structure and logic: This was the most serious weakness Sprewell brought to a team. It was also his greatest strength, and the one thing the Knicks may have needed most.

The Great Western Forum was filling up uncharacteristically early on March 28. The poseurs and potentates arrived promptly and took their seats at courtside for the nationally televised game between the league's two biggest markets and midseason disappointments.

Shaquille O'Neal and Kobe Bryant had engaged in a slapfest before training camp started, and Dennis Rodman had officially brought the circus to town. Kneading the sharpshooter Glen Rice into the mix was merely another obstacle for a team badly lacking in chemistry. The Los Angeles Lakers were almost as discombobulated as the Knicks.

Rodman was missing practice routinely and left the team before a recent road trip for "personal problems." He went to gamble until dawn in Las Vegas while his team fell apart in Sacramento.

The Sunday of the Knicks-Lakers game was shaping up as the perfect day to depict Rodman as a buffoon, an attention-starved thirty-seven-year-old child who needed the NBA more than it needed him. The day before, he had arrived seventy-five minutes late to practice. The night before, he told Coach Kurt Rambis he was too stiff to go back into a game in the fourth quarter because he had been sitting on the bench too long. His teammates were mortified and were almost waiting for the Lakers to send him back to Carmen Electra, Jay Leno, and the World Wrestling Federation for good.

It said a lot about the state of the league and the Lakers that

Jerry West, the respected general manager whose 1970s silhouette is used as the NBA logo, would even consider signing a cross-dresser to be their power forward. West dismissed the notion but the Lakers' owner Jerry Buss had gone over West's head to acquire Rodman, leaving one of the NBA's premier franchises looking a little desperate. After all, Dave Checketts would never gamble on Rodman, would he?

"I'm sure there is an element in New York that would really love him," Checketts once said. "As far as I'm concerned, I think it's awful. I really do. When I saw the picture of him showing up on the motorcycle with the makeup job, I just couldn't believe this is what it has come to. I guarantee you that as long as I'm running the New York Knicks, he will not be on this club."

The Garden president had cleansed the locker room of Anthony Mason in 1996, and had shocked most of New York when the Knicks acquired Sprewell. But Rodman, it seemed, was from a different universe altogether. Checketts was outraged by inflammatory comments that Rodman made against Mormons in 1997 during the finals in Salt Lake City, and had never hid his distaste for the multi-tattooed but uni-dimensional player.

But these were different, desperate times. Before Rodman signed with the Lakers, Grunfeld did the unthinkable: He placed a call to Rodman's agent, Dwight Manley. If Sprewell fell through, the Knicks wanted the Worm to know that all was forgiven. Yes, there was some trepidation that Dennis would spend more time at the topless club Scores than at practice, but they were willing to discuss taking that chance.

The Lakers were not imploding on the court, anyway, having gone 19-11 entering this game. But they were all over the map on offense and they didn't seem to care on defense. Veteran point guard Derek Harper, New York's respected leader during its 1994 Finals run, had essentially become a baby-sitter. As bad as the Knicks were playing, the Lakers were viewed as an even greater enigma. They had already gone through one coach this season, the recently fired Del Harris, and the honeymoon was about to end for Rambis.

So, there were two struggling franchises in front of the NBC cameras on a Sunday afternoon, vying for the right to be considered the most overrated team. You knew it was going to be a war, especially when Shaq made some recent comments directed at union boss Patrick Ewing, whose labor career O'Neal probably wanted to see end like Jimmy Hoffa's.

It did not matter to O'Neal that Ewing was a hard worker who was leading the players' fight against the owners. O'Neal had lost almost as much salary as Ewing during the lockout, and had been privately hoping to exercise an escape clause in his contract after the season to set himself up for yet another monster payday, as if the $121 million deal he signed with the Lakers in 1996 was chump change. But the new labor agreement prevented O'Neal from hitting the jackpot yet again, and he was even more outraged at how long the fight had gone on. He blamed Ewing and his Georgetown brethren Alonzo Mourning and Dikembe Mutombo.

"He's somebody I really don't like," O'Neal said in *Sports Illustrated* that week. "Especially since the lockout. Let me tell you this: Patrick and his Georgetown boys messed up the lockout. Georgetown is supposed to be a five-star university. Yeah, right. That's why he and 'Zo were trying to play lawyer, trying to intimidate billionaires like Paul Allen [co-founder of Microsoft and owner of the Portland Trail Blazers]. Please."

O'Neal came out angry for the game, but only managed to outscore Ewing 21 to 20. Meanwhile, Rodman dusted off his annoying-player manual, baiting Kurt Thomas into losing his senses with 2.4 seconds left in the third quarter. He and Thomas became entangled under the basket, their arms locking. Thomas was so enraged at Rodman's antics that he simply threw Rodman to the ground and almost set off a melee. "Rodman! Rod-man! Rod-man!" the Forum crowd chanted as Thomas was ejected from the game. Earlier in the game, Thomas and Rodman had each been assessed a foul for excessive contact, and Thomas told one referee, "If he kicks me again, I'm going to have to protect myself." Rodman scored seven points, grabbed 12 rebounds, and blocked a Patrick

Ewing dunk attempt. The Lakers won 99–91, and all was well again in Los Angeles—for the day.

Just like the old days when Rodman was with the Bulls, Dennis antagonizes, the Knicks retaliate, and guess who's laughing in the end? With the Lakers ahead by three points with six minutes left, the animosity grew when O'Neal forced his way into the paint and ferociously dunked over Dudley, who actually caught O'Neal in his arms. His reward for bracing Shaq's fall? O'Neal shoved the ball in his stomach, knocking Dudley on his ass. Dudley got up and, from thirty feet away, the worst free throw shooter in league history fired the ball at O'Neal's head and struck his leg. Dudley was gone, too.

"There is a time to retaliate," Chris Childs said. "We picked the wrong time."

In the middle of it all was that irascible character with the peroxide blond hair, the tattoos, and the mischievous grin. For a change, he was making life miserable for the other team instead of his own. But this was one of his few L.A. highlights; a couple of weeks later, the accumulated effect of a series of Rodman episodes forced the Lakers to release him.

The Knicks were no longer interested in Rodman's services. With Ewing hurting, Sprewell unhappy in his role, and Van Gundy and Grunfeld bickering, they had enough headaches of their own.

7
"BACK UP THE TRUCK"

Allan Houston quit on the play—there was no other explanation.

The Hornets were routing the Knicks at the Charlotte Coliseum on the night of April 7. With 4:08 left in the third quarter, the Knicks' shooting guard was stripped of the ball by Eddie Jones on one end of the floor, and he backpedaled slowly on defense on the other. Without laying a finger on the Charlotte guard, Houston allowed Jones to go in for a layup.

Houston's lack of desire ate Van Gundy up, made him wonder what had happened to his once-proud team. He began lecturing Houston as he walked off the court and back to the bench.

"What the fuck is going on?" he said to Houston. "Why didn't you put him on the line? Are you kidding me, Allan?"

Houston wasn't the only culprit; his teammates were as emotionally out of that game as their inconsistent shooting guard. On a night they badly needed a win, the Knicks fell behind 29–12 after one quarter and lost by 24 points. And these Hornets were not to be confused with Michael's Bulls. David Wesley. Eldridge Recasner. Charles Shackleford and the geriatric Chuck Person. Derrick Coleman was out with a sprained left ankle. At the end of the game, Anthony Mason, out for the season with a torn biceps muscle, was laughing and clowning at the end of the bench.

"Are you losing the team?" Gus Johnson, the Knicks' radio play-by-play announcer, asked Van Gundy.

"I don't think I'm losing the core guys," Van Gundy said. "I don't know where everybody weighs in on that."

The Knicks were now 18-17, and 4-12 on the road. They were in tenth place in the Eastern Conference with fifteen games to play. With only the top eight teams advancing to the playoffs, the draft lottery seemed like a more realistic goal. For the first time since the 1986–87 season, the Knicks were on the verge of missing the postseason, and they knew it.

Ewing called it the most depressing night of his career. Johnson, his voice almost cracking, apologized to the head coach after the game. Ewing bristled when a reporter asked if the team had quit, and Houston added that everyone, except Van Gundy, was to blame.

"As much as you want to say everybody is at fault, if anybody is not at fault it's Jeff," he said. "All he does is prepare for the game. Coming from a coach's son, that's all he can do. He can't go out there and play for us."

Amid this sea of discontent stood a 6-5, corn-rowed beacon of optimism—or absurdity, depending on your point of view. If Houston looked out of it thirty minutes earlier on the court, Sprewell seemed like he came from a different galaxy this night. Standing in the middle of this basketball morgue after most of his teammates had licked their wounds, Sprewell had a What, me worry? look about him.

"Being in sixth place with fifteen games left, that's a lot of time," said Sprewell, oblivious to the Knicks' actual standing in the conference, tenth. "We don't have a lot of time, but we have enough time to make a run here. So I'm not throwing in the towel yet. I know we're down, but we got to get over it. You can't stay down. That's the attitude I have."

"You seem kind of unfazed by all that's taken place," one observer said.

Sprewell shrugged his shoulders. "I've played on losing teams before. I know what it takes. A lot of these guys haven't experienced times like this, and I have. We can't think championship right now. I think we have to take it game by game and think, 'Hey, let's get in. And let's build on that.' I've said it before: I don't see the elite teams in the East being that much better than us, especially when we're playing well.

"I'm staying optimistic about everything."

Though Sprewell seemed genuinely concerned about turning the team's fortunes around, most observers thought he was clueless and, frankly, not of this earth.

Less than two years ago, Johnson sat in this same locker room after the Knicks had swept the Hornets in a first-round playoff series. Johnson hit the deciding 3-pointer and gained a good measure of redemption against his former team. The Knicks were the hottest team in the league then, headed on a collision course with Chicago before they lost their heads against Miami and threw the season away.

But on this April 7, Johnson must have been wondering what had happened to this franchise. How did everything get so bad so fast? "Two years is a long time," he said. "We've got some different players than we had then. A lot can happen in two years."

The season would be over in a month, and everyone but Sprewell seemed to understand the implications of this demoralizing loss. He acted like some wise, old sage had entered their midst, saying something to the effect of, *"I can lead you. We're on my turf. We're losing. The unpromised land is near. I can get us a lottery pick."*

The game had the same Chicago feel to it from three weeks earlier. How many more bad losses could the coach survive before the Knicks made a change? They were treading water, all their liabilities coming back to haunt them. Every trade for a troubled soul. Every missed workout in the off-season by the labor-pained franchise center. Every bit of awful chemistry on the court.

By the first week of April, the Knicks were nearly unwatchable. Instead of complementing each other, Houston was picking up some of Sprewell's quick-trigger tendencies, throwing up bad shots with more than 15 seconds left on the 24-second shot clock.

In the first eight games that Ewing, Sprewell, and Houston played together, the Knicks were 2-6, with Ewing averaging more than 20 points and Sprewell and Houston at about 14 points apiece.

To beat good teams, Van Gundy still had to rely on Ewing. A week before the Charlotte disaster, Sprewell and Houston had combined for 35 points in a one-point win over Indiana—but it was Ewing who carried them, pouring in 37 points and gathering 15 rebounds in a team-high 40 minutes. On a bad leg.

Ewing, battling Father Time, had about an eighth of a tank left in April. Van Gundy was taking a huge risk playing the franchise center so many minutes in the regular season. But these were the facts: He needed the wins, and Ewing was too proud to ask out of the lineup.

Childs and Ward were up to their old bad habits, with the former railing at the officials and the latter having trouble stopping his opponents. Worse for the fans, the Knicks were as beleaguered—and predictable—as ever: Ewing on the blocks, physically unable to go around his man. Houston on the perimeter, trying to create a shot with his passive body language. Sprewell out of control, not waiting for screens or teammates to cross midcourt before shooting the ball.

The reality for Grunfeld and Van Gundy was that the Knicks needed what neither of them could give them: time.

The problems of playing well in this truncated season were not restricted to the Knicks. Most NBA coaches had feared the worst as the labor dispute dragged on: With no legitimate practice time to make all the pieces fit and with the proliferation of nagging injuries as a result of so many players not working out the prior seven months (made worse by the compressed schedule), the golden era of Stern's great league was about to end with a thud.

In their quest not to have the players lose another week of salary, Stern and Billy Hunter, the executive director of the players union, decided to cut short the training camps and add lost games to the schedule. This trade-off led to some of the most God-awful basketball imaginable.

Scores in the 60s and 70s were the norm those first few weeks. The Sonics' Vin Baker, still trying to shed the extra pounds he carried around in Atlantic City for the charity game, missed his first 18 free throws to begin the season.

Ten years earlier, all but one team averaged more than 100 points per game, with the Knicks pouring in 116.7 points per contest—third best in the league.

"We were scoring 117 points per game, the Garden was packed, and we were winning, that's all I cared about," said Rick Pitino, the Knicks' coach then. "The thing is, they say you can't play playoff basketball that way. And I disagree, because the Lakers were the hottest team with Magic and they were scoring a lot of points. We were playing West Coast basketball on the East Coast. And that's what this is all about, winning and entertainment."

Sacramento was the only team to average more than 100 points in 1999. Much of the blame over the past decade could be heaped on the marketing of Jordan, whose dunks became part of the nightly highlight reel. Jordan could do everything—shoot, defend, rebound, and take and make the clutch shot. But his image was tethered to his famous logo, flying toward the basket for a dunk while defying gravity. It was not long before kids on every American playground tried to be Air Jordan, forgetting medium-range jump shots and concentrating solely on the dunk and the 3-pointer.

The league's statistics mirrored the change in style. Shooting percentages declined, 3-point attempts were up, and the sublime choreography of teamwork had all but disappeared from the game.

By acquiring the greatest freelancer known to man, the Knicks seemed to be contributing to the mess.

Rumors of Van Gundy's imminent demise circled the press room after the Charlotte loss. Would he get whacked tomorrow? Would he last past Atlanta two nights later? Or would Grunfeld wait and drop the guillotine when the Knicks returned home that Saturday?

Either way, it seemed just a matter of time. The coach could not afford another blowout loss. He needed a win, any kind of win, to keep the vultures away.

With an off day between games, the Knicks knew they were about to be clobbered by the seven newspapers that cover the team for all home and away games. The *New York Post*'s Kevin Kernan, the beat-hardened reporter who would often stun the players by walking into the locker room with a Hawaiian print shirt in the middle of winter, made that abundantly clear. He telephoned Van Gundy in his Atlanta hotel room to let him in on a little scoop: Kernan and, by association, the *Post,* was firing the coach for the third time in three years on its back page the next morning. Van Gundy was caught off guard by the call, and figured he was empathizing with Kernan when he told him, "I understand, it's your job and the paper you work for." Kernan cut him off, saying, "No, I believe you should be fired."

Grunfeld was not exempt from having his job performance criticized either, having been ripped in the *Times* and the *Daily News* for much of the season. The day of the Hawks game, *News* columnist Filip Bondy and *Times* columnist Harvey Araton took their swings, blaming Grunfeld for putting together such a flawed team. Grunfeld was easily as culpable for the team's failures as Van Gundy, but the coach usually gets the axe first.

Ten days earlier, Ewing tried to put an end to the Van Gundy speculation. He telephoned Checketts, lobbying on the coach's behalf. By the end of that conversation, Ewing had received assurances from the Garden president that Van Gundy was safe for at least the rest of the season.

"Ain't nothing going to happen," Ewing said. "I spoke to Dave and he guaranteed me that nothing is going to happen. Jeff is the coach I want to play for. I'm not playing for Phil Jackson. Phil Jackson can take his ass back to Chicago."

Talk of the Knicks' being interested in the former Bulls coach had been around forever. But with Jackson unemployed and playing pickup ball minutes from his new home in Woodstock, New York, most observers realized that Jackson was one phone call away from his dream job.

The specter of Jackson always kept Van Gundy on his toes. And each time the ghost of Big Chief Triangle got closer, Van Gundy found a way to get a win.

That morning in Atlanta, he ran the Knicks through an uncommonly grueling ninety-minute practice. Hours before they would meet the Hawks, the Knicks were scrimmaging and going hard. It was odd, because NBA game-day routines are usually very consistent: forty-five-minute shootarounds, which consist of walking through plays and light shooting drills, at about 10:00 A.M. (Most players believe that the shootarounds started because coaches did not want their team partying late into the night; it gave them a reason to wake up and start their day.) After the shootaround, players usually eat lunch and take a nap before arriving at the arena between 5:30 and 6:00 for a 7:30 game.

Van Gundy's strategy at least got it through the players' heads that another crisis was at hand if the Knicks looked bad against the Hawks. Checketts had spoken by telephone with reporters from the *Times, Daily News,* and the *Post* before the game. Shooting down speculation that a rift existed between the coach and the team president, Checketts blamed overzealous reporters for starting the rumors. "I don't think there's a problem," he said. "At this point, and not just because of the Charlotte performance, we have to say that everybody needs to be on alert," Checketts continued. "I don't think anyone can say they're safe, including me. I approved the moves we made. I'm more than a little disappointed. This is probably the most frustrated I've been with the Knicks. It's a situation where we put together a tremendous amount of talent.

"Maybe the expectations were unrealistic. I'm coming down on everyone. All twelve players, Jeff and the coaching staff, and Ernie and his staff. I've known of a lot of talented teams that didn't click. And I know of a number of highly compensated teams that didn't make the playoffs. This is a proud, storied franchise and what I see happening is unacceptable. I'm not going to single anybody out. But no one here has tenure, so to speak. That's the law of the jungle in New York."

At the Georgia Dome, Grunfeld held an impromptu press conference to address his and Van Gundy's future. Grunfeld had been keeping a low profile since the March 14 NBC report involving the possible firing of Van Gundy. Two days earlier, he went on the country's largest all-sports radio station, WFAN in New York, and said in an interview that Van Gundy's job was safe.

No one believed Grunfeld, least of all the coach. Deep down, he knew Grunfeld wanted him out.

If the law of the jungle was to prevail, few doubted that Checketts could draw on tremendous survivor instincts. Hired by Paramount to run the Knicks in 1991, he had weathered three ownership changes in as many years. After Paramount was taken over by Viacom, ITT Cablevision bought the Garden and its assets in 1994. When ITT became the object of a hostile takeover soon after, Checketts again survived.

Checketts is a tall, well-coiffed man of forty-four with steely blue eyes and a thick thatch of brownish-blond hair. He resembles less a corporate executive than a ski-resort mogul from his native Utah, one of those former instructors from out on the slopes not born but hatched inside the Alpine cave where all the ski gods come from.

He looks you straight in the eye when he talks, says your first name often during conversation, and makes you feel like the most important person in the room when you ask a question.

Political office or used-car sales could have been his calling had professional sports management not beckoned. In a town consumed with image, he was often seen as the shining Anglo from the West who could do little wrong.

He had learned from the best in the business. Checketts owed much of his start in the NBA to Commissioner David Stern, whom Checketts befriended in 1983 while working for Bain Associates in Boston, a financial consulting firm that was interested in purchasing the Celtics at the time.

One day that spring, uninvited and full of grandiose ideas, Checketts met with then–deputy commissioner Stern in his Midtown Manhattan office. They debated the state of the game. "I was just twenty-six, and all of a sudden we're in his office arguing," Checketts said in the *Daily News*. "I'm yelling at him. He's yelling at me. About the new drug agreement, the new salary cap, about why there are franchises nearly bankrupt, about why anyone in their right mind might pay $20 million for a team in those days."

He began to view Stern as a father figure—and a very valuable reference on the résumé. On Stern's recommendation Utah owner Sam Battistone installed Checketts as vice president of the Utah Jazz on August 1, 1983. At twenty-seven years old, he was already a player in an NBA front office.

Checketts climbed the corporate ladder in Utah, but his ambition often grated on Larry Miller, who purchased the team from Battistone. Checketts resigned in 1989 to become the Denver Nuggets' general manager, but within weeks he bailed out on an ill-fated ownership team in Denver headed by Bertram Lee and Peter Bynoe.

He worked in the league office for nearly two years and— again on Stern's recommendation—was hired to run the Knicks in 1991. Their symbiotic relationship even spilled over into the league's labor struggle; Checketts helped put forth ownership's proposals to the players. It was in those closed-door negotiating sessions that the less-appealing side of Checketts surfaced.

Gone was the smiling veneer, the kind and deeply concerned Mormon missionary raised in Bountiful, Utah. Checketts became irate at union lawyers during a bargaining session in December of 1998. At one juncture, the young attorney Ron Klempner began trying to shoot down a claim made by Checketts regarding the league's proposal. Suddenly, Checketts spun around in anger, eyed Klempner and exclaimed, "You don't know what the fuck you're talking about!"

The gathering of players and owners in a conference room of the Omni Hotel in Manhattan looked on in stunned disbelief. Danny Schayes, the journeyman center, looked at Miller, the Utah owner, who is Mormon, and quipped, "You really ought to look into canceling Dave's Mormon membership card."

When it came to the bottom line, he could be nasty and profane. But then, at the Garden he had to be.

Since 1994, Cablevision had become a media colossus. Headed by Charles Dolan, the chairman, his son James Dolan, the president, and vice chairman Marc Lustgarten, Cablevision had spent $3 billion to acquire several companies and expand its core business to include sports, entertainment, and retail properties. It is one of two cable systems dominating the New York area, along with Time Warner.

Its facilities included the Garden and Radio City Music Hall, and it controls cable TV rights to seven of the nine major pro sports teams in New York, including the Knicks and Rangers. Having failed in a bid to acquire the new Cleveland Browns franchise, Chuck Dolan and his conglomerate were also negotiating to acquire the Yankees from George Steinbrenner and the Mets from Nelson Doubleday and Fred Wilpon. By the beginning of 1999, Cablevision's stock market value had shot to $12 billion—$4 billion of which was owned by the Dolans.

They had not reached such heights by sitting quietly while things went wrong.

However much they were saying Van Gundy was safe, the comments of Checketts and Grunfeld revealed that their support was wavering. They would not stand for another debacle. Nor would Van Gundy.

Just as they had in Phoenix two weeks earlier, the players

recognized the sense of urgency. They were stoic, serious, and focused.

Whether it was the day off or the ninety-minute practice that worked, the Knicks came out with force. Sprewell and Camby combined for 27 points, 10 rebounds, and 8 assists off the bench, and Ewing added 16 points.

Childs committed no turnovers in 27 minutes and shut down Mookie Blaylock in the fourth quarter. "This was humongous," the 6-foot-2-inch point guard said after the Knicks controlled the Hawks in an 86–78 victory. "This one we had to have."

Speaking with a front tooth missing after he took a forearm from 7-foot-2-inch Dikembe Mutombo, Childs's resolve began to embody his team's. "You'll see the next time we play them," he said afterward. "I'm going to call Don King. I put that on my grandmother. I'm going to get him back. I might not be able to reach him and his mouth, but I'm going to get him back."

Childs visited the dentist before the Knicks met the Nets on Sunday in the Meadowlands. He received a false tooth. And that morning, Grunfeld received a kick in the teeth courtesy of the Sunday *New York Times.*

The paper's aggressive beat reporter, Selena Roberts, had written a scathing story on Grunfeld's spending habits with the Knicks. Following a money trail that began with the Charles Smith deal, Roberts detailed Grunfeld's personnel foul-ups since he was promoted to general manager. The graphic accompanying the story didn't exactly help, either: Framed as if they were hanging in an art gallery were color pictures of the players the team president had rewarded with outlandish contracts, under the heading, "The Grunfeld Collection."

It is one thing to hang in effigy on the back pages of the *Daily News* and the *Post,* an ignominy that came with the territory; it is quite another to be belted by the newspaper you know your well-heeled bosses at Cablevision are reading. You could just imagine members of Charles Dolan's family, passing the sports section to the media tycoon who presided over the multinational conglomerate: "Chucky, who is this Ernie Grunfeld chap, and why is he wasting all your money?"

Grunfeld was in trouble. He needed his guys to start delivering. Camby answered the call against New Jersey by scoring a season-high 19 points. Van Gundy was starting to show more faith in the young forward by rewarding him with more minutes, and he could not argue with the results.

The Knicks handled the Nets 93–78, and two nights later they roughed up Iverson and the Philadelphia 76ers 91–72. Camby and Sprewell combined for 31, and Kurt Thomas was beginning to find his legs. He contributed 18 points, most coming on soft rainbow jumpers.

Yet every time the Knicks took a giant step, it hurt. Especially when that step belonged to Ewing.

He played only 12 minutes in the win over the Sixers, leaving the game when he reaggravated his left Achilles tendon. New York's hopes for its first four-game winning streak since February went down hard in Washington the next night, as they lost to the lowly Wizards in overtime without Ewing. The Knicks followed that performance with another fourth-quarter meltdown, even though Houston caught fire against his former team for the first time in Detroit.

In four previous games for the Knicks at the Palace of Auburn Hills, Houston was a combined 11-for-44 with 11 turnovers. He appeared tentative and passive against the Pistons; he did not respond well in front of a crowd still holding a grudge over his '96 signing with New York. This was the soft side of Houston that would sometimes surface. But in this game he showed signs of breaking the Detroit hex. He scored a team-high 23 points, but the Knicks played the final seven minutes as if they were trying to clinch ninth place in the conference. They scored a mere 10 points in the fourth quarter, and Sprewell was awful at both ends of the floor in the Pistons' 80–71 victory. Sprewell missed 10 of 13 shots, and he committed yet another boneheaded defensive blunder with 1:05 left. Leaving Pistons reserve Jud Buechler alone behind the 3-point line—much as he had forgotten about Milwaukee's Dell Curry five weeks earlier—Sprewell got caught in a screen as Buechler put the dagger in the Knicks.

"We just fell apart," said Ewing, who missed his second straight game. "We got out of sync. We were doing things well for the entire game and then we just stopped."

The losing streak reached three games the next night at the Garden, and Grunfeld was not sleeping any better. Oakley had come back to haunt him again, delivering hip checks, forearms, and the most clutch and savvy of rebounds in the final seconds.

At one point in the game, the 6-foot-9, 240-pound Oakley collided with Childs near the midcourt line and momentarily knocked the diminutive guard out of the game.

"Both of us went for the ball, a Mack truck and a Volkswagen," Oakley said in his own inimitable way. "Which one do you think I'm drivin'?"

With Camby (zero points, four rebounds in 20 minutes) napping in the final 12.7 seconds and the Knicks down by three points and needing a stop, the veteran player he was traded for reached around Camby and grabbed an offensive rebound. If each matchup between the two represented a referendum on the trade, this one felt like a stake through the heart of the man who made the swap.

The Knicks were on the brink again, and not just because of how badly they looked on the court. Before the Toronto game, Charlie Ward's religious beliefs suddenly got in the way of his job as a floor leader.

Dave D'Alessandro, the *Newark Star-Ledger*'s beat reporter, observed Ward giving Houston a copy of a *Wall Street Journal* editorial written by former Green Bay Packer Reggie White. A friend of Ward's who shared his fundamentalist Christian beliefs, White had raised the issue of whether female journalists should be banned from male locker rooms.

"Players and their spouses should try and put a stop to this policy, go all the way to the Supreme Court, if need be," White wrote. "I just hope that if it happens, one of the exhibits before the court isn't a film of Reggie White singing in the shower."

When Selena Roberts of the *Times* got wind of the literature being distributed, she confronted Ward. He had pressed a major hot button, given the fact that many female journalists had covered the team on a regular basis during Ward's career in New York.

In the 1999 season alone, Barbara Barker and Johnette Howard of *Newsday,* Lisa Olson of the *Daily News,* and Sara Smith of the *Village Voice* had spent considerable time interviewing Knick players before and after games. For Olson, it touched an ultrasensitive nerve.

While covering the New England Patriots for the *Boston Herald* in 1989, Olson was waiting to interview a player in the New England locker room. Two minutes into the interview, a small group of Patriot players that included tight end Zeke Mowatt emerged from the showers, removed their towels, and made suggestive and outright lewd comments to Olson.

"Is this what you want to see?" said one player.

Several players, Olson later learned, were upset because they believed the day before she was lingering in the locker room and playing the part of a voyeur rather than a journalist. In fact, she had been kept waiting by two players who were receiving treatment in the trainer's room.

She received no sympathy from then–Patriots owner Victor Kiam, the Remington Razor king, who referred to Olson as "a bitch." Months after the story became page-one news in Boston, Olson relocated in Australia to distance herself from the firestorm.

Ten years later, White wrote that Olson had instigated the incident. And now, having returned to the United States to start over, she was being haunted by that awful episode again.

The Knicks did not need this kind of publicity, especially after an unsubstantiated report in *New York* magazine a month earlier in which Larry Johnson was said to have exposed himself in the locker room to Lori Hamamoto, the PR director. It went on to say that Johnson played a silly and perverted game to try and get Hamamoto to see him naked. Both Johnson and Hamamoto vehemently denied such an incident took place, but people were talking about it.

It became an altogether embarrassing allegation for the franchise.

Grunfeld never acted with any urgency in such matters. His failure to do so—his reluctance to involve himself in off-the-court matters that arose on his watch—began to weigh on Checketts's mind as the team faltered.

On and off the floor, the Knicks' world was spinning out of control. And not even their emotional touchstone, Ward, could bring them back. He had other battles to fight.

"My whole thing wasn't about people coming in and looking," Ward said, trying to explain himself while digging a deeper hole. "My whole thing is, when you start having male and female in the same place, things happen. Accidents happen. Even being a male. It's embarrassing for everyone."

Ward kept dialing the hotel operator, asking that she connect him to the rooms of several teammates at the Atlanta Ritz-Carlton. But after a few rings, he invariably ended up leaving voice-mail messages.

"Bible study's going on in my room right now," he said in the messages. "If you get this in time, come on by."

Dudley was in his room and eventually took the elevator down and shuffled into Ward's room, where he joined Ward, one of Ward's longtime friends, and a reporter. Houston and Williams, who usually attend the study groups with Ward, were out taking part in the Knicks' other major pastime, golf. And most of the other players were simply not interested in spending their off day before a game against the Hawks discussing scripture with the team's starting point guard.

"I think the team we had last year I did have a big influence on because a lot of guys wanted to start having Bible study," Ward said. "We had more guys coming to Bible study. Now, we have a lot of new guys. And they're going their own separate ways. And no one wants to really stand up for Christ in the way of saying, 'Hey, I'm going to live for Christ and live for Christ only.' It might not equate into wins, but having praying brothers on this team really helps."

Whether it was Bible study on the road, chapel services at Madison Square Garden, or the ostentatious public prayer at midcourt with his teammates and other players after each home game, Ward, from his first days with the Knicks, had tried to balance his enthusiasm for his religious beliefs and the professional obligations of playing point guard for the team.

Raised in the Southern Baptist Church, Ward was baptized in fifth grade. His parents were educators who raised six children. He views his first year in college as a turning point in his convictions. Ward said his immediate family prayed for him after he suffered a serious knee injury, and that, in effect, "God delivered me from my injury."

But with his comments about the role of women and the danger of their locker room presence, he was beginning to be viewed as a Christian extremist, going to his right harder off the court than on it. It didn't help Ward's cause that White was one of his spiritual confidants.

White, an ordained minister, was invited to speak to the Wisconsin legislature in March of 1998. His nearly hour-long speech included remarks on homosexuality, race, and slavery that turned the Assembly's applause to stunned silence.

Among his most outlandish remarks, White said the country has gotten away from God, in part by allowing homosexuality to "run rampant."

"Homosexuality is a decision, it's not a race," White said. "People from all different ethnic backgrounds live in this lifestyle. But people from all different ethnic backgrounds also are liars and cheaters and malicious and back-stabbing."

In a speech aimed at portraying ethnic diversity as the way to unify, White drifted far off course. He went on to stereotype ethnic groups, saying that God gave each race certain gifts. Blacks, he said, are gifted at worship and celebration. Whites are good at organization, White said: "You guys do a good job of building businesses and things of that nature, and you know

how to tap into money. Hispanics were gifted in family structure, and you can see a Hispanic person, and they can put
twenty, thirty people in one home." The Japanese and other
Asians are inventive, he said, and "can turn a television into a
watch." Indians are gifted in spirituality, he noted.

Ward defended his friend and was prepared to take the same
public backlash.

"When you start talking about lifestyles—like Reggie White
did—people aren't going to like it," Ward said. "Why? Because
you start getting into individuals. Male-female. Gay, straight,
lesbian. Drunk, nondrunk. People feel like, 'He doesn't have
the right to judge me about my lifestyle.' He's not judging you.
He's giving you the word of God on your lifestyle. And it's not
right. And people always want to say, he hates women or he
hates men or he hates gays. No, he doesn't hate that person. He
hates their lifestyle.

"People always say, 'It's a lifestyle and I was born this way.'
You weren't born that way. It's a choice and we all have choices
in life. And you chose to be with the person of the same sex.
That's why God created man and woman; they're different.
They have something we don't have; we have something they
don't have. That's why he created us, so there's a challenge for
us in life. When you decide to be with the same sex, there is no
challenge because you've decided to be with the same thing.
That's why a lot of divorces happen, because we're different.

"It's a choice. Just like, you can choose Christ or choose not
to have Christ in your life. Once you start reading the scrip-
tures, the word will convict your lifestyle. There is no biologi-
cal or chemical reason for being gay. We always want to make
everything scientific."

Ward was on a roll now, going on about society and the root
of its problems.

"Who's behind the country? Definitely not the Lord. You got
bombing here, bombing there, Satan on the Internet. You got
Satan everywhere. They took prayer out of school and they
wonder why we have all those killings. Not saying that if prayer

was in school it wouldn't happen, but we have so many problems in this world and so much access to Satan that it's destroying our country."

While developing from a role player into the team's floor leader, he lectured Patrick Ewing about his profanity. He even talked to married teammates about being seen with other women on the road.

"If someone is trying to help you become better—if you're married and you're out on the road messing around—anyone that comes up to you and says, 'That's not right,' you should take that advice," Ward said. "A lot of times you look at the messenger and say, 'You're no better than I am,' but we should open our heart to everyone."

Ward had encountered trouble at both ends of his life's formula. In trying to justify a new $27 million contract, he instead had regressed as a player, his inconsistency in running the team one of the chief reasons the Knicks were struggling just to make the playoffs.

Team officials and teammates have always been guarded in talking publicly about Ward and the impact of his beliefs and advocacy. But management began expressing concern that Ward's insistent outspokenness had become something of a distraction for him and the team. In particular, Van Gundy was uneasy with Ward's comments regarding God favoring the Knicks because of their faith. Even the religious Checketts spoke to Ward about proselytizing in the locker room.

"That's why God placed me here," Ward said. "I never imagined myself being in New York. It took me a while to understand what his sole purpose for me being here was. First and foremost, it was to get the message across through the way I live and my lifestyle. And also to be challenged by everyone: the press, teammates, coaching staff, everyone." Unapologetic, Ward railed against the rap music his teammates listened to in the locker room. "My job is to try to sanctify the locker room," he said. Ward said he recognizes that his thoughts and encouragements have been met with both respect and annoyance by his teammates.

Ewing had grown weary of his advice. "Whatever it was, I found myself doing it in excess," Ward said. "I saw it was hurting him and turning him away. Then again, it could have been helping him. I would talk to him about his lifestyle, cursing and all that other stuff. Just trying to help him as a man."

In Dudley, Houston, and Williams, Ward had his emphatic defenders. "Whenever a person is more righteous than the next, he becomes an easy target," Dudley said. "That's what's happening to Charlie right now."

Ward was vilified for many of his comments and was the butt of many jokes because of his convictions, which, frankly, scared people. But at least he was walking the walk. Happily married to the attorney Tonja Ward, he had sworn off alcohol, profanity, and promiscuity a long time ago. And on these scores, he was beyond criticism.

Meanwhile, some of the same columnists who were passing judgment on Ward were absolving Darryl Strawberry, the Yankee slugger who over the winter was arrested in Florida on charges of soliciting a prostitute and drug possession—the same Strawberry who was once charged with spousal abuse and had been suspended from baseball for substance abuse.

But Straw played nice with the media. He claimed to have found religion, was outgoing and personable. And for that, he was usually given a favorable hearing in the court of public opinion. It was a common double standard.

"I was reading something the other day," Ward began, "where it asked, 'Have you made any enemies today?' It said anyone can be a friend because it's easy to be a good Joe if you do what the world says. But if you're a man of God and you're living in this ungodly society—where people are cursing, fornicating, and doing all these things—you should make enemies. They're not living according to the word."

In the end, Ward was as worried about his team's religious convictions as its playoff chances.

"All those unbelievers," he said when asked who might be headed for eternal damnation. "It's real. People want to say it's hell on earth now, but it's nothing [compared to] what God has

told us about heaven and hell. Hell, you're going to be in agony
for a long time. I don't know where they're going, but all I can
do is bring them closer to Christ and give them my understanding. I can only worry about myself and I can only share with
them the information about Christ. If they choose not to accept
that, then that's on them. But I hope they don't wait till the last
minute. A lot of them say they're going to wait until the last
minute and give their lives to Christ, but no man knows the
hour."

With the loss to the Raptors, the Knicks
fell to 21-20. The grand experiment had blown up in management's and the coach's faces, and all over the metropolitan area
this overpaid bunch of underachievers had frayed the nerves of
their fans more than their opponents.

They hit their nadir two nights later in Philadelphia. On
April 19, that same 76er team the Knicks had beaten by 19
points six days earlier brought them back down to .500. Matt
Geiger abused Ewing, outscoring him 22 to 11, and Iverson
made Ward and Childs look silly, crossing over them for 20
points.

The Knicks scored a mere 11 points in the third quarter, 17
in the fourth, and saw Ewing miss a potential game-tying
jumper with 30 seconds left—his fourth missed shot of the season with the game on the line.

"There are times when we have these dazed looks, like we're
not capable of getting it done," Childs said after Philadelphia's
72–67 win. "Teams feed off that."

Houston said: "It feels like we don't have an idea sometimes."

They had fallen into a three-way tie for ninth place in the
East with Toronto and Charlotte. Devoid of confidence or much
of a clue, they could take solace only in that their season would
be over in eight games.

As usual, the Knicks had attracted a large contingent at
Philadelphia's First Union Center. These Knicks fans either
lived in South Jersey or made the two-hour drive from New

York because, as any New Yorker knows, it's easier to get tickets to a Knick game in Philly than it is at the Garden. With WFAN's signal coming in loud and clear along the New Jersey Turnpike on the ride back, the several thousand who attended the game could hear overnight host Joe Benigno from midnight to 5:30 A.M. Speaking for the masses of disgusted fans who found it difficult to like much about this team, his thick Bronx accent boomed through the speakers:

"I've had it with this team! Back . . . up . . . the . . . truck! I want dese guys out of hea. Patrick Ewing, let's get rid of him. Allan Houston, the most overrated guard in the NBA! Sprewell, out of here. Chris Childs, Charlie Ward. When are we going to get a point guard? It's time. Ernie Grunfeld, Jeff Van Gundy, Dave Checketts. They all gotta go!"

8

ERNIE'S LAST SUPPER

Dave Checketts called Ernie Grunfeld on the night of April 20 and asked if the team president could meet him for dinner at Gregory's Restaurant in White Plains, New York. The Knicks had three days off before Friday's game against Charlotte, seventy-two hours for the Garden president to salvage the season.

Nervous times were ahead for everyone, except maybe Grunfeld. With eight games left, what could he possibly have to fear?

Beyond their business association, the two men had been friends since Checketts took over the Knicks a decade ago. They grew the franchise together and their families were close. When Grunfeld was asked to play a word-association game in 1997, for "Checketts" he came up with, "A good man and loyal friend."

Grunfeld was unsure of Checketts's motive for meeting him that night, but he felt he had little reason to be worried. Sure, Grunfeld and Van Gundy were bickering and not on the same page. But with only eight games left in the regular season and the Knicks still a slot out of the eighth and final playoff spot, Grunfeld figured their dinner conversation would entail fixing the myriad leaks, plotting the team's future, and figuring out what to do with Van Gundy.

Checketts wanted desperately to make the playoffs, especially after the Rangers collapsed in the final two months of the NHL season. With the Knicks clearing an estimated $2 million per playoff game, the Garden president needed those extra dates to fill the coffers.

Checketts's approval rating was starting to slip. During Wayne Gretzky's emotional farewell at the Garden, Rangers general manager Neil Smith was showered with boos upon his introduction. Checketts saved himself that fate by making his way onto the ice driving a jet-black Mercedes the team was presenting to Gretzky for his contributions to the game—with Gretzky's father riding shotgun in the car, an announcement that brought cheers.

And now the Knicks' management's grand off-season scheme had exploded in front of his eyes. As much as Grunfeld and Van Gundy had to answer to him, Checketts had cable television moguls to whom he was accountable. Neither the Knicks' play nor the feud between the coach and GM placed Checketts in a favorable light. Whatever vestiges were left of the sharp young executive who took over the Utah Jazz at age thirty-two were beginning to fade.

Earlier that day, Grunfeld sat in his office and tried to sound upbeat. Of the Knicks' chances of making the postseason, he said, "These eight games are huge. We're obviously in a playoff fight." He refused to discuss his future, deflecting even the gentlest of inquiries.

"Ernie, do you think you and Jeff deserve a full season to make this work?" he was asked.

"I don't want to get into that," he replied.

It was widely believed that if Van Gundy was to be fired, Grunfeld would not survive either. So Grunfeld had as much riding on the season's final two weeks as the coach. Or at least he believed he had two weeks.

Grunfeld later said the furthest thing from his mind as he drove to the restaurant that evening was that his job might be in jeopardy, that Checketts's asking for a meeting might be the NBA equivalent of a mob setup.

Gregory's is a quaint, upscale eatery—a little, old, white, three-story stucco house converted into a restaurant years ago. Gregory's was convenient because it's centrally located between Checketts's home in New Canaan, Connecticut, and Grunfeld's home in Franklin Lakes, New Jersey. With a predominantly Italian menu, it had become the favorite dining spot of many celebrities. The A-list included Frank Sinatra, Dean Martin, and Liza Minnelli on separate occasions.

Bill Losapio, the owner, gave Checketts and Grunfeld their favorite table that night, a secluded spot in the middle of an enclosed porch. Knowing the two men well from their frequent visits, Losapio brought them out a half-order of penne vodka pasta to split as an appetizer.

For ninety minutes, they discussed the future of the team—especially Sprewell, Camby, and Van Gundy. After they were through with their entrées and most of the restaurant had emptied out, Losapio brought them biscotti and fresh fruit as a dessert.

"Ernie, I'm sorry," Checketts began, "but I have to let you go."

"Yeah, right, Dave," Grunfeld said, laughing.

After an awkward pause, Checketts looked somberly at Grunfeld and said, "No, I'm serious, Ernie."

"Dave, you can't do this to me," Grunfeld said. For the next two hours, Grunfeld pleaded for his job and debated the move with Checketts, who listened intently and gave his reasons over and over. It was an awkward spot for Checketts, who claimed that his bosses had wanted Checketts to simply call Grunfeld in twenty minutes before he was supposed to report to work that day and ask him to clear out his office. He felt this was a more humane way to fire someone.

In the *Journal News* of Westchester, columnist Ian O'Connor saw it differently. "In the middle of dessert," he wrote, "Grunfeld found out he was the main course."

Checketts wanted to give Van Gundy every possible opportunity to make the playoffs, and he felt by removing Grunfeld that some of the stress-induced paranoia the coach was feeling would be alleviated. If the Knicks could not salvage their dreadful season, no one else could be held accountable but the coach.

Before they left Gregory's that night after what turned into nearly a four-hour dinner, Grunfeld's loyal friend picked up the tab.

The next morning, Checketts drove to Purchase College to bring Van Gundy and the team up to speed. He informed them of Grunfeld's "reassignment" to special consultant, and reinforced his desire to make the postseason.

"The number one lesson I learned from Red Holzman was that you had to be on the same page all the time," Checketts said. "And everybody in the organization had to have that. Red stood for class, dedication, staying together, and he stood for winning. That spirit is not going to be lost, in spite of the fact that we lost him."

He then addressed several sensitive issues that Grunfeld would never have thought to discuss with the players. He told Charlie Ward not to use the locker room as his pulpit. He told Larry Johnson that if the allegation of Johnson exposing himself in the locker room were true, he would face disciplinary action. He warned of fines, but the players viewed his bluster as more show than substance.

That morning, the *New York Post* had run a story in which Sprewell's agent, Robert Gist, ripped Van Gundy and Grunfeld. He claimed they were misusing his client (in other words, Gist wanted Sprewell to start).

Checketts took Sprewell aside at practice and told him he was fining him $25,000 for his agent's comments. Though the sheriff had clearly come to town and laid down the law, the players felt Checketts was grandstanding. He could make threats all he wanted, but what could he really do other than trade them? They still had their guaranteed contracts, and on the face of it, the Sprewell fine almost seemed ludicrous. He was going to lose $25,000 for something he did not say? The players union would have a field day filing a grievance over that one.

News of Grunfeld's demotion began to leak out Wednesday afternoon, and Checketts called a press conference for 5:00 P.M. at the Garden. It was held in the arena's rotunda, a vast open area at the opposite side from where the players enter the court. Used for large media gatherings like the Big East Tournament and the NBA playoffs, it is also where the elephants are housed when the circus comes to New York. Every major Garden employee was in attendance. Checketts, appearing somber and wearing a dark suit, walked up to the podium. After saying how hard reassigning Grunfeld was given their personal history, he outlined what had gone wrong under Ernie's watch.

"There were critical people in the organization who did not support the mission, and there was division clearly," he said. "And for that I hold him and myself responsible. I'm not making this guy a scapegoat for the mistakes I may have made. I approved things he did. I tried in every way to support the steps he made. Even knowing that much of the responsibility for where we are is mine, on a day-to-day basis I was not in the chair to know what was really happening."

Van Gundy had survived the power struggle for the moment, but if he could not siphon a playoff appearance out of his team, he, too, was going to be dining at Gregory's soon. Phil Jackson's name was out there; the Nets had contacted him, and the Lakers were poised to make a run. With Grunfeld out of the way and Van Gundy and his team in trouble, the Jackson-to-the-Knicks rumors were about to come to fruition.

"There are no winners in today's announcement," Checketts said. "No, this is not a show of confidence in anyone." Asked about Jackson, he added, "I know where you're going with that. I'm not going to speculate. Jeff is the head coach."

The next day a number of columnists began calling for the heads of Van Gundy and Checketts, portraying Grunfeld as a sacrificial lamb.

The media, which had taken up sides, were an integral part of this circus. When the team won, Grunfeld was vindicated by many columnists because his off-season gambles were finally paying off. But in the next paper, you could read about how with Grunfeld out of the way, Van Gundy finally had time to mold this disparate group of personalities and talents together. Or how Checketts knew this was going to work out all along.

The Garden brass read every word, dissecting stories as if they were the Pentagon Papers.

In most large American media markets, the local sports television reporter is viewed as an important figure; the job has a celebrity quality attached to it. But in New York, it was the printed word that ruled. Mike Lupica, the nationally known columnist from the *Daily News,* could still get managers fired. Peter Vecsey, America's most recognized basketball columnist, could run a player out of town. And Harvey Araton, from the *Times,* could eloquently turn a Teflon star into a hoodlum in 800 words or less. Newspapers were still the most powerful medium in the city.

The players all take great pride in informing reporters that they don't read anything written about them. Yet whenever you wrote anything overly critical, the players would make sure you heard about it.

Interestingly, Sprewell may have been the exception. You could carve him up, and he did not blink. Perhaps he had no choice but to develop thick skin during his exile from the league, a period that featured negative stories in every publication in America about his horrible act from December of 1997. He was indifferent about criticism, but was still very accommodating when it came to interviews. Sprewell did not mind talking to you today, because he couldn't care less about what you wrote yesterday.

Never was this more apparent than after a scathing *New York Times Magazine* article that portrayed Sprewell as a player who marched to his own beat—ignoring convention, his teammates, and structure so he could essentially play basketball in his own private universe. The story appeared on May 2, the week the playoffs would begin, when the Knicks were just beginning to find some cohesion on the floor.

It generated endless debate about Sprewell's impact on the franchise, and may have been the most provocative and widely read story about the player during the season. After two weeks

of interminable analysis—talk-show arguments, hate mail, and
unflattering comments from fans at the Garden—the author of
the article, a coauthor of this book, finally approached Sprewell
and asked if he had any problem with anything written in the
story.

"I'm sorry, I just haven't had a chance to read it," he said
earnestly. "You know me, I just never look at the stuff. Thanks
for asking though."

Some players might have just said that; with Sprewell, it was
unquestionably the case.

Jeff Van Gundy was among those not
buying his boss's explanation for why Grunfeld was fired. Although the coach accepted his share of the blame, he said that
losing—and not a rift between him and Grunfeld—caused the
front office shakeup.

"I've learned a couple things about being here," he said.
"When you lose, it's ugly. If we would have won more, there
wouldn't be a need to blame anyone. The unfortunate part is
that losing caused this. If we win some of those close games,
everybody has their job. What's reported as a feud is way over-
stating it. I even read that Dave said there was division. If there
was, losing caused the division. It was not the division causing
losing, that's for sure."

Van Gundy was not out of the woods, but it was clear Checketts had taken sides. On the one hand, it absolutely mortified
him to demote the man who in many ways had been his touchstone in New York since he took over the Knicks—Grunfeld,
the family man from Queens who had more tenure with the organization than anyone in the front office. On the other hand,
Ewing and Larry Johnson had lobbied hard for the coach, and
Checketts was worried that if he fired Van Gundy his hopes of
making the playoffs would disintegrate. Who knew if Ewing,
his left Achilles tendon throbbing, would not just shut it down
for the final eight games and return next season?

If Checketts had considered firing Van Gundy, his options on the sideline were good ones: Don Chaney, the former Celtic who had been a head coach in Houston and Detroit; and Brendan Malone, the former Toronto coach who had overcome prostate cancer surgery a year earlier and promptly returned to the bench. Both were great teachers of the game and well liked among the players, and either one could have taken over. But out of loyalty to Ewing and to his own gut feeling, Checketts decided he would not meddle in the locker room any further.

With Grunfeld, a former teammate of Ewing's, out of the picture and Van Gundy still at the helm, the franchise center pledged his allegiance to the coach and the team. "We definitely have to play for ourselves and for Jeff," Ewing said. "The bottom line is, we have to win."

They would try to make the playoffs under the watchful eye of Checketts, who had announced that for the first time since he ran the team in the early 1990s, he would be traveling with the Knicks for the remainder of the season—whether it was eight games or more. He had appointed himself interim team president and effectively took over the day-to-day operations of the club.

Over the season's final two weeks, he planned to speak with the players individually and gauge where the team was under Van Gundy. From Ewing to Brunson, the third-string point guard, he wanted input. His methods were a stark contrast to those of Grunfeld, who rarely reached out to the players in the same concerned manner as Checketts.

Whether it was Van Gundy's ill feelings toward Grunfeld or that Grunfeld was simply viewed as a management guy, the battle created a wedge in the organization. Players such as Allan Houston and Marcus Camby genuinely liked Grunfeld, but Ewing, who had been around the longest, had his suspicions. Grunfeld often seemed irked that Van Gundy, whom he had given the job after firing Nelson, earned more than his own annual take of $750,000. Not surprisingly, Grunfeld's name surfaced in connection with several job openings around the NBA; whether it was Denver or Golden State expressing passing interest, the reports always seemed to be Grunfeld's way of getting another bump from the Knicks—a negotiating technique used successfully by players, coaches, and, yes, the media.

Holding court in the Garden corridor before a game, Grunfeld often shook hands like he was running for office. Friendly and personable, he became known as good old Ernie. In a profession where it's not uncommon to put your job in front of your family, Grunfeld always maintained perspective; he was always more proud of the accomplishments of his teenage daughter, Rebecca, and his son, Dan, than anything he or his team achieved.

But his suspicion of the media often made him come across as insecure. He sometimes felt they were out to get him. He was consumed with how he was represented in newspapers, often asking inquisitive reporters over the phone, "What's your angle here? Where are you going with this?" In a 1997 interview, he lamented the perception that he was "just a dumb jock from Queens" instead of the architect of the franchise who knew the salary, strengths, and weaknesses of every player in the league.

His insecurities seemed unfounded. After all, how stupid could a guy who climbed the ladder be? From marginal player to radio color man, assistant coach, general manager, and then, finally, team president, Grunfeld had ascended quickly in the organization. Overpaid contracts, questionable signings, and all, he had presided over a perennial playoff team that came within a game of winning it all in 1994.

Why did he lose his job? Beyond what Checketts felt was a lack of institutional control, he thought Grunfeld had become obsessed with firing Van Gundy. Likewise, Van Gundy became obsessed with the thought that Grunfeld wanted him out. Clearly, Grunfeld had overestimated his friendship with Checketts—but he had also underestimated Van Gundy's intelligence and strong bond with the players.

While Van Gundy was perceived to have swum with the corporate sharks, the real man-eaters were the players. However much executives want to run things, stars wield the ultimate power in today's NBA. Van Gundy's support from the key players made all the difference. Grunfeld believed he was safe because of his relationship with Checketts, the suit above him. But Van Gundy had the loyalty of the majority of the team, the only constituency that mattered.

On the day after Sprewell was fined and Grunfeld was sent away, Sprewell sauntered into practice at Madison Square Garden twenty minutes late. It would not have been a big deal, except that there were several hundred employees of American Express and twelve reporters watching during a rare open practice. Sprewell had forgotten about the public workout and had gone to Purchase; realizing no one was there, he hightailed it to Midtown Manhattan. He was not fined for his tardiness—and even if he had been, the money was not going to come out of his own pocket.

AND 1, the Pennsylvania-based basketball shoe and apparel company, had signed an endorsement agreement with the Knicks guard two days earlier. It was just the latest example how Sprewell's image was on the comeback trail. Fired by Converse and ostracized by the sports world after choking Carlesimo, he had become an instant star at the Garden. Fans rose from their seats as he ripped off his warmups and reported to the scorer's table to check into the game.

Sprewell's appeal in New York crossed all social, economic, and racial lines. Like Lawrence Taylor with the Giants or Darryl Strawberry with the Mets and Yankees, the feelings in New York toward Sprewell were time-tested: As long as you perform, fans would look the other way when it came to off-the-field transgressions. Sure, Sprewell was still widely perceived to be a thug for his actions more than a year ago. But he was *their* thug. And that's what attracted AND 1 to Sprewell.

The deal was yet another example of the image-making forces at work in the NBA. Ever since Nike began its association with Michael Jordan in 1984, the role of the shoe companies had been expanding in the league.

Jordan's enormous popularity—the fact that his charisma

and presence, as portrayed in the early Nike spots directed by
Spike Lee transcended sport—ushered in the era of NBA Superstar as Global Celebrity.

From Shaquille O'Neal to Gary Payton, by the early 1990s
every team seemed to have a commercially identifiable face.
The league salivated as players rose to rock-star status.

That evolution kept marketing executives on constant watch
for the next Jordan, and soon even the most obscure players
were signing endorsement deals with sneaker companies, just
in case.

It was not long before the time players spent filming commercials and making special appearances began to grate on
team officials and coaches. Many of them believed the players
were more loyal to their product lines than their teams. For the
1992 Dream Team, featuring Magic Johnson, Larry Bird, and
Jordan, that loyalty superseded even patriotism; before heading
to the medal stand to receive their gold and hear the national
anthem played in their honor, they took time to zip down their
Reebok warmup tops to conceal the logo, thus making sure
their own brand identities were not compromised.

One of the most telling scenes of the new priorities involved
David Falk, the agent responsible for projecting Jordan's image,
discussing a deal for Allen Iverson with Reebok executives after
Iverson was drafted in 1996. "Allen doesn't have to be a great
player," Falk told the executives around a conference table. "He
has to perform great."

Before O'Neal left Orlando for the Los Angeles Lakers in
1996, facetiously discussing what he wanted from a new team
he said, "I just want to play the game, drink Pepsi, and wear
Reebok."

In recent years, with sales sliding backward, many shoe
companies severed their ties with NBA players. O'Neal was one
of the first casualties, and soon the seven-figure sneaker deal
had all but disappeared. At the same time, off-court scandals
and criminal charges left many stars with dwindling endorsement opportunities.

But AND 1 was different. To the fledgling company, NBA

malcontents were misunderstood artists. The unsavory pasts of some of their clients fit right into the marketing scheme. Pump up the player whom every parent detested, and what do you get? A bunch of rebellious teenagers buying Sprewell apparel for no other reason than to piss off Mom and Dad.

The company's clients included such upstanding citizens as Chris Webber, detained abroad in the off-season on charges of marijuana possession, and Vernon Maxwell, the hothead who missed the playoffs with the Hornets in 1998 because he had to serve time on a drug charge. Mad Max was also suspended for ten games in February of 1995 for running up into the stands to physically confront a heckler in Portland.

AND 1 came onto the scene five years ago catering to the hip-hop playground set. Beginning with a line of "in your face" trash-talk T-shirts, they expanded to shoes and other apparel.

"AND 1 and Latrell Sprewell come from the same place," said Seth Berger, the founding partner and president who along with co-founder Jay Coen Gilbert had become the latest white businessmen to package urban street culture for profit. "Our roots are at the playground level, where ballplayers talk smack and have the game to back it up. With his charisma, his attitude, and his All-Star game, Latrell is a natural for our brand, and we're lucky to have him."

Berger and his company had embraced Sprewell's image, that leave-me-alone-and-let-me-play-ball attitude. In many ways, Sprewell had taken on the establishment and won. He had become a counterculture hero in the world's largest media market. He was a natural, in-your-face pitchman.

Early on in the season, his No. 8 jersey had become a hot-selling item at the team's store on the Garden's second level. John Starks's No. 3, meanwhile, was on sale for half price. It did not take long for the team's unofficial mascot and lifelong fan, Spike Lee, to accept Sprewell as one of New York's finest; he, too, traded in his faded blue Starks jersey for No. 8.

"He fits the perpetrator to a 'T,'" Lee said through a voice thick with sarcasm. "The corn rows. The scowl. What's interesting, though, is he's very articulate. People would think he's another thug the NYPD has to protect us from. Look, I love his heart. I love the way he goes up and down the court. Sometimes, though, when he gets the ball, it doesn't matter how many guys are on him, he's going to shoot. And he makes up his mind, 'I'm shooting,' and that's it. I just wish he wouldn't be so quick to pull the trigger sometimes."

Lee also led the get-off-Spree's-back contingent when it came to Sprewell's past. "Even Jay Greenberg in the *Post* had a line, 'Van Gundy must have had a good meeting with Sprewell because there were no scratches on his neck.' I mean, when are they going to let that stuff die? He was wrong, but that book's been written and now it's closed."

Sprewell was upset about the fine that day at practice, claiming Gist had misrepresented him. "One thing I don't need, and that's more controversy," he said. Checketts's penalty also cast Sprewell in the role of locker room martyr; among the outraged players was union chief Ewing, who said the players association would discuss appealing the fine.

But Berger and AND 1 jumped at the opportunity for more publicity, announcing that it would pick up Sprewell's $25,000 tab. "We got Latrell's back," said AND 1's Jay Coen Gilbert. "And we want him to concentrate on playing basketball and helping the Knicks get into the playoffs."

It was a marketing stroke of genius, and it stole a lot of Checketts's thunder. If he was looking to make a point with Sprewell that he could get tough with him, the move had backfired. For the cost of a decent-sized advertising spot, AND 1 reaped a campaign's worth of publicity at Checketts's expense. In a league where arbitration lawyers, unions, and sneaker companies were part of the landscape, Checketts's old fashioned disciplinary tactics were doomed to extinction.

In the post-Grunfeld era, the Knicks finally found an intangible they'd been missing all season: luck. Three days after the team president was reassigned—against the Charlotte team that had humiliated them two weeks earlier—the Knicks led by as many as 18 in the third quarter on their way to a 110–105 victory.

Ewing nearly lost his cool when he absorbed a shove from Derrick Coleman. He was about to retaliate when Ward stepped in like the boxing referee Mills Lane and pushed Ewing to safety. Ewing was so irate he took a swing at Ward and later apologized for his outburst. "I just wanted to play the good guy as usual," said Ward.

Ward's quick response ended up saving the Knicks down the stretch. The Hornets erupted for 35 fourth-quarter points and were trailing by only 104–102 with 24 seconds left when Ewing scored on a runner over Coleman that bounced around the rim four times before falling in.

If Ewing had made that shot four days earlier in Philadelphia, maybe Grunfeld would still be the president. Either way, the center had finally caught a friendly bounce in the final seconds.

"That's the shot I was criticized for the other day," he said. "That's the shot I've been shooting my whole career. It's my shot and I'm going to take it." Ewing's 26 points and three blocked shots had put the Knicks in a tie with Toronto for the final playoff spot.

But the win came with a price. Ewing's Achilles tendon was hurting again, and he could not physically bring himself to play in that Sunday's crucial game at Miami.

For all the euphoria over last season's Game 5 win in the first round, the Knicks had suffered some of their most deflating losses at the decrepit Miami Arena in the city's impoverished Overtown section. And more than any other regular season game in South Florida, they needed this one.

You would never have guessed that from the first three quarters, which featured the Ewing-less Knicks standing and watching as Alonzo Mourning dominated inside. He scored 27 in those first three periods.

Miami was blowing the doors off the Knicks, 55–35, early in the second half. Even the most loyal and optimistic fans turned off NBC's telecast to enjoy a spring day in New York. They never could have imagined what was about to unfold.

A desperate Van Gundy went to a more athletic lineup, inserting his top three reserves, Sprewell, Camby, and Childs, to team with Johnson and Houston. Over the last one and a half quarters, Van Gundy essentially used a six-man rotation, as Kurt Thomas, who had spent the first two years of his career in Miami, transformed into that stone-cold presence he once talked about in the locker room.

Bodying up Mourning, crawling inside his brain like Charles Oakley always did, Thomas held the brutish, 6-foot-10 Heat center to a measly two free throws over the final 19 minutes. During one sequence, Thomas drew a charge against Jamal Mashburn and then baited Mashburn into a foul on the ensuing possession that nearly precipitated another Heat-Knick brawl. Thomas and Mashburn were both assessed technicals. The game may have looked like a lost cause, but at least the Knicks were finally going down with a fight.

The score was 73–58 with seven minutes left. "Give-up time for some teams," Johnson would later say.

But Miami scored only one point over the next four minutes as the Knicks' defense stiffened. And then it happened.

Sprewell hit two free throws. Thomas set Camby up for a dunk. Sprewell and Thomas each made a pair of free throws. After Mourning hit one of two foul shots, Houston dropped in two straight pillowy jumpers over a defenseless Dan Majerle. Suddenly the sullen and quiet Knick bench came alive.

Miami's lead was incredibly down to four when Thomas fouled out with 2:47 remaining. He did not want to leave the floor after playing the most productive 33 minutes of his season. He stared at referee Joey Crawford, who said to Thomas, "Don't give me that stupid fucking look."

P.J. Brown's two free throws made it 76–70, but the Knicks had one run left in them. Houston's two free throws with 1:58 left drew New York to within 77–74.

The Heat came up empty on their next two possessions. Moments later, with 56 seconds left, Johnson and Houston ran a pick-and-roll play with Johnson moving behind the 3-point line on the right elbow. Houston kicked it out to Johnson with the shot clock running down, and Johnson buried the shot.

Tie game.

Tim Hardaway, a renowned Knick killer on par with Michael Jordan and Reggie Miller, had had enough. He coolly dropped in a bomb from 26 feet away at the top of the arc on the next Miami possession with 39 seconds left, Miami's first field goal in more than seven minutes. The Knicks called timeout, and the ball rolled toward Van Gundy, who picked it up and smacked it in disgust before looking in disdain at Hardaway.

"Unfortunately, we've seen that before," Van Gundy said.

That one big shot seemed to swing the momentum, to bury the Knicks for good.

But after the timeout, Houston drove the middle of the lane, drawing Mourning and Brown. Out of the corner of his eye, he spotted Camby streaking in along the left baseline. A quick pass around the trees resulted in an easy two-handed dunk by Camby, who drew a foul on Mashburn. Camby made the free throw to complete the three-point play and knot the game at 80-all, six seconds after Hardaway's shot had seemed to put the game away.

He would try again. But this time, Hardaway's turnaround jumper on the next possession was short. Childs chased down the rebound and was falling out of bounds with Brown on his back. It was incidental contact, but the referee gave the Knicks a small gift by calling Brown for pushing.

By sinking both free throws with 20.1 seconds left, Childs stunningly gave the Knicks the lead in a game they trailed by 20 less than two quarters before.

Miami's final possession ended with Mourning missing a jump hook in the lane with 10 seconds left. The rebound was knocked out of bounds to Miami, and the Heat went back to their franchise center. This time, he passed to a cutting Mashburn underneath the basket. Mashburn lost his dribble, and Childs and Hardaway dove to the floor for the loose ball with

0.6 second left in front of the Knick bench. As soon as the ball was tapped, the buzzer sounded and the Knicks celebrated as if they had just won a playoff series.

"We stole this one," said Camby, who finished with 15 points and proved he could play against a physical team like Miami. "We just didn't want to give up."

Johnson was the spiritual leader that day, scoring 23 points on 10-of-13 shooting from the field. He also provided perspective afterward. "There is no time to celebrate," he said to the players in the locker room. "We have to think about Charlotte. We've lost like this the whole year. That's why we're in this position."

Checketts watched the whole scene unfold from ten rows up in the arena. "You just played the best four-point game of your life," he told Kurt Thomas. NBC's cameras captured a pensive Checketts watching as the Knicks were on the verge of annihilation. Later, he said he was not worried when the Knicks fell behind by 20.

"I never felt they were blowing us out," he said. "I felt like the shots were going to fall, and we were going to have a chance. But that was some ending. It's great being around these guys. They want to get it done."

They parlayed the improbable Miami victory into another win the next night at Charlotte. Streaking to a 30–16 first-quarter lead, they held off the Hornets in the final minutes and won 91–84.

Camby was monstrous, blocking six of his seven shots in the second half. Sprewell scored a game-high 21 points, including a tough, pull-up jump shot with 47.7 seconds left to effectively end Charlotte's comeback bid. And in Ewing's absence, Dudley came up huge, too; he scored seven points, grabbed 12 rebounds, blocked three shots, and scored on the most un-Dudley-like of shots, a wild, double-pump reverse layup that was half Kobe Bryant and half Georghe Muresan.

"Every now and then I break something out," Dudley said.

Nineteen days earlier, the Hornets had blown them out and their season was on the precipice. Now they were 24-21, a game and a half ahead of Charlotte and Toronto for the eighth spot. They had a long way to go, but the mood in the Charlotte Coliseum that night was a far cry from that of the despondent group who showered and dressed there on April 7.

Up next was a short flight to Atlanta, a favorite city for many of the league's black players because of its abundance of Southern hospitality, black-owned restaurants and nightspots. Dudley tried to persuade Johnson, who took more time than any of his teammates to leave the locker room, to hurry up.

"Why you in such a rush to get to ATL, Duds? I didn't know that was your city."

Dudley smiled as Childs cracked, "He must be in a rush to get to his hotel room to watch a movie."

The next afternoon, Johnson, Childs, and their teammates had the day off. Van Gundy was beginning to feel a little better about his team. Even the beat reporters and columnists assigned to cover this season-altering road trip were given a controversy-free day.

Two road wins had taken the heat off the coach, and for the moment no one was saying how structurally damaged the Knicks were. Maybe they would not have to completely refurbish in the off-season.

Dudley even had time to make it up to Ward's room for Bible study in the afternoon. There, they discussed everything from the Book of Mark to the miracle win in Miami. Van Gundy could talk all he wanted about God not taking sides, but Ward felt otherwise. He referred to the comeback triumph over the Heat as further evidence of intervention by a higher authority. "I've been in comebacks before, but I haven't seen anything like that," he said. "That was a clear example of how God confirms that things are going to work out if you have prayer warriors on your team."

Barry Watkins, the communications director for the Garden and Checketts's right-hand man, organized an outing at Turner Field that evening for the traveling broadcast and print media.

Checketts returned to New York for the day, and Van Gundy never leaves his hotel room the night before a game to dine with reporters, so it was up to Watkins and the team's two PR officials, Weiller and Hamamoto, to entertain.

The night included a lavish and large buffet in the club restaurant, followed by a Braves-Pirates game. Joining some of the same people who were calling for Checketts's and Van Gundy's heads two weeks earlier, Watkins formed a $1 buy-in pool to guess how many pitches would be thrown in a half inning. It made for decent if awkward camaraderie. Everybody played nice for the evening.

The Knicks had won two big games without Ewing, whose Achilles tendon needed the rest. The more dismal the team's long-term playoff hopes looked, the more Ewing's health became a topic for discussion. Did it make sense to shut Ewing down for the remaining six games, with the hope that he would be rested and ready by the time they got to the first round—if they made it there? Shuffling him in and out of the lineup did not exactly help the team's chemistry. His day-to-day status mirrored that of Larry Bird at the end of his career; as great as Bird was, his balky back became a distraction for the Celtics his last two seasons.

So Checketts decided to tread on hallowed ground, asking Van Gundy whether Ewing should remain sidelined until the playoffs began. "I threw it out just to say, 'Is it worthwhile just resting him now?'" Checketts said. "But I think in Jeff's view—and in Patrick's view—if he can help us, if that one extra game can make a difference, I think we have to have it.

"I'm not giving up on the season when I say this by any stretch, but Patrick needs a good off-season when he's not sitting at the bargaining table and he doesn't have that load on his mind. But saying all that, I still believe that if we can get him at 80 or 90 percent of what he's capable of doing and get a good playoff position, there isn't anyone or anybody we can't beat."

With a home game against Philadelphia coming up the following night, Ewing elected to sit out against the Hawks. His good buddy, Mutombo, took advantage of his absence by pro-

ducing 18 points and 18 rebounds in Atlanta's 76–73 win. Indicative of the bad basketball still being played, the two teams
combined for an NBA-record low 19 points in the third quarter.
Sprewell went off for 29 points, including a wild running
3-pointer with 2.4 seconds left to cut the lead to one.

The shot would have meant more had the Knicks not been
burned by a questionable call with 9.5 seconds left. After Johnson hit a 3-pointer to cut the lead to one, referee George Toliver
inexplicably whistled Houston for a foul away from the play as
Atlanta was taking the ball out of bounds.

Toliver ruled that Houston was holding the Hawks' Steve
Smith. The foul was costly because in the final two minutes of a
game, a foul during a dead-ball situation results in one free
throw plus possession. The play was a noncall in any close
game, and Van Gundy was beside himself. He said he had not
seen a foul called like that in ten years. And the official who
made it actually had the Knicks to thank for some financial as-
sistance a year ago.

Toliver was one of more than a dozen referees targeted by
the Internal Revenue Service for downgrading first-class flight
tickets to coach, pocketing the difference, and not reporting the
income. He was indicted, pled guilty, and was dismissed from
the NBA for a year. During that time, the Knicks contracted
with Toliver to referee their training camp games in Charleston,
South Carolina. Van Gundy wasn't expecting favors in return,
but with the team's season and his job on the line every night
he could have used the normal noncall.

Their four-game winning streak over, the Knicks returned to
a charged gathering at the Garden. Fans were starting to wonder if their team had turned the corner, but they were brought
back to reality 10 minutes into the 76ers game. With Ewing
playing, the Knicks missed their first 11 shots and fell behind
23–8. A cascade of boos rained down from the rafters.

Sprewell finally got on the board on a short turn-around
jumper in the post moments later. Allen Iverson and friends
didn't know it, but the game was over after that seemingly
harmless shot. In the next 37 minutes, the 76ers scored 47

points to Sprewell's 30, and New York cruised to an 85–70 victory.

It wasn't just his numbers, but the way he was scoring: Two open-court dunks within 14 seconds of each other at the end of the third quarter—emphatic, two-handed jams that left him scowling after each one—turned the Garden into a madhouse and became the first four of an 11-point binge by the energized guard. He nailed a running 25-footer with the shot clock running down to start the fourth quarter and bring the crowd to its feet.

He had scored 80 points in three games, relishing the sixth-man role as if it were his birthright. But he still wanted to start.

"It's amazing when you're watching him," Camby said. "When he scores in bunches, it's like a video game. When he gets the rock, he can go. He can go for 50 if given the time."

Rescuing the Knicks from a potentially devastating loss, Sprewell's contributions helped New York move to 25-22 and one and a half games ahead of Charlotte for the last playoff spot. If the Knicks won one of their final three games, the Hornets and Raptors would have to win their final four games to eliminate New York.

The Knicks were not totally cured, as shown by their 23-point loss at Indiana three days later. Unable to match up with the Pacers, the Knicks were abysmal from start to finish. Going into the season's final two games against Boston and Miami, they not only needed to secure a playoff spot but they wanted to avoid Indiana, certain to be the number two seed behind Miami in the East, at all costs in the first round.

The Knicks had not beaten the Pacers at dilapidated Market Square Arena since January of 1997, having lost seven straight on Indiana's home floor. The Pacers' experience and size were too much for the Knicks, not to mention their starting center. Ewing resembled a cardboard cutout against Rik Smits, who blew by a flat-footed Ewing for a dunk during the game.

"We need two more wins, so I have to play," Ewing said afterward.

With Charlotte losing that same night and Toronto out of the picture, the Knicks needed only to beat Boston at home the next evening to clinch a playoff spot for the twelfth straight season.

Sore, tired, and his pride hurt by all the talk that he might be a detriment to the team, Ewing summoned his resolve and his skills against the Celtics. He scored 27 points, grabbed a season-high 19 rebounds, and carried the Knicks past Boston 95–88.

With one game left in the season, they were in.

"I don't listen to anything y'all write," he said. "I've always believed in myself. And when I stop believing in myself and don't think I can play this game at a high level, that's the day I'm going to retire."

Van Gundy was relieved to have locked up a playoff spot, but he was incensed at the Garden fans who groaned each time Ewing caught the ball in the post, dribbled, and began his monotonous journey to the basket. In perhaps his finest moment of the season, they still would not appreciate him.

"Patrick's will to be great superseded his health," Van Gundy said afterward.

Amid the malcontents in the crowd were a small faction of people who in the final seconds began chanting, "We want the Heat! We want the Heat!" But before the Knicks could set up a meeting with Miami in the first round of the playoff, they had other business to take care of with Riley's team on the final night of the regular season.

The Knicks had a lot to gain by losing on May 5. A Miami victory would ensure that New York would not have to face Indiana, and instead would create a Knick-Heat postseason matchup for the third straight year. But Philadelphia also controlled the Knicks' fate.

If the Sixers defeated Detroit in a game that began at 7:00 P.M. that night, it would render the Knick-Heat game at 8:00 P.M. meaningless. Philadelphia would secure seventh place if it won and New York would automatically fall into the eighth spot.

Playing the paranoid control freak to the hilt, Van Gundy demanded that the Garden's scoreboard posting out-of-town games be turned off. He didn't want his players distracted by what was happening in the Sixers-Pistons game. Plus, he was playing to win, even if it meant the Knicks would face Indiana and most likely first-round elimination.

He kept the injured Ewing out of the starting lineup, but the other four regulars stepped onto the floor. Riley, meanwhile, was clearly looking to avoid facing New York in the first round. He started his junior varsity. Mourning did not dress. Hardaway did not play. The starting lineup included Duane Causwell at center, Voshon Lenard at shooting guard, and Rex Walters at the point.

Much to the dismay of their fans, the Knicks were winning easily. After everything they had been through, they were blowing perhaps their one shot at moving past the first round.

But ninety miles south, Allen Iverson would give them the sweetest reprieve imaginable.

The Pistons, holding a two-point lead with 13 seconds left, were inbounding the ball when Jerry Stackhouse appeared to be intentionally fouled by Philadelphia guard Aaron McKie. To Stackhouse's shock, no call was made by referee Tom Washington. Stackhouse lost the ball, Iverson scooped it up like a cornerback, and sank a rainbow jumper with eight seconds left to force overtime.

Finishing with 33 points, Iverson then hit two clinching free throws with 28 seconds left in the extra period to send his team leaping up to sixth place—and the Knicks to Miami.

Riley wasted no time in stoking the pre-series embers. "This series is beyond everyone's control," he said. "This is preordained. It's the way it has to be. This is something that the gods want to take care of."

Van Gundy and his team were beginning to find an identity, but so many issues were still left unresolved. Sprewell had only appeared in three playoff games; Camby was a postseason virgin, and Ewing's health was a monster question mark. And then there was Van Gundy's future with the club: He seemed to be a first-round knockout away from the unemployment line.

Before the Miami game, Checketts spoke candidly about his team.

"I don't like being the eighth seed," he said. "I don't like not winning the division. I don't like not having home-court advantage, at the very least, in the first round. And I won't accept it for having the payroll we have."

Checketts was happy about the Knicks avoiding a first-round date with Indiana. Earlier he had said he did not feel New York matched up well with the Pacers, a theory that Van Gundy did not buy. He thought management was again selling the team short, and that the Knicks should never fear any opponent. After all, Bird was coaching, not playing.

"It's not the first time we disagreed and it won't be the last," said Checketts. "I said this after Indiana beat us in the playoffs [last year]. I didn't think we had enough size and rebounding to match up with them. We didn't make changes for the sake of change. We made moves that didn't come together at the start of the year, but now have a chance to come together."

Even if the architect of those changes had to be sacrificed to make it happen.

9

MIAMI MIRACLE, THE SEQUEL

The season was about to expire, and Latrell Sprewell had dribbled himself into a corner. Trapped 25 feet away on the right wing, the Knicks' season would most likely hinge on a circus shot in front of the Miami Heat bench.

Terry Porter, the veteran Heat guard, was flailing away at the ball. He suddenly knocked it free, and the ball rolled right through Sprewell's legs—barely missing his right heel—and out of bounds with 4.5 seconds left.

Trailing by a point and with no timeouts remaining in a decisive Game 5, an animated Jeff Van Gundy signaled for the Knicks to run a play called simply Triangle Post. Sprewell was about to inbound. His teammates were lining up to run the play. Miami Arena was on its feet.

"One stop!" Alonzo Mourning, the Heat center, yelled to his teammates. "One stop, that's all."

Within moments, years of intertwined history and animosity would reach a climax.

On the eve of the 1999 playoffs, the Las Vegas bookmaker Danny Sheridan installed the Knicks as a

25,000-to-1 shot to win the championship. A trailer park in a tornado had a better chance of survival.

But the players were giving themselves more than just a shot in the best-of-five first-round series. This was Miami, New York's mirror image and nemesis the past two seasons. If they learned anything from their incredible comeback two weeks earlier, the Knicks knew the Heat were as flawed as they were.

Their previous two playoff series had come down to a decisive game, and were marred by fights that gave birth to the league's most unsavory rivalry.

So they had history, too. Each side felt a grave injustice had been committed in separate seasons, though the real reason for their misfortunes had more to do with their inability to control their emotions.

Two years earlier, it wasn't the Heat that beat the Knicks; it was their own stupidity. New York was leading the second-round series three games to one, about to collide with the Bulls, when the infamous Game 5 melee in Miami—ignited by P.J. Brown and Charlie Ward—led to multiple suspensions for the final two games.

In 1998, they again could not govern their passions. Pat Riley's face was ashen when he realized his best player, Mourning, had taken himself out of the most crucial game of the season by trading punches with Larry Johnson at the end of Game 4, a transgression that carried an all but automatic suspension for the fifth and final game.

Ewing was still recovering from wrist surgery and had to miss the whole series, but now the Heat's force in the middle would be out of Game 5. "You just blew the season," Riley said to Mourning as he was escorted off the Madison Square Garden floor.

(The most enduring and comic image from that fight, which happened in front of the Knicks' bench with just 1.4 seconds left, was of Van Gundy running onto the Garden floor between the two and eventually clinging to Mourning's leg like a Chihuahua nipping at a mailman's trousers.)

New York's blowout of Miami in Game 5 helped avenge the

'97 debacle, and it opened up a huge personal wound for Riley, whose relationship with Van Gundy would change forever.

"What Van Gundy said the other night was wrong, when he said he's 'embarrassed for the Knicks, the NBA, and the Heat,' " Riley said. "He should not be embarrassed for us. The only one who was out of control the other night was him. Totally. Why didn't he go after Larry Johnson? The rule is, you go after your guy. I've been in some piles myself. And I've always tried to find my guy."

Head coaches are permitted to leave the bench to break up a fight, but Riley was blaming Van Gundy for heightening the tension between the two teams. Of course, he also told the *Miami Herald*'s Dan LaBatard, " 'Zo should have punched that motherfucker [Johnson] in the face."

It was classic Riley, pulling out all the motivational ploys to spur on the troops. But that he would disparage Van Gundy, whose brother, Stan, served on Riley's Miami staff, outraged his one-time pupil.

Van Gundy was especially hurt by a comment from Riley regarding their relationship, when Riley said that winning is more important than friendship. Van Gundy could not believe how the man he looked up to had turned on him. Riley had referred to Van Gundy as one of his "few loyalists still left in New York" when he left the Knicks for the Heat in 1995, and Van Gundy believed that loyalty extended beyond the court. But now he began to see a side of Riley he had heard and been warned about, yet never wanted to believe. The Winner Within, to take the title of Riley's best-selling book, had become the Whiner Without— without regard for anyone or anything in his path.

Beating the Heat, and Riley, in '98 led to an awkward moment for Van Gundy, because he could not share his greatest coaching moment to date with either his brother or his mentor. But the victory did convince the organization and fans that the diminutive coach could escape Riley's immense shadow; he was not just Pat's personal assistant.

Following in the footsteps of the coach with the second highest winning percentage of all time was not easy. While it was flattering to have his coaching style compared to Riley's, Van Gundy faced personal comparisons to the most stylish sideline tactician in sports. In 1996, the *New York Post* published a tongue-in-cheek graphic to show how Van Gundy could not hold a candle to Riley. From clothes to hairstyles, the newspaper poked fun at Van Gundy's appearance—a ridiculous tale of the tape that brought his wife to tears.

From either insomnia or from watching hours of game film, the bags under Van Gundy's eyes indeed sometimes seemed too large for the overhead compartment. But some in the media were just mean-spirited. The *Chicago Tribune* columnist Bernie Lincicome once wrote that Van Gundy needed to go a little lighter on the formaldehyde. "The national poster boy for nerds," was how the *Miami Herald*'s Greg Cote described the coach after the Mourning incident.

"We've heard them all," said Kim Van Gundy. "From, 'He looks like a funeral home director' to comments about the dark circles under his eyes. One of the papers ran a fashion comparison between Pat and Jeff, making fun of Jeff's suits because they're bought off the rack. I mean, this is a guy I've gone out with since I was fifteen years old. It hurts for a lot of reasons, but mostly because I buy his suits."

The *Newsday* sports cartoonist Richard Harris Jr. could not draw Van Gundy without depicting him in a cheap, unkind way—exaggerated receding hairline, droopy eyes, deathly facial pallor. It made you wonder, if Van Gundy were of African-American, Hispanic, or Asian descent, would his physical appearance take such a beating? Was it somehow politically okay to make fun of little white coaches who paid their dues and beat the odds to survive in a profession dominated by former players?

"Somebody made a comment that Phil Jackson looks like Theodore Kaczynski," said Jeff Nix, the Knicks' assistant coach. "Well, he does, but what is a coach supposed to look like? Does George Karl look like a coach? Does Rick Majerus look like a coach? There is no blueprint. I think what has happened here and in college is that everyone is so into individual marketing. What's the image of your coach? Jeff Van Gundy has been defying stereotypes for a long time."

He learned early that image can count more than experience and potential. After the Providence College coaching staff was fired in 1988, Pitino placed a call on Van Gundy's behalf to the Naval Academy to recommend him for the job of head coach. "That guy told him that I was very good, but that he thought I was too short. I was shocked by that. It raised my awareness that some people are shortsighted enough to think that you get respect based on how you look.

"Okay, so I don't look like Pat Riley. Neither does anybody else in the NBA. Get over it."

At first glance, the Knick-Heat rivalry embodied all that was wrong with the NBA. Unimaginative offense. Violence. And those pathetically low scores. Yet had it not been for those two regrettable fights, the perception would be different. Their genuine dislike fostered some of the NBA's fiercest competition, however tainted.

"We don't like them, they don't like us, so let's get it on," said Tim Hardaway before Game 1. "I hate the Knicks. Absolutely hate them. That's just the way it is."

The Heat finished with the best mark in the Eastern Conference, but were a vulnerable number one seed. Hardaway, the All-Star point guard, had a creaky knee. Mourning had historically shown too much deference to Patrick Ewing, his Georgetown mentor, through the years. And no one considered the Knicks your typical, happy-just-to-be-here eighth seed.

Riley was the architect of the Showtime Lakers that dominated the 1980s. In Miami, he built a team that became a carbon copy of the Knicks: Flawed center. Aggressive defense. Strong rebounders. And a lot of anonymous role players playing key minutes.

The Knicks always said the two teams mirrored one another, and maybe that was true for two seasons. But this Knicks team was different. With Sprewell and Camby, they were more explosive and athletic. They believed the Heat could not keep pace.

By Game 1, that much was evident. Allan Houston drew a favorable matchup against Dan Majerle, the veteran guard with chronic back problems who walked around the court like a woozy prizefighter about to drop from a barrage of punches. Houston, who hit his first five shots, exploited Majerle for 22 points. And those playoff neophytes, Sprewell and Camby, played like postseason veterans. They combined for 33 points off the bench, including 22 from Sprewell.

In the first half, Camby threw down a vicious dunk in Mourning's face. As Mourning lay there stunned on his back, Camby came back to earth, planted his feet and glared at him.

Sprewell made the thirty-six-year-old Porter look forty-six. One sequence in the second quarter revealed the changes in style: Stealing the ball on one end of the floor and racing toward the basket, Sprewell had his path cut off by a charging Mourning. Undeterred, he somehow contorted his body in midair, ducked under Mourning, and converted a reverse layup as the Heat center nearly disemboweled him.

"I knew it was going to be physical," Sprewell said after the Knicks routed Miami 95–75 on its home floor. "But I haven't torn a ligament or ripped anything. So I'm going to be out there. It's going to have to be something serious to keep me away from this kind of action. I'm loving it."

Miami's silver lining was in the box score next to the center position, where Mourning had outscored Ewing 27 to 9. Ewing did have a game-high 15 rebounds, establishing himself as the man in the middle these Knicks needed. He was still a threat to score, but he also seemed content taking a back seat on offense.

The Big Fella, role player. The plan was working.

Checketts even alluded to the notion in a *Sports Illustrated* article that week, agreeing that the Knicks' biggest challenge was to define a new role for Ewing and that it was time for Ewing to relinquish his mantle as the first option on offense. "That has to happen," he said.

Ewing was angry about the remark, feeling that Checketts had addressed an issue with the media that should have been kept in-house. He felt somewhat betrayed. "They must be getting ready to send me somewhere," he said. "Do you know where I'm going?"

Given the circumstances, the controversy barely registered on the Knicks' crisis meter. After going up 1–0 in the series, they suddenly had a free Saturday night in Miami.

If the players grew excited about the prospect of going to Atlanta, they positively loved Miami. South Beach bustled with neon, fashion models, restaurants, and nightclubs. Coconut Grove, where the team's hotel was located, was another all-night fiesta. Women were everywhere, walking around in provocative blouses. Some were escorted by men better-looking than Antonio Banderas. Others were just escorts, period. The Mayfair House hotel, where some of the Heat players resided, became a hot spot in the 1980s when Madonna began staying there. The entire area soon became a huge tourist attraction, replete with jewelry stands, the Gap, Planet Hollywood, and any derivative of a rum punch you could order. Spring Break in Coconut Grove went from January to December.

The players enjoyed the atmosphere, mainly because they could walk the streets without causing a ruckus. They were noticed, all right; some wore Knick T-shirts and caps just to make sure. But everyone in the Grove was too self-important to make a fuss over a bunch of tall black men who might or might not make more money than they did.

Van Gundy knew how much the players enjoyed South Florida, which is why he made sure to get them out of bed before 11:00 A.M. on Sunday.

The main topic at practice that afternoon was, of course, The Phasing Out of Ewing. Sprewell was so bold as to say, "I think the big guy knows there are players here who can take the load off his shoulders somewhat."

Ewing was growing tired of the analysis, especially after a victory. It showed when the longtime, loquacious NBA writer from the *Chicago Sun-Times*, Lacy Banks, inquired in his own eloquent way whether Ewing should concentrate more on asserting himself defensively.

"You sound like you're from New York," Ewing said to Banks, smiling.

More than his shots in the offense, Ewing's main concern was his nagging left Achilles tendon. He would not admit it, but his left foot was throbbing so badly he wondered whether his body could hold up during the postseason. In the first round, having only one day off between games meant the Knicks could play as many as five games in nine days.

Ewing's frustrations mounted on Monday night in Game 2. He wasn't moving his feet, and twice during the first half Van Gundy had to take him out because he simply could not guard Mourning.

Ewing sulked both times he was substituted for, once throwing his head back in disgust when he realized he was coming out. He was pissed off, defiantly exiting the court as if Van Gundy had been cheating him out of minutes all season. Sprewell had never pouted in this manner with the Knicks.

"Join the club," Van Gundy said of Ewing's reaction.

Ewing led the team with 16 points and 15 rebounds, but Mourning dominated him by going for 26 points. After the Knicks closed to within 59–55 with a minute left in the third quarter, Mourning sank two free throws and then Ewing sank New York by picking up an offensive foul on one end and foolishly goaltending Porter's errant jump shot.

Sprewell and Houston were roughed up, producing just eight field goals and 10 turnovers. Even Van Gundy was reminded how quickly a series can change. In the second half, as he walked toward the midcourt sideline to yell out a play, a Heat fan several rows back screamed, "Hey, Jeff, you know Phil Jackson is watching this game back in New York."

Van Gundy laughed. "You're probably right," he said.

Miami evened the series, winning 83–73 and playing as aggressively as any Riley team with its back against the wall.

As the series shifted north, New York was buzzing over the

possibility of closing out Miami on the Garden floor. Two weeks earlier, a postseason appearance was in jeopardy; now the Knicks were two victories away from improbably advancing to the second round and sending Riley home prematurely again.

Moreover, the winner of the Heat-Knicks series would match up against either Atlanta or Detroit in the East semifinals—a scenario that both teams salivated over. The Hawks and the Pistons were both regarded as mediocre and not much of an impediment to reaching the conference finals.

Van Gundy was concerned his players would have a false sense of security playing at the Garden, a venue where the fans can turn on the Knicks in an instant and where they sometimes turn passive down the stretch of close games.

The game started out the way Van Gundy had feared: Miami led by as many as eight in the first quarter and was ahead 37–33 after Mourning hit a jumper with 4:41 left in the first half.

But over the next 11 minutes, the plodding Knicks of the last decade disappeared forever. They were replaced by the vision Grunfeld, Checketts, and Van Gundy had in January, a more athletic group that could get its points in transition as well as in the half-court offense.

In one of the most devastating runs in playoff history, the Knicks outscored Miami 32–2 between the end of the second quarter and the middle of the third.

At one juncture, they scored 19 unanswered points. Converting turnovers into dunks, Sprewell was one of eight players to score during the onslaught. He and Camby set the pace, flying past Miami—just as Grunfeld, sitting at home watching the games on television, had envisioned.

The Garden was ecstatic, serenading the Heat coach with the familiar chant of "Riley sucks! Riley sucks!" It seemed unfair and shortsighted: It should have included the entire Heat team, which scored a paltry 73 points—the lowest ever by a Knick playoff opponent.

Hardaway, who was held to under 10 points for the second

straight game and seemed to be hobbling on his bum right knee, went face-to-face with referee Mike Mathis in the final quarter and was ejected.

"We got run over by a freight train," said Brown.

Some definite trends were beginning to emerge. The Knicks' bench, with Sprewell, Camby, and Chris Childs, created a frenetic energy that exploited the Heat's aging warriors. Camby, the player who'd posted a DNP this year against the Heat because Van Gundy didn't feel he could handle the matchups, put up a nice line: 13 points on six-of-eight shooting and nine rebounds in 29 minutes. Maybe he couldn't absorb a Mourning elbow, but then, he didn't need to. He could jump over the Heat like no Knick forward of recent vintage. His inspired play gave support to those who believed that Van Gundy had buried him on the bench early in the season only to spite Grunfeld.

The coach could not win. Figuring he had brought the young forward along perfectly, he was now getting ripped for Camby's playing well.

"Earlier in the year, it was just a coach's decision," he said. "I thought he handled himself terrifically. I thought he handled coaching well. I thought he handled people trying to infiltrate his mind with negative thoughts well. I think he's handled everything well this year. And when he's earned his time, he's played well."

Camby was treated like a conquering hero in his first-ever playoff game at the Garden, a 97–73 rout. Sprewell, who led all scorers with 20 points, elicited a loud cheer the first time he rose from the bench, took off his warmups and checked into the game.

But the loudest ovation that night was reserved for a surprise visitor. John Starks stood in the walkway leading from the locker room to the court. Caught on the scoreboard screen, Starks was on the verge of tears when the crowd suddenly got out of their seats, stood, and roared.

There was something right about the symmetry. The player whom Starks was dealt for had become beloved by the fans, but they still felt a lot of sentiment for the player who had given them so many wonderful postseason moments.

"Johnny Rocket," Van Gundy said, smiling, as he passed Starks on his way to the refrigerator in the locker room to pick up a Diet Coke after the game.

"What's up, Jeff?" Starks said.

"You coming back for Game 4?"

"I'll be here."

Starks lingered with his former teammates until the last player, Johnson, left. However much it killed him not to be playing, he was officially on the bandwagon. Never mind only a 2–1 series lead in the first round; Starks was already handicapping the Knicks' hopes of reaching the Finals.

"You guys can beat Indiana," he said to Johnson after everyone had cleared out.

"Jalen Rose is going to be tough," Johnson said. "He worries me. But our bench is pretty strong."

Starks shook his head. "You guys'll be all right."

Meanwhile, down the corridor in the Heat locker room, Riley's team was on the brink again.

Looming was Game 4 and the unthinkable—another first-round elimination at the hands of his former employers. If it was to be a referendum on Miami's season, it was also a referendum on the Riley Way. Maybe building a team of aging warriors and making them believe was not enough anymore.

"Everything we've worked for, everything we've talked about is on the line," he said at the next day's practice. "We have an MVP candidate, veteran warriors on this team, one of the greatest clutch players in the history of the NBA with Tim Hardaway, role players that help us win games on a regular basis, we have a great defensive foundation . . . we are a winning team.

"This is the team that got me here, this is the team that will get me over the top—or we're all going to go down together."

"I don't know what it is," said Brown. "It's just amazing to see how well they shoot, how well they play against us. You would think they're the number one seed and we're the number eight seed. We're kind of back on our heels. They have an amazingly high level of confidence when they play the Miami Heat. And it's been like that almost every game. I don't know what it is."

Riley, the team president, stubbornly believed in his veterans, enough so that he did not give Riley, the coach, a bona fide third offensive option in the off-season. He thought Golden State asked too much for Sprewell, and left the Knicks to the bidding. He made overtures to the Lakers about Eddie Jones and Elden Campbell and explored several other deals, but never pulled the trigger to upgrade his team offensively.

"We're into building a team," he said. "We went through the season with this basketball team because we wanted to see it whole in the playoffs, and if this is what I've seen in the playoffs, then we've got a lot of work to do.

"We are a winning team. We're a good program. We're building something good down there. But this isn't good at all. It doesn't mean anything to win three Atlantic Division titles if we lose in the first round."

On the morning of Game 4, Van Gundy did not resemble the coach of a streaking team headed to the second round. He looked almost morose. All of New York had the Knicks 48 minutes away from eliminating Riley's team, but Van Gundy approached Game 4 from the worst-case scenario.

Knowing the Knicks have never handled prosperity well, he could see them losing two straight games. Their season would be over and so would Van Gundy's ten-year coaching career with the franchise.

"I feel almost nostalgic," he said after the team's morning workout prior to the game. "This could be the last time I ever make the drive to the Garden. Do you know how many times I've made that drive?"

He was standing in the stairwell outside the gymnasium at Purchase College, around the corner from the school's trophy case where Van Gundy usually holds his daily press briefings.

Reflective, he added, "There are only two things I regret. One is Game 5 against Miami [in '97] when we got into the fight. If that doesn't happen, we end up in the conference finals. I'll take responsibility for that. The other is that all I ever wanted to do is coach. And nothing else. But this year . . ."

His voice trailing off, what Van Gundy did not say was that he engaged in the kind of survivalist behavior he came to abhor at the Garden. He ultimately won a war with Grunfeld that made him neither proud nor feeling much like a victor.

For a brief period when he was trying to save his own job, he was just another suit carrying out his own agenda. Privately, he had made sure the media and Checketts knew his side of the Grunfeld dispute.

Van Gundy did not want to direct that attitude toward the players, instead warning the Knicks that Miami was playing for its season, that the Heat would summon everything they needed to take the series back to South Florida.

"You know that team, you know the way they're coached," said Johnson. "They're coming out for a fight, a dogfight."

The Knicks were ready, building an 11-point third-quarter lead that left Childs chest-bumping Allan Houston during a timeout after a wild Knick run. The tremors could be felt inside the Garden and inside Riley's head. For a moment, he actually looked nervous.

Stan Van Gundy was irate. He threw a clipboard to the floor and began cussing out the Heat players. He could not believe they were letting his brother's team dance on their grave with more than a quarter of basketball left.

The Heat answered with seven straight points, and closed to within 62–58 by the end of the period. That unbelievable run by the Knicks in Game 3? Miami issued payback in Game 4, opening the final period by outscoring New York 23–4. Hardaway finally recaptured his range, knocking down two long 3-pointers. Porter even found the Fountain of Youth, burying clutch long-range jumpers.

Miami won going away 87–72. For the third straight season, they would go the distance.

"I made a statement prior to the series that a higher being has brought these two teams together," Riley said.

One by one, the Garden crowd, so unshakably jubilant only a half-hour earlier, quietly shuffled out into a humid Manhattan spring night.

On Saturday morning, the Knick players were dreading the trip to Miami for Game 5. They realized what a grand opportunity had been wasted, and that the Heat was suddenly rejuvenated. Van Gundy noticed the woe-is-us persona immediately. Following a light practice at Miami Arena that afternoon, he addressed the team's mood.

"We have to guard against what happened two years ago," Van Gundy told his players. "We lost a tough game at home in Game 6, and then we came down here and it carried over into the first quarter of Game 7. When you're up 11 in the second half—and you're up four going into the fourth—all you need is 12 minutes of great basketball to close out the series. If you don't get it done, you have the possibility of a hangover.

"We can't be down or frustrated or unhappy that we're back here, or that we're thinking of it as a lost opportunity. We have to look at it as the opportunity to play in a deciding game, where you really find out about people and teams. We have to turn the frustration into anger and do anything it takes to win."

After practice, Van Gundy, dressed in blue denim shorts and a white Knicks T-shirt, took his customary stroll along the CocoWalk toward his favorite restaurant, Johnny Rockets—a retro 1950s burger-and-shake joint. Not that a deluxe cheeseburger and fries would put a dent in his wallet, but he had to wonder if this would be his last meal on the Knicks' dime.

The night before Game 5, the players had their own self-imposed curfew. Resisting the temptations of a perfect, 75 degree evening, they remained holed up in the luxurious Grand Bay Hotel. For all the social activity going on, they may as well have been in Cleveland in the dead of winter.

The game was scheduled for 12:30 P.M. that Sunday. All of the Knicks were present and accounted for at Miami Arena by

10:30 A.M. Outside the building, fans clad in red Heat T-shirts were already lining up at the entrances. The Heat marketing department distributed clackers, an annoying contraption that sounded like a million crickets on steroids.

Inside the cramped visiting locker room at the decaying arena, the Knicks sat stone-faced. Larry Johnson, Marcus Camby, and Chris Childs watched film of Game 4. Ewing sat on a table in the trainer's room. His left Achilles tendon was hooked up to an electrostimulation machine. Most of them listened to their portable CD players. A handful of writers milled about, not knowing exactly what to ask. *Do you think today's a big game?* was not at the top of the list.

You really had no reason to be in there, other than to gauge the mood of the team. And as clichéd as it may sound, that fifteen-by-fifteen crackerbox had the feel of a heavyweight championship fight moments before the long walk to the ring.

The clackers greeted the Knicks as they took the floor for pregame warmups. Since Riley's arrival, Heat fans have saved their most venomous behavior for New York. But that afternoon, the decibel level reached new highs, and kept growing with each Heat basket.

Miami drew first blood, opening the game with a 21–8 run. The Knicks looked terrified and about to throw away the series. Mourning rubbed it in, hitting a short bank shot and then mocking his old adversary, Johnson, by pointing to his right arm, which he had formed in the shape of an L.

Johnson had introduced the Big L at the end of the regular season. After each made 3-pointer, he flashed his trademark gesture to the crowd. Some viewed it as a self-congratulatory act, further evidence of why you shouldn't like the Knicks.

Instead of Larry, the Big L now stood for Losing Badly.

Van Gundy searched for answers, first inserting Sprewell for Kurt Thomas four and a half minutes into the first quarter with New York trailing 10–3. But it was not until he summoned Childs from the bench and took out a lethargic Houston with 4:43 to play in the first quarter that the Knicks began to make their move.

With Charlie Ward, Sprewell and Childs were part of a three-guard offense that quickly erased an 18–8 deficit.

Childs hit a jumper as soon as he was inserted. Sprewell followed with a three-point play and then Ward dished to Ewing for a dunk. Before Riley knew what happened, the Knicks had scored 13 straight points to tie the game at 21. They had survived the first-quarter gauntlet, something they had not done in Game 7 of the '97 playoffs.

Down four at intermission, tied at 60 at the end of three quarters, the Knicks somehow dug themselves another hole early in the fourth. Mourning converted a three-point play over Camby. After Ewing sank a 15-footer, Majerle and Voshon Lenard converted back-to-back 3-pointers. Those shots gave Miami a 69–62 lead with less than 10 minutes left.

Ewing was running on fumes, having strained his left rib cage early in the third quarter. It was painful to watch him run, loping downcourt as if he had just been sucker-punched in the gut and was wearing a prosthetic on his left leg. The Knicks looked no more healthy than he did.

But Houston gradually began to bring them back. He dropped in two jump shots during a 7–0 run that tied the game. Mourning scored on the other end to break Miami's five-minute silence, but Childs came up with another huge shot. His 3-pointer from a few steps left of the top of the key gave New York its first lead at 72–71 with 4:05 left.

Points were at a premium over the next two minutes. Jamal Mashburn gave the Heat a one-point lead by hitting two free throws with 3:42 left. Neither the Knicks nor the Heat scored on their next two possessions.

Johnson finally hit a short jump shot to put New York back in front with 2:21 left, and the battle was back on. Mourning energized the building with a jump hook. After Childs missed a 3-pointer, the Heat center had a chance to extend the lead. But first he would have to go around his old friend.

Mourning was being touted as an MVP candidate for the '99 season; for the first time in his career, he had surpassed Ewing as the more productive center. And at times during the series, he went past his elder with relative ease. Now, he had one last test to pass.

Isolated against Ewing on the perimeter in front of the Knicks' bench, Mourning tried to fake Ewing up in the air before driving left, hoping to blow by the thirty-six-year-old, slow-footed Ewing along the baseline.

Ewing somehow found some lateral movement left in his aching legs. He beat him to the spot, sealing off Mourning's drive and forcing him into a 24-second violation.

The old man was not going away, and neither were the Knicks. With a minute left, Ewing's jumper hit the back of the rim and bounced out. Porter grabbed the rebound and was fouled.

His two free throws gave Miami a three-point lead at 77–74 with 58 seconds left. Given Miami's ability to close out teams defensively in the final minute—a Riley hallmark—the Knicks were desperate for points.

Battered as he was, Ewing delivered. He rebounded a Sprewell miss under the rim, drew a foul, and made two of the most clutch free throws of his career with 39 seconds left. Trailing by one, the Knicks needed one stop.

It was Sprewell's turn to star. He produced the biggest defensive play of the game with 24.9 seconds left. Hardaway was driving and trying to create a scoring opportunity when he lost control of a high dribble. A gambling Sprewell slapped the ball away and then began dribbling over the midcourt line as 15,000 people gasped for air.

The Knicks had a chance.

During a timeout, Van Gundy set up a play for Sprewell that looked mistimed and awkward from the start. He began his dribble at the top of the circle, going wide to his right, and eventually winding up in front of the Heat bench with an aggressive Porter bodying him up.

After Porter slapped the ball out of Sprewell's hands with just 4.5 precious seconds left, the call for Triangle Post went out.

The play called for Ewing to set a screen for Houston, the first option, at the top of the key. If that didn't work, Ewing would have to find a way to get up a shot or get to the line.

When the referee handed Sprewell the ball, he slapped it to start the play. Instantly, Houston, guarded by Majerle, ran a perfect curl around Ewing. Houston caught the pass right of the top of the key. With Majerle tracking him, Houston took two dribbles toward the basket.

Lifting off on his right leg from the foul line, he threw up a leaning one-hander that appeared on line but short. The ball grazed the right side of the rim, kissed the backboard, and dropped in.

Bedlam.

Houston sprinted to the other end of the court, stopping at the baseline to punch his fist into the air. Most of Miami Arena was dead quiet, and Riley resembled a ghost. Van Gundy appeared numb as well, and was not buying into destiny yet with eight tenths of a second remaining.

The Heat's last shot came from Porter, who somehow took a dribble, pump-faked, and launched a 35-foot prayer that hit the backboard and bounced away—all in 0.8 second. The Knick bench stormed the floor, circling Houston and Ewing and anyone else dressed in orange and blue.

Chris Rock, the 5-foot-something comedian, joined in the sea of emotion, high-fiving any professional basketball player from New York he could reach.

Van Gundy, the lifer, could not even enjoy the moment. He was screaming, "No fuckin' way! No fuckin' way!" in the direction of referee Ed F. Rush. He could not believe Porter was allowed to get a shot off in that amount of time. Only when assistant coach Brendan Malone grabbed him and embraced him did he snap out of his momentary insanity and realize what had happened. By God or Houston or someone, his Knicks were headed to the second round.

The son of a coach had saved the coach's job.

It came down to one shot, a wounded duck that easily could have bounced out and sent the Knicks into off-season disarray.

It came down to making or missing, just like Van Gundy always said.

"We got a good roll today," said Charlie Ward. "It sent chills up my spine."

Houston had salvaged a bad game and a season by hitting the game-winner. But Ewing was the primary reason they were moving on. He dominated Mourning for the first time in the series and led the Knicks with 22 points and 11 rebounds, summoning courage and grit from another decade.

"Mr. Body Breakdown came through," Van Gundy said.

Said Childs, "What he did moved me."

The surreal locker room scene included Checketts hugging players, Johnson's booming voice echoing playfully from the shower, and an almost adolescent Sprewell, bouncing around like a kid on a sugar high.

"There were a lot of hugs and a lot of emotion," he said. "It says a lot about the character of this team. The guys never quit."

When the celebration ended, Checketts held an impromptu press conference in a small room across the hall from the locker room. He said he had not made his mind up about Van Gundy's future.

The coach was down the hall in an empty room, telling reporters he would not talk about his job security. When they left, Stan Van Gundy entered the room and the two brothers embraced.

Riley conveyed his congratulations a day later, and wished Van Gundy and his team the best. The two had spoken once after a regular-season game in '99, burying the hatchet from the past seasons.

For once, Knicks-Heat was a good, clean fight.

10

HAWKS AND OTHER BIRDS OF PREY

The new AND 1 commercial began with the striking image of Latrell Sprewell sitting in a barber's chair, having his large Afro braided into corn rows. With Jimi Hendrix's rendition of "The Star-Spangled Banner" playing in the background, Sprewell's voice intones, "Some people say I'm America's worst nightmare." As the grainy salon footage continues in the thirty-second spot, he looks chillingly into the camera. "I say I'm the American dream."

Now he was in everyone's living room, as defiant as ever. This wasn't Coca-Cola's "I'd Like to Teach the World to Sing" or Gatorade's "I Wanna Be Like Mike." Sprewell was the antihero. Bigger. Badder. Blacker.

In New York City, the cutting protest to old-school values sold well. Across America, however, the ad reaffirmed every uncomfortable feeling you had about him. He was capitalizing on the martyred image. There were no shades of gray. You either loved him because he thrilled you with his play, or you loathed him because he stood for everything reprehensible about modern professional sports.

The contrast was stark and obvious. He was the most popular player among the fans at Madison Square Garden. "They love him," said Marcus Camby. "He's one guy that really has crowd control."

On Court TV, his name was being mentioned in the same breath as a triple murderer. When a white homicide victim's co-worker addressed the court during a sentencing hearing, he talked about how his friend was a true role model. "Not like this guy," he said, looking at the convicted black teenager. "Not like the role models they have today, like Latrell Sprewell."

Some reporters and commentators had reconciled Sprewell's angry past with his awesome future. Others refused to accept a player who seemed to have no structure in his game and but one thing on his mind: getting his. Either way, he had come to the right place to begin a new life.

Nearly thirty years earlier, a Philadelphia urban legend joined Red Holzman's selfless Knicks and created quite a media stir of his own. In a February '99 issue of the *Village Voice*, the author Nelson George insightfully compared Sprewell's arrival in 1999 to Earl Monroe's in 1971.

Nelson wrote that the warm memories of the Holzman championship teams were obscured by "the commotion the arrival of Earl Monroe created in '71. Aside from being the star of the archrival Baltimore Bullets, the Pearl was the harbinger of undiluted black street style's arrival in the NBA. Monroe, known to folks in his native Philadelphia as 'Black Jesus,' was the landlocked Dr. J, the man who brought jazzy syncopation to the floor game. The ABA merger was four years away when his Monk-esque dribbling and dazzling 'J' had the Garden faithful up in arms. There were columns then about him spoiling the Knicks' rhythm. In truth, Monroe's creativity often carried an injury-plagued and aging team during its last two Finals appearances."

Monroe blended in seamlessly. The jury was still out on Sprewell, who was waiting for the Knicks to adapt to him. Still, a veteran of three playoff wins, he had helped the Knicks into the second round.

Where Ewing looked old and sore, Sprewell looked like the preseason had just ended.

The Atlanta Hawks, who had just finished their own grueling, five-game series against Detroit, had the same dilemma that had bedeviled Miami: how to stop this suddenly athletic team with boundless energy and renewed confidence. A New York team that could run and jump in May? Who were these impostors?

Forty-eight hours after Houston's pulse-stopping shot changed their travel plans, the Knicks came to Atlanta with a simple mission: get out of the second round for the first time in five years.

The Knicks were rolling, blending the new (Camby and Sprewell) with the old (Ewing, Houston, and Johnson), and about to face a team that was much more vulnerable than Miami. The Hawks were a team of three stars—Dikembe Mutombo, Steve Smith, and Mookie Blaylock—and little else.

They had the league's all-time-winningest coach, Brooklyn native Lenny Wilkens—one of only two people to be inducted into the Hall of Fame as a player and as a coach. But on the floor, they were hurting. The Hawks were missing forward LaPhonso Ellis, who underwent hernia surgery earlier in the season, and power forward Alan Henderson, who was out for the season because of blurred vision in his left eye.

Wilkens was forced to start reserves Grant Long and Tyrone Corbin and bring inexperienced young players like Chris Crawford and Anthony Johnson in as substitutes. Wilkens did not have much to work with.

Still, Van Gundy fretted. He always does. Smith's perimeter game bothered him, the way the 6-foot-7 shooting guard could post up smaller guards and shoot over anyone he wanted. Blaylock, the point guard, could hit the 3-pointer regularly and had earned a reputation as a great thief in the backcourt. So quick were his hands that he could change games defensively. Mutombo was a robot in the post, but a prolific shot-blocker and rebounder. The Knicks feared the angular, sharp elbows of the Congo native most.

You cannot venture into the Land of Mutombo without running into one of Dikembe's elbows, a major source of consternation and sutures around the league. The players wanted them banned, and NBA officials wanted them to at least be padded.

The 7-foot-2 Mutombo was an intimidating force, known for wagging his index finger after blocking a shot—like a parent scolding a child: *No, no, don't do that.* He had a thick accent, sounding like James Earl Jones playing the part of an African king. Glib, personable, one of the most charitable players in the league and media-friendly, it was hard to believe he came from the same guarded program as Ewing.

But Mutombo was no innocent on the court. The Nets' Jayson Williams and Vitaly Potapenko of the Celtics had both had their noses broken, courtesy of Dikembe. Childs had lost a front tooth a month earlier. On the same night, Mutombo caught Marcus Camby in the throat and drilled Larry Johnson's head.

Dikembe professed not to know what the fuss was about. He has a tendency to play with raised elbows. Whether it's intentional or simply the awkward movement of a big man is open for debate; either way, it was a valuable psychological tool. Like a wideout hearing the footsteps of a closing free safety, players driving to the basket saw and felt Mutombo and had to steel themselves to absorb the inevitable blow.

"There's been a lot said because of the Chris Childs accident, and the New York media pumped it up," Mutombo said. "People want to change my game and I don't know why. They know that I'm dominating in the middle. It is a problem for some people for the fact that I'm a defensive force and offensive force."

The Hawks were having a new downtown arena built, so they rented the cavernous Georgia Dome for the second-round series. The Dome had accommodated 62,046 for Jordan's last game in Atlanta on March 27, 1998. For playoff games, the seating capacity was considered 34,821.

Little more than half that, only 18,513, showed for Game 1,

and the building seemed to be teeming with Knick fans. Some had flown down from New York, knowing that airfare and a ticket to the game would cost less than buying a ticket from a scalper outside the Garden. Also, many native New Yorkers had become Atlanta transplants because of their corporate jobs; employment was plentiful in Ted Turner's jewel of the South. Unfortunately for the media tycoon, Hawks fans were not.

Not only were there many thousand vacant seats, but love was hard to come by for the home team. Predictable, half-court-oriented, the Hawks didn't generate any kind of excitement. For a change, that was left to the Knicks.

Houston and Sprewell detonated for a combined 65 points in Game 1, the most by a Knick playoff tandem in eleven years. Whether they were dunking on the break or squaring up from all over the perimeter, the two guards each set career playoff highs and tormented Wilkens's backcourt. It was an ominous sign for the few Atlanta faithful.

"Everyone said we couldn't play together," Sprewell said following the 100–92 win. "Now, people are saying we complement each other."

And the Knicks ran through Atlanta with a hobbled Ewing playing just 17 minutes due to foul problems. Unable to move well laterally, he grew frustrated and was nearly tossed from the game in the third quarter while arguing a call with referee Ted Bernhardt.

Beyond Ewing's health, there were other problems percolating. Sprewell scored 17 points in the first half, and was visibly upset when he sat for the first nine minutes of the second half. He glared at the head coach when Van Gundy finally told him to enter the game with 3:04 left in the period and the Knicks up 79–64.

The Knicks had just won a playoff game convincingly, a reason for locker room harmony. And now Sprewell was rolling his eyes about the coach's substitution patterns?

"Him and the eleven other guys," Van Gundy said. "If he comes out of the game and he's upset, join the list. I think we had an off-guard [Starks] here before that I had a few problems with about that. Patrick Ewing, the guy who supposedly likes me the most? There was one game when he was madder than a hornet. So guess what? Join the crowd. He may have a problem with me, but I have no problem with him. He's fine. He's very coachable.

"I think it starts because he keeps being asked the same question, 'Do you want to start?' He says, 'Yeah, I do.' The answers have never changed. The questions just never stopped."

Sprewell did not publicly air his complaints. But if he had one, he found an old ally in the Coach Is Screwing Me Club. Camby was also upset after playing just 10 minutes. He had played the good soldier all season, but now he was visibly upset about his diminished role in Game 1. As reporters filed into the locker room afterward, he sat there dejected, airing out his grievances to Larry Johnson but within earshot of everyone.

It did not help matters that Camby's agent, Alex Johnson, was seated in the same area behind the Knick bench as Charles Oakley. Oakley, attending his first Knick playoff games in civilian clothes, quickly drew the media's attention. The Camby camp learned that Van Gundy had left tickets for Oakley, which only helped bolster their conspiracy theory: With Oak back in the building, Coach was trying to disrespect Marcus.

"I wouldn't say [Marcus] is discouraged," Sprewell said. "I would say, though, he's probably like me in the sense that I would want to start and I would want to play a lot."

Van Gundy's reading of the whole evening was different. He did not want to make an issue of playing time; he was more concerned that Sprewell had allowed Crawford, a playoff neophyte, to explode for 20 first-half points, most of which came in transition, with Sprewell watching from a safe distance.

"Even though players would never admit it, when you're coming from losing situations, you develop bad habits," Van Gundy said, choosing his words carefully. "You're not going to admit it, but it's there. What Latrell has done this year, I've been shocked a guy can be this good after being out that long."

Van Gundy drew a parallel with Derek Harper, who came to

the Knicks from the moribund Mavericks and nearly became the Finals MVP in 1994. Harper agreed he had picked up bad habits. Sprewell, however, was not about to agree with the coach.

"He hadn't really watched me enough to know how I competed and how I played," Sprewell said. "Even though we were losing I always tried to go out and play hard and try to win. Everybody has bad habits. Nobody is perfect. Everybody has their downfalls."

Had the discontent come while they were falling apart, it would have made for more off-court drama and might have splintered the fragile team psyche. But game by game, the Knicks continued to improve. And the squabbling was by now old-hat. Everyone knew Sprewell wanted to start and Camby wanted to play more. But arguing with success was tough, especially the kind of success Sprewell and Camby were having.

Two nights later, with Game 2 still in the balance, Camby placed his own distinctive mark on Knicks playoff history with a play as dynamic as John Starks's dunk over Jordan and Pippen. The score was 62–58 with 7:28 left in the fourth quarter, and the Hawks needed a huge defensive stop. Camby received a bounce pass from Chris Childs near the free throw line and eyed the rim. He took one power dribble and lifted off approximately eight feet from the basket. For a brief second, he seemed to be suspended in air, daring Mutombo to challenge him.

With his right arm cocked and his eyes level with the basket, the agile young forward force-fed Mutombo a thunderous slam. One of the most athletic plays in franchise playoff history, that dunk rocked the Georgia Dome and became the defining moment of the game.

Camby let out a primal scream after the flush and then began mocking Mutombo, waving his right index finger at Dikembe.

"That dunk," said Ewing, "was vicious, man, just vicious."

Camby's explosion was part of an 11–4 fourth-quarter run by the combination of Camby, Sprewell, Childs, Dudley, and Johnson, and it ended Atlanta's bid to knot the series. The Knicks won handily again 77–70.

Camby got his minutes, playing 27, scoring 11 points, and grabbing 13 rebounds. Sprewell was equally awesome, taking turns scoring 31 on most of Atlanta's roster. He went to the foul line 19 times, hitting 16 free throws.

Mutombo and his elbows were no longer feared. For the first time since the Miami miracle, the Knicks were coming home to the Garden, just two wins away from an improbable date in the conference finals. Nothing could penetrate their confidence.

Dave Checketts's secret was out, and he was nowhere to be found. And Checketts had every reason to hide.

On the morning of Game 3 in New York, the press room at the Garden was humming with gossip and intrigue. Reporters were working the phones, snooping around, trying to get some kind of confirmation, any kind, of a bombshell that had hit newsstands that morning.

In the Sunday edition of the *New York Times,* it was reported that Checketts, the Madison Square Garden president, had had a face-to-face meeting with Phil Jackson to discuss the possibility of Jackson's becoming the club's next coach. The *Daily News* also reported the meeting.

According to the story, Checketts, Jackson, and Jackson's agent, Todd Musburger, had met at an undisclosed location in the New York metropolitan area in mid-April before Grunfeld was fired. The meeting was arranged by an intermediary, who Jackson later revealed to be presidential candidate Bill Bradley, Jackson's former Knick teammate and close friend; Jackson was spending time helping the former senator raise funds for his campaign.

The three spoke informally for nearly two hours, but no job offer was made.

Barry Watkins, Checketts's spokesperson, was engulfed by reporters demanding to know if the story was true, if Checketts was covertly trying to replace Jeff Van Gundy.

Watkins, one of the more likable people at the Garden, had

his share of brushfires to extinguish during his years as a Rangers public relations director, including the messy departure of coach Mike Keenan after the Rangers won the Stanley Cup in 1994. Now, for the senior vice president of communications—the Garden's top PR job—this nightmare was just beginning to smolder. The timing could not have been worse.

The last thing the Knicks needed was a distraction. They were playing well and had weathered every controversy en route to their surprising postseason run. When Checketts dismissed Grunfeld and took over the reins, his mission was to provide a healthy, focused working environment. Instead, he was beginning to resemble George Steinbrenner in the late 1970s when Billy Martin managed the Yankees and Reggie Jackson presided over right field—another meddling executive who could not help himself.

This was bad, and Checketts was making it worse. He decided not to attend Game 3. As a devout Mormon, he made it a point to observe the Sabbath. He had also promised his family because of his busy schedule that he would set aside Sunday as a day on which he would not work. He did not attend Game 5 against Miami in 1998—but he did make exceptions, including Gretzky's last game in April. And only a week earlier, he was in Miami for Game 5 against the Heat.

Checketts issued a denial through Watkins early that morning before Game 3. During NBC's pregame show, analyst Peter Vecsey called the report "bogus." Van Gundy's fifteen-minute pregame meeting with reporters drew a record crowd. The questions, rattled off as if they were being asked at a White House press briefing, had nothing to do with the Hawks or Ewing's health.

"Did you see the story in the paper today?"

"I'm not talking about this," Van Gundy said. "Every time I'm honest, it comes back to bite me."

"Do you even want to come back here next year?"

"Don't even go there," he snapped.

Van Gundy had known in his gut that Jackson and Checketts had probably talked. In fact, he could not blame his boss for trying to pursue the most-sought-after coach on the market. Jackson's agent had spoken to six teams, and the Nets had already made a lucrative offer that started at $7 million per year. Plus, there was the persistent rumor that the Lakers would make a run at him. It wouldn't be prudent for someone in Checketts's position *not* to contact Jackson for a preliminary conversation. Still, just when Van Gundy finally thought he could stop worrying that his next loss would be his last, the subject had been revived, with the added annoyance that the latest threat was his greatest nemesis.

If he could not get validation from management, at least the fans cared. The story was the talk of the arena. When the Knicks' public address announcer Mike Walczewski prefaced the player introductions with the words, "The Knicks are coached by Jeff Van Gundy," the Garden erupted in applause.

It had been a strange and eventful morning, and an even crazier afternoon.

The Knicks took a commanding 3–0 lead in the series, cruising 90–78 in Game 3. And the best center on the floor wasn't even from Georgetown; the Ewing-Mutombo matchup took a back seat to the pride of Yale.

Chris Dudley checked into the game, walking shoulders first, looking like John Wayne about to rope a calf. "Do-right," as the players affectionately called him, outscored two of the best centers in the game, posting career playoff highs of 14 points and 12 rebounds. Foul-prone, offensively challenged, the worst free throw shooter in league history, Dudley took on cult-hero status for one afternoon.

"Dud-lee! Dud-lee!" they were chanting in his honor in the fourth quarter; the crowd gave him two standing ovations—one for making a free throw, and another when he fouled out of the game in the final minutes. The last time he remembered people standing, cheering, and chanting his name? "You mean, besides my wife?" Dudley said.

While Dudley was schooling the Hawks in the fourth quarter, the Checketts-Jackson saga was taking another wild turn. NBC's sideline reporter Jim Gray tracked down Checketts over the phone and got him to admit that he had contacted Jackson. But it wasn't as awful as the papers were saying. Checketts said the two had only spoken through a third party, that there was no meeting. He did admit Jackson was interested and that "we left it at that and said, 'We'll see you at the end of the season.' "

The Garden president, known for his honesty and integrity throughout his tenure in New York, suddenly had some explaining to do. Not only had he reached out to the former Bulls coach, but he had lied. He had told Van Gundy the story was untrue, and had issued the same blanket denial to Ewing.

Checketts even went so far as to deflect some of the attention away from Jackson. According to Gray, Checketts revealed that the former Knick Doc Rivers and former Charlotte coach Dave Cowens had also contacted him. But the misdirection play backfired. By now, everyone knew the truth: Checketts wanted Jackson.

"It shocks me," Ewing said in the locker room afterward. "I'm not playing for Phil Jackson. There's no way. They can trade me if they get Phil."

Poor Watkins. He was constantly readjusting and tweaking the story, trying his damnedest to stop the bleeding. Watkins assured the media that Checketts would address the issue prior to Game 4 Monday evening, giving him twenty-four hours to get his story straight.

Van Gundy could not believe the commotion over the story, how it put the game in the background. He knew how the coaching profession worked, but he still had a genuine feeling of betrayal. He always believed Grunfeld was out to get him. Now his level of mistrust with management reached an all-time high. He chose his words carefully after the game while painting Checketts further into a corner.

"Dave told me it's not true," he said after the game. "He told me just the opposite. Dave has never lied to me."

He sounded cold and calculating. Van Gundy and the media now had Checketts on the ropes.

On Monday, a month and four days after he demoted Grunfeld, Checketts faced the music again. White, hot lights beamed from the back of the rotunda area, every camera was poised to roll. Reporters, columnists, TV anchors, Garden personnel— everyone wanted to hear what Dave had to say.

The scene had a very Clintonesque feel to it. You were half expecting the first words out of his mouth to be, "I did not have contact with that man, Mr. Jackson."

For the second time in two days, Checketts changed his story. This time he came clean, admitting that a face-to-face meeting with Jackson in April had taken place and that he had lied about it to Van Gundy, the papers, and the fans. Contrite, somber, Checketts offered apologies to everyone and proved once more how smooth and genuine he could appear during a crisis.

Somewhere in Miami, Pat Riley had to be smiling. Checketts had portrayed him as a carpetbagging operator when Riley had worked out a deal with Miami behind the scenes while still under contract with the Knicks four years ago. Looking back, maybe Riley was just getting them before they got him.

"There was nothing that came out of the meeting, other than getting acquainted with a guy that I felt was a tremendous option for us," Checketts said of Jackson. "If anything, what I did was err on the side of protecting everyone. I regret that I lied about it. For misleading Jeff, I feel deeply sorry and I told him that."

Checketts would not rule out further talks with Jackson once the season was over and again refused to give Van Gundy a public endorsement. Before the news conference, Checketts walked into Van Gundy's office across the hall from the Knick locker room. He explained himself as best he could to the coach, who did not condemn Checketts for meeting with Jackson: "He's the boss. He can talk to whoever he wants to talk to."

Rob Ades, the flamboyant agent for Van Gundy whose background as a labor lawyer meant he always believed the establishment was screwing the little guy, went on the offensive.

"I'm embarrassed for Dave," Ades said. "He made himself look like a fool. Phil's good, he's very good. But he can't coach the Lakers, the Knicks, and the Nets and run Bill Bradley's campaign at the same time."

For all the bizarre happenings, Van Gundy emerged from the shark tank as the organization's martyr. Checketts's clandestine meeting had given Van Gundy Grunfeld's mantle. His approval rating soaring, Van Gundy became the symbol for the beaten-down, underappreciated workingman. He was being treated like dirt, his boss was lying to him, and he didn't even have Saturdays off.

On WFAN, the all-sports radio station, callers were ripping into Checketts and voicing support for the little guy, who just happened to be making $2 million a year. First up was Don Imus, only the most popular on-air, early-morning personality in America.

"Did you hear about that chump Checketts, lying to his coach about meeting with Phil Jackson?" Imus said. "He's a lyin', Mormon-sucking, yuppie weasel, that's what he is."

Two days later, Checketts tried to repair his image by going on with WFAN's Mike Francesa and Chris Russo. He was a regular on the *Mike and the Mad Dog Show,* a sports staple for every junkie in the tri-state area.

Checketts hoped this would be his chance to reconnect with the public. Instead, Francesa and Russo backed him into a corner.

"Dave, why don't you just give Jeff the job right now and end the speculation?" Russo finally said.

As Checketts tried to explain himself, he made Van Gundy again look like the mistreated worker on the assembly line. And impossible as it seemed, he had made himself look worse.

But the support that mattered most to Van Gundy was in the Knicks' locker room, where the players had his back. Maybe Sprewell and Camby weren't going to carry him off on their shoulders, but the majority of them were in Van Gundy's corner.

Van Gundy received a raucous ovation before Game 4, as the Knicks went for the sweep and their first five-game winning streak of the season.

Houston had his second huge close-out game, scoring 19 points and getting the Knicks off to a quick start. They led 19–10 with three minutes left in the first quarter and 25–18 heading into the second.

Banged-up body and all, even Ewing smelled blood. The old warrior had his best game of the series, ending with 17 points and nine rebounds. Mutombo, proud but ineffective, shook his head in disgust. This was easier than the Knicks had expected.

In the fourth quarter, with the Knicks about to hold the Hawks to a playoff-low point total in a 79–66 win, the Garden began chanting, "Sweep! Sweep! Sweep!" Moments later, the crowd got more creative. "We want Reggie! We want Reggie!" referring to that longtime Knick playoff demon, Indiana's Reggie Miller.

But in the final minutes, an unfamiliar chorus began to reverberate through the building, a loud and throaty chant never before bestowed upon a Knickerbocker basketball coach.

"Jeff Van GUN-dee!" "Jeff Van GUN-dee!"

Kim Van Gundy, seated in her usual spot five rows up from the floor directly across from her husband's bench, began sobbing uncontrollably. Ewing gave her a thumbs-up from his courtside seat. It was one of those touching moments at the Garden, a time when you forgot about the game and remembered a coaching family's perseverance.

All those days of wondering where their three-year-old daughter, Mattie, would start school. The Miami brawl. The daily reports Jeff would be fired if the Knicks lost one more game. Grunfeld wanting him out. Checketts courting Jackson.

For a brief moment, this maddening existence was worth it for the Van Gundys.

The coach, who had always claimed he did not hear the crowd, appeared numb. Had he spotted his wife, he would have broken down, right there in front of 19,763. As it was, he was choked up and near tears. He reached for his Diet Coke on the scorer's table and composed himself.

Asked afterward if it was the greatest night of his career, he said, "There have been some great highs since I've been here and some great lows. I had some big nights at McQuaid High, but you probably don't want to go back that far. Those were some exhilarating wins . . . for the thirteen people that saw them."

Atlanta was knocked out. Four more wins, and the Knicks would be in the NBA Finals for the first time since 1994. Twenty-one and twenty-one was but a memory.

In a noisy, jubilant locker room, Van Gundy's team began ribbing him about the chant. He took it in stride, laughing and breaking up the room in his own self-effacing way.

"Jeff Van GUN-dee! Jeff Van GUN-dee!" the players chanted.

"Usually," he told them, "the next word after my name is SUCKS."

11

BABY STEPS AND A FINAL LEAP

Allan Houston nonchalantly walked onto the court, grabbed a basketball from a rack, whipped a one-handed bounce pass to Chris Childs, and took another ball for himself. He surveyed the dome-shaped arena and began swishing jump shots from different spots on the floor.

The Knicks had come out to shoot around prior to Game 1 of the Eastern Conference finals in Indianapolis, and their starting shooting guard could hardly believe all the blessings in his life.

Most of his thoughts were with his wife, Tami, who was expecting the couple's first child any day now. His team, monstrous underdogs against Larry Bird's Pacers, had shown so much resiliency in their playoff run, and much of the success was due to Houston. Their inconsistent, unsure player from the regular season had become a supremely confident and clutch player—the cool customer who knocked out Miami with 0.8 second left, then shot down Atlanta by averaging 18 points per game.

Consummate teammate. Father-to-be. And a shot at playing in the Finals. A long shot, maybe, but with everything coming together for him personally and professionally, no goal seemed unreachable.

It was a drizzly spring day in Indianapolis, basketballs were bouncing, and Market Square Arena was beginning to swell with people and possibility . . .

A drizzly spring day in Indy, with basketballs bouncing and Market Square filling up for the big game.

It was 1980. The Louisville Cardinals were moments away from meeting Larry Brown's UCLA Bruins in the NCAA championship game, and an eight-year-old kid with a cardinal painted on his right cheek was sitting next to his mother, Alice, cheering on his idols.

Big Al, that was the nickname for the gangly son of Wade Houston, Denny Crum's assistant coach. Wade's kid was Louisville's unofficial mascot, hanging with Dr. Dunkenstein, Darrell Griffith; the late Derek Smith; Scooter and Rodney Mc-Cray; and that high-flying Cardinal team. They liked him so much that Big Al got to ride the team bus back to Louisville after the Cardinals captured their first national title.

"Big Al's Used Cars is what they used to call me," Houston said. "I had a lot of nicknames. I got pretty abused."

He grew up with the Louisville program, from Griffith, the McCrays, and Milt Wagner all the way to Pervis Ellison, Tony Kimbro, and LaBradford Smith. When Houston was thirteen and traveling with the team to a preseason tournament in Hawaii, Crum didn't have enough healthy bodies to practice so he enlisted the help of the young Houston, who was dribbling the ball on the sidelines.

"He had to do everything the players did," Wade said. "The court was dirty and we had to sweep it, so Denny told him, 'If you want to practice, you better start sweeping.' Allan was very nervous. He threw the ball all over the gym."

One day Crum threatened to have the team run wind sprints if Houston could not make seven of 10 free throws. He knocked down eight.

Growing up, he had connections all over Louisville. When he turned two years old, Houston's doorbell rang and there, standing on the front porch, was the greatest gift of all: Muhammad Ali had come over to wish little Al a happy birthday—just three weeks after having his jaw broken in the ring by Ken Norton. Houston's mother was a childhood friend of Ali's, who lived down the street on Grand Avenue in Louisville's West End section.

"Not many kids can say Ali came to their house on their birthday," he said. "A couple of years ago I saw him and wanted to get his autograph. But when I went up and introduced myself, he smiled and asked me how my parents were."

Some encounter, the most prolific trash-talker of all time and one of the most humble souls in professional sports.

Houston grew up respectful of his elders and authority, qualities that separate him from many of his NBA peers. And yet, overlooked in his somewhat privileged childhood and his year-round basketball instruction, was another form of education, one that came straight from the asphalt. Shawnee Park, where the inner-city kids ran day and night on a court with weeds muscling up through the concrete, was no place for a soft, suburban teen.

"I wanted to experience an atmosphere where if you scored on somebody enough they were going to try to take your head off," he said of his indoctrination to playground ball. "I had to get tougher, but I don't think that has anything to do with my personality. A lot of my friends were bused from the city to my school. I hung out with these guys all the time, and when we played basketball we played hard. I never played nice. I don't think I could get to this point if I didn't have any desire or intensity."

A sad but true NBA perception: If you're a pleasant person, your peers and critics think you don't have the balls to go strong to the basket and withstand hard, physical play. You unfairly earn a label as a player who shuns contact and can easily be taken out of his game.

David Robinson, San Antonio's great and equally gracious center, got the same rap. Other than his sometimes passive body language on the court and his notorious slow starts at the

beginning of each season, Houston's reputation was largely un-
deserved; his numbers kept improving as the season wore on,
and he saved his best performances for the postseason.
Houston's scoring average in the playoffs topped his regular
season average four years in a row.

Finally, during the '99 playoffs, he was beginning to build a
résumé as a big-game player. People now saw a resolve in Houston that had gone unnoticed early in his career. In reality, it
was always there.

Sons of coaches are inherently unselfish and team-oriented,
and more often than not they play the point guard position.
Houston was a natural scorer; he needed to learn to be greed-
ier. Like his former teammate John Starks, the trigger-happy
Sprewell, and, say, Reggie Miller.

The comparisons between Miller and Houston were inevitable as the Knicks prepared to meet Larry Bird's streaking
Pacers, who were unbeaten in seven playoff games. The shooting guard matchup would be pivotal.

In 1996, the Knicks cleared salary cap room to bid for the
best free agent class in NBA history. Needing a backcourt
scorer, they passed over Miller and Steve Smith for the young,
still unproven jump-shooter from the Detroit Pistons. Miller
was hoping to at least use the Knicks for contract leverage in
his negotiations with Pacer management, but Houston ruined
that the first day free agents were allowed to sign by agreeing to
a $56 million, seven-year deal.

Grant Hill was livid that Houston had not given the Pistons
a chance to counter, and skipped Houston's wedding that
summer along with many of his Detroit teammates. Hill found
out about the deal through Miller, his Olympic teammate,
while the Dream Team was in Indianapolis for an exhibition
game.

"I ran out of my room and started running down the hallway
of the hotel, yelling, 'Your guy signed with the Knicks! He just
screwed up my negotiations,'" Miller recalled. From that day
forward, Reggie took pleasure in reminding the media that he
felt Starks was the best shooting guard on the Knicks, and also

enjoyed the challenge of matching up against Houston, a player he felt was inferior to himself.

If Ernie Grunfeld took heat for acquiring Camby early on, he absorbed a steady stream of criticism over nearly three seasons for choosing Houston over Miller. The usual refrain went something like, Why didn't Ernie just fork over the money to Reggie, the man who had run a knife through more Knick play-off dreams than perhaps even Michael Jordan?

And now they were facing off again, for the conference title.

The Knicks and Pacers had met in four of the last seven postseasons, with each team winning two se-ries. Miller always seemed to provide incredible drama, never more stunningly than when he single-handedly shot the Knicks down in Game 1 of the 1995 conference semifinals.

In what would be Riley's farewell playoff in New York, the Knicks had a six-point lead and the game in hand with 16.4 seconds to go. Somehow, Miller scored eight points on two 3-pointers—one of them off an inbounds steal in which Miller stepped behind the line as soon as he gathered the loose ball—and two free throws to swipe the game and leave the Garden crowd in utter shock. The Pacers would go on to win in seven games.

The year before, Miller exploded for 25 of his game-high 39 points in the fourth quarter of Game 5, taunting Spike Lee and crawling beneath Starks's skin on NBC. Starks head-butted Miller earlier in the series, and their heated matchup became must-see TV. Theirs was truly a bitter rivalry. Starks's famous temper vs. Miller's needling disposition.

During a regular season game in 1995, they went nose-to-nose on the court. So incensed was Starks afterward that when a reporter wondered why he had let Miller get into his head, Starks got a frightening look in his eye. "I'm goin' to cut his dick off and make him eat it," he said.

Forty-five minutes after the game in a near-empty locker room, he was still possessed.

They would eventually embrace after a hard-fought series and over the years gained a mutual respect for one another, especially after Starks adopted a more Christian lifestyle. But Miller would have the final say on the floor, coldly stealing another Knicks season in 1998.

With New York seconds away from tying the conference semifinals at two games apiece, Miller was left open on a broken play. A few steps in front of a screaming Lee, he let fly a 26-foot 3-pointer with 5.9 seconds left that sent the game into overtime. Indiana won that game and the series in five games. The next morning's *Daily News* detailed the Knicks' agony: On the cover was Starks's head bowed underneath the word CRUSHED. On the back page, photographer Keith Torrie captured Reggie's release and a frantic celebrity row behind him. "Killer Miller," read the headline.

And here he was again in Game 1, squaring up behind the arc while all of New York prayed for him to miss.

The Pacers had put Milwaukee away in three games and Allen Iverson's 76ers in four straight before meeting the Knicks. Determined not to get blown out early, the Knicks led by as many as nine points in the first quarter.

The lead would change hands 17 times, with crucial stops and huge shots on both ends in the fourth quarter. But just as Indiana seemed ready to put New York away, the Knicks overcame a five-point deficit in the last two minutes, 10 seconds.

The run began when Ewing drove around another wounded and sore center, 7-foot-4 Rik Smits, and scored on a short jump shot. Houston, who led the Knicks with 19 points, put Smits out of the game with six fouls moments later, then made both free throws. After Mark Jackson missed his second high-arching jumper from a few feet away, Ewing was fouled in the act of shooting by Antonio Davis. He made both, free throws that quieted Market Square and gave the Knicks an 88–87 lead with 51.3 seconds remaining.

Jackson made a free throw on the other end to tie the score, but he missed the second. Ewing grabbed the ball as Davis reached over his back harmlessly. The whistle blew, the Pacers were furious, and Ewing, who had dropped in those pressurized free throws in Game 5 against Miami, was about to sink another team in the clutch. With 29.4 seconds left, the Knicks led 90–88.

Only a Miller 3-pointer could destroy them. He came around a screen on the left elbow, in front of the Knick bench. Shadowed by Houston and with Ewing running out at him, Miller rushed the shot. It barely caught the side of the rim with less than 13 seconds left.

Childs concentrated and made two free throws with 12.4 seconds left. Antonio Davis answered with an uncontested dunk four seconds later to give Indiana a chance. Childs then missed one of two, leaving the door open with 6.7 seconds remaining.

With Indiana needing a three to tie, Childs bottled up Jackson in the left corner. Jackson's foot was on the 3-point line when he released the last shot of the game. It never hit the rim. The Knicks had held on for a pulsating 93–90 victory, and Market Square Arena went silent.

The Knicks had not only ended an 11-game win streak by Indiana, they had won their third straight Game 1 on the road— becoming only the third team in NBA playoff history to achieve the feat. They had taken Indiana's best shot, and still managed to get up and steal home court advantage.

Ewing scored six of New York's last nine points, finishing with 16 points and 10 rebounds in 40 painful minutes. The injury that had bothered him since March 1 was growing more severe each day. It was not just about his skill and savvy anymore; his pain threshold and stubbornness were helping the Knicks win games.

The Pacers were feeling duped. Leading up to Game 2, they questioned the severity of Ewing's injury and wondered if the Big Fella wasn't just playing possum. Jackson and Bird, both friends of Ewing, facetiously suggested that Ewing was milking his injury for all its emotional worth. After all, didn't that jalopy just log 40 of a possible 48 minutes? How hurt could he be?

Two nights later, during pregame warmups, Ewing felt a ripping sensation in his Achilles tendon as he jogged around the court. He quickly retreated to the locker room to have his left ankle retaped. He was limping even more noticeably during the game, straining himself just to get back downcourt.

He played like his sneakers were nailed to the floor. Unable to move side to side, he could not help his team defensively or on the boards. Meanwhile, the Knicks had reverted to early-regular-season form. Falling behind by 17 in the second quarter, they managed to trim the lead to 11 at intermission.

Jackson finally got untracked, exploiting his mismatch against Childs and Charlie Ward. He would use his rump to back them down in the post, and then either score on easy jumpers or pass out of the double-team to teammates streaking to the basket. But the Knicks rallied behind Houston, Sprewell, and Childs.

Their offense accounted for most of a 19–2 run that gave New York a six-point lead with 8:25 left. But Jalen Rose, the Pacers' multifaceted sixth man, subdued the Knicks by scoring seven of Indiana's nine straight points. The sinewy, left-handed 6-foot-8 guard was the perfect answer to Sprewell, slashing, creating, and burying short turnaround jump shots along the baseline.

New York was not done. The Knicks used a 6–0 run, capped by two Ewing free throws with 45.5 seconds left, to go back in front 86–84. But that was their last stand. Antonio Davis mowed over Camby underneath the basket, which seemed to be a clear offensive foul—only referee Dick Bavetta called Camby for the personal, giving Davis the bucket that tied the game plus one free throw with 31.1 seconds left.

Davis failed to convert the three-point play, but after a failed Knicks possession that ended with Houston dribbling into a turnover, Miller closed the door. Using a simple head fake to get Childs off his feet along the left baseline about twenty feet away, Miller barely drew contact as he released a shot with 2.2 seconds remaining. The whistle blew again.

Childs was beside himself, but he clearly bit on the fake. Miller went through his customary routine before he goes to the foul line, sprinkling a powdered rosin mixture on his hands, rubbing them together and taking his sweet-ass time to step up and take the first shot. However annoying the whole drawn-out process was to opposing fans, it was remarkably effective. He made two to break the tie.

Out of timeouts, the Knicks were forced to go the full ninety-four feet. Ward cleared the cobwebs from his quarterback days at Florida State and threw a bullet to Ewing, who had pushed off on Antonio Davis to get free a few steps left of the free throw line. The play was designed for Ewing to catch and pass to Houston or Sprewell on either wing, but he was so wide open, he elected to shoot.

His wide-open jumper hit off the back iron, giving Indiana an ugly 88–86 win. Eighty-four free throws, 68 fouls, and 33 turnovers later, it ended with a Knick collapse.

"Aaahhh!" Ewing screamed at the Market Square rafters. The Pacer fans, as vicious and mean-spirited as any fans in the league, mocked him as he walked off the court. Even Miller could not resist a classless jab at him in the postgame press conference. With Ewing waiting for Miller to finish his session at the podium, Miller talked about how games often hinge on making or missing in the final seconds. Looking over at Ewing, he said, "Isn't that right, Pat?"

Ewing had no rejoinder in the interview room, and he would have no opportunity to respond where he'd have preferred to, on the court.

Dr. Norman Scott broke the bad news the next morning. "Pat, you have a partial tear of the left Achilles tendon just above the ankle," the Knicks team physician said.

"You're kidding," Ewing said, knowing that Dr. Scott did not joke about these things.

After all the physical anguish, the franchise center was finally done for the season.

A magnetic resonance imaging test that morning at Beth Is-

rael Hospital North Division in lower Manhattan had revealed
the injury. Ewing tried to convince Scott to allow him to play;
throbbing foot and all, he realized that at age thirty-six he
might not have another chance at a championship ring.

The Knicks were seven wins away from a title, and he figured, *What the hell. I played the last three months in pain.* But
after further consultation with Scott, he realized, "If my
Achilles ruptures completely, it would end my career."

The ripping sensation he had felt prior to Game 2, Scott con-
cluded, had done Ewing in. He played 26 minutes in excruciat-
ing pain. The next morning, he would be fitted for a walking
boot that he would have to wear for the next six weeks.

That afternoon, Van Gundy got on a conference call with the
news media and sounded like he had lost a family member. He
broke the news to his players and gave them the day off. "Today
will obviously be a down day for our team," he said. "Patrick
has won a lot of personal awards. But the reason he plays now
is to win a championship."

Ewing put on a brave face the next day, gathered the team
around in a huddle, and demanded one favor. "Get me my
ring," he told them. Inside, though, he was hurting. Who knew
if he would be this close to a title again? He wondered if he was
jinxed, one of those star-crossed players for whom it was never
meant to be. Dan Marino. Karl Malone and John Stockton.
Ernie Banks. Great Players Who Never Won a Title was not the
kind of list he wanted to make.

He never had a chance to fully recover from reconstructive
wrist surgery, and now he had a bum leg. The lockout scars
were still fresh in his mind, too. He was perceived to have lost a
labor war. Throw in the fact that a segment of Knick fans still
believed Ewing's presence was dragging the team down, and he
did not exactly feel the confidence of a future first-ballot Hall of
Famer.

Van Gundy understood that Ewing's pain was more than
physical. The coach was incensed at the mere suggestion that
Ewing's absence might actually help his team. He lashed out at
the media and fans the morning of Game 3.

"I'm listening to the radio and reading and people are saying, 'What has Patrick done in this series?' Well, let me just tell
you if anyone wants to know. He had 16 points and 10 rebounds in Game 1. I think he had six or eight in the last two
minutes, and he's also the guy that ran out at Reggie Miller and
made him miss. But other than that he didn't do a damn thing.
In Game 2, he didn't play much but he still got the hoop that
cut it to two and the two free throws that put us up two. But
other than that he didn't do anything. So he really hasn't
helped us in this series."

For Van Gundy, Ewing's absence meant a certain amount of
tinkering. Against the most brutish, experienced, and talented
team in the East, the Knicks were down to an eight-man rotation of role players, streak shooters, and foul-prone big men.
For all of Ewing's defensive liabilities against Smits, his ability
to create his own shot in the final minutes or draw the foul
would be missed.

The obvious move was to insert Dudley into the starting
lineup, and encourage Sprewell and Houston to start running a
more up-tempo, end-to-end game. Above all, it meant Camby
was on the spot. His minutes were bound to increase. The
young forward with arms that went on forever would finally get
to test his agility against the muscle of Antonio and Dale Davis.

"I still can't believe they traded Oak," Scottie Pippen, that
renowned Knick analyst, said earlier in the season. "Marcus
Camby? He's got some talent, but the Davis boys will crush
him."

Camby was eager for the opportunity. All season he had
heard how his lithe, 225-pound frame would not survive a
seven-game series against the brawn of the Davises. Oakley had
been outplayed the year before, and he had experience and
toughness on his side. Camby was a stick in a forest of red-
woods.

"I'll go up against anybody," he said. "That's just who I am.
The Davises are big and strong, but so is everybody in the
league. I can play against anybody."

Meanwhile, Ewing swallowed hard. Making sure his tailored

suits were pressed, he was about to become the world's tallest cheerleader.

The Ewing saga was not the only subplot as the series shifted to New York for Games 3 and 4 on Saturday and Monday. Antonio Davis was calling Kurt Thomas a "dirty player," adding, "Either the referee has to step in and take care of it or we'll take care of it. One or the other."

The emotional ante kept rising, and soon an endless flow of forearms and elbows would follow. Would the Knicks once again be goaded into belligerent self-destruction, or could this new breed remake the team in their own athletic, souped-up image? For the first time in eleven years, they would go into a playoff game without Ewing, Starks, or Oakley.

As the clock wound down, Larry Johnson simply relied on instinct. He launched a desperation shot, a 30-foot heave as the buzzer sounded.

All net. All even.

The Garden went ballistic. The first quarter had ended, and Johnson had found a new toy.

Over the course of the season, Johnson had gained more confidence in the 3-point shot. Van Gundy had encouraged him to take it, especially with defenses allowing him to roam free on the perimeter. In the first two series, he had attempted and made more shots from beyond the arc than Sprewell and Houston combined.

He had hesitated to square up from that far away for most of his career. When the NBA moved the line back from 22 feet to the original 23 feet, 9 inches in 1997, Johnson was even more cautious.

Even as he established himself as one of the league's premier players in the early 1990s, all many people ever remembered about Johnson were those final, fleeting moments against Duke in the 1991 NCAA semifinals.

The image is indelible. Johnson, the player of the year on one of the most talented teams in college history, stood out there in a trance on the right wing with his UNLV Runnin' Rebels trailing Duke by two points. He had a clear view of the basket with a few seconds left, had a chance to be the hero and send UNLV to its second national final.

Instead, he hesitated, passed off to Anderson Hunt with almost no time, and his teammate forced up a wild, off-balance shot to end the game.

Eight years later, his teammates and coaches were still urging him to take the shot. By Game 3 against the Pacers, he had no other choice.

Johnson's first 3-pointer tied the game at 17. And with Camby (21 points, 11 rebounds, and four steals) emerging as a force, the Knicks entered the fourth quarter knotted at 69 with the Pacers. Johnson went to the well again with 10:50 left, improbably banking in a 3-pointer with the shot clock running out.

The Pacers trailed by four points when they embarked on an 18–6 run. Smits finally caught fire, scoring six of his 25 points during the spurt. With only 3:21 left, the Knicks trailed 89–81. The pendulum had all but swung back toward Indiana.

Moments later, the Knicks were somehow back in the game. Childs started a 7–0 run with a huge 3-pointer. Sprewell knocked down a jumper. And Camby, who made only 55 percent of his free throws during the regular season, brought the Knicks to within one by converting two pressure foul shots with 13.8 seconds left.

Jackson appeared to ice the game when he hit two free throws with 11.9 seconds left. Down 91–88, the Knicks set up a play for Houston. Ward would inbound at the scorer's table, and Houston would come off a screen and launch a 3-pointer if he was open. If not, he would drive to the basket for a quick two, the Knicks would quickly foul and hope for one more possession.

But Derrick McKey, the Pacers' defensive specialist, foiled their plans. He blanketed Houston, forcing Ward to find any open man before he was hit with a five-second violation. Johnson wisely came to the ball. When Rose tipped the entry pass, the ball was momentarily free. Using his body to block out Antonio Davis, Johnson quickly gathered it in.

He faced up Davis twenty-five feet away on the left wing, in front of the Pacer bench. He dribbled twice to his left and then pulled up with 5.7 seconds left. Pump-faking once, Johnson rose for the shot as the Garden rose with him. Davis had put his hand lightly on Johnson's hip, but not lightly enough for referee Jess Kersey not to call the infraction.

Kersey's whistle blew as the ball settled gently into the net. You could almost hear Marv Albert, the legendary voice of the team, bellowing his trademark line.

"Yes!!! And the foul!"

Delirium consumed the building, and the Knicks were almost as shell-shocked as the Pacers. The chance for a four-point play began in front of Coach Bird, whose Larry Legend moniker was on loan for the afternoon.

Johnson, in disbelief, ran to midcourt and embraced Sprewell. Then Childs, the feisty point guard, ran over and told him to hold off on the champagne for a few moments.

"Hey, you've still got a free throw to make," Childs said.

"Okay, Chris, you're absolutely right," Johnson replied. "Let's calm down."

Johnson composed himself, walked back downcourt, breathed deeply, bent his knees, and followed through on the most important foul shot of his career. Good. His 26th and final point of the game had given New York a 92–91 lead that held up when Jackson's one-handed runner in traffic fell short at the buzzer.

He ran into the crowd along the Seventh Avenue baseline. Mobbed by teammates, Johnson caught Spike Lee in his arms. Another 20,000 or so of his closest friends stayed and partied in the building, not wanting the moment to end.

"Here you are in New York, hitting a shot like that, Spike, the Garden crowd, and you're like, 'Say, that's pretty big,' " Johnson said.

Ewing's injury had received most of the headlines, but Johnson was quietly playing in pain as well. His left knee was strained, and he could barely push off of it. If his teammates were marveling at his clutch play, they were even more impressed by his ability to ignore his health problems.

Jerry Tarkanian watched from his hotel room in Portland, Oregon. Johnson's former coach at UNLV remembered how much criticism Johnson took for passing up the shot against Duke. So many times Johnson has deferred in that situation, passed off because he either did not want to take the pressure of losing the game on himself or he genuinely believed a teammate had a better chance to win it.

"I don't think he had any demons left because he's won so many games at different levels," said Tarkanian. "But after he makes it, it's pretty easy to think back about that. On his voice message the week after we lost, he said, 'Hi, this is Larry. I'm not home right now. And, yes, I should've taken the last shot.' "

No one was prepared to call it destiny, but you got the feeling something special was happening to the Knicks. If it wasn't Iverson beating the Pistons in overtime on the last night of the regular season to ensure a Knick-Heat matchup in the first round, it was Houston's Game 5 winner in Miami. They kept parlaying their good fortune into more, and it all manifested itself in Johnson's four-point play.

Even the nonbelievers were converting. Van Gundy sought out Ward and told him to keep up the good work. "Keep talking," the coach said. "If you've got a direct line to Him, use it."

Van Gundy, the pragmatist, was not about to get caught up in the magic. After replaying Game 3 and watching the Pacers dominate his team for nearly all of four quarters, he decided to mess with success and make a lineup change.

"We caught a miracle," he said. "We all know it. You need one if you're going to keep moving on. But you can't rely on it. We were dominated in the game. It was great that we hung in there and won. . . . Anything's a gamble right now. I know I would have made the change if the miracle hadn't happened.

Miracles happening don't change what I think we need to do to win the series."

Sprewell would get his wish: He was going to start for only the fifth time all season and the first in the playoffs.

Van Gundy's brainstorm was a huge risk and a source of endless debate. Why now? Sprewell had been playing well off the bench, however grudgingly he accepted the role. From a basketball standpoint, it made sense to protect Dudley and Kurt Thomas from foul trouble against the Pacers' big men. But chemistry-wise, the decision was questioned widely.

The Knicks were up two games to one on the most potent team in the East. They had just won a dramatic game. They were only 1-3 with Sprewell as a starter, including a blowout loss to the Pacers on April 4. It also meant Johnson would have to sacrifice again, moving from small forward to power forward—a position where he's undersized and uncomfortable.

But then, Sprewell's shining moment had arrived. Breakaway dunk after breakaway dunk, his popularity was growing exponentially during the playoffs. In Atlanta, the cheers for him after scoring were louder than they were for Steve Smith. In New York, they could not stock his No. 8 jersey on the shelves fast enough. In Game 3, he was paid the ultimate tribute when the Knick City Dancers bounded out onto the Garden floor during a timeout in the first quarter for a routine: Every member had braided cornrows, just like Spree. "I thought it was cute," he said.

The Garden was already rocking by the time Game 4 started. The announcement of Sprewell's name during player introductions brought the noise to a crescendo. He came out in force, bumping chests with teammates who had formed their usual human gauntlet leading out from the bench to the floor. His contorted face formed a menacing scowl. His cornrows were flopping. It was quite a scene. And it was the only memorable Knick moment of the night.

Rose scored 19, knifing through every Knick defender. Chris Mullin, Sprewell's teammate at Golden State, had 18 points and victimized Sprewell repeatedly with up-and-under moves, hesitation jump shots, and everything in the arsenal he used to school Sprewell in practice when they were Warriors.

Sprewell, battling a head cold, was abysmal on both ends. He finished with only 12 points, missed eight of 14 shots, committed three turnovers, and fouled out.

"The whole game was like we were stuck in mud," Sprewell said after the 90–78 loss. "We were doing a bunch of different things to try to get ourselves going. Nothing we did seemed to work. I guess it didn't work because we lost. But the series isn't over."

To old-school purists, Game 4 represented a one-night revenge against the Gen-X player. Mullin, thirty-five, was the slow-footed, pasty white kid from St. John's via Brooklyn's Xaverian High School. He played as much with his head as he did his body, forging an All-Star career after winning a battle against alcoholism his first years in the pros. A product of the playgrounds, he was one of a select group of white players accepted by the vast majority of black NBA players. He could not defend, but he could still stroke the 3-pointer and even in his advancing age his game still had a lot of panache to it.

He had gotten out of Golden State, too, but in a much more conventional way than Sprewell. Mullin went to management and quietly asked to be traded and was granted his wish when the Pacers traded for him prior to the 1997–98 season. His career was all about professionalism and class, and it made you wonder what kind of injustice it would be if Sprewell made it to the Finals before a thirteen-year vet who had done things the right way.

But that was just perception. In reality, Mullin had taken Sprewell under his wing and had played a role in Sprewell's ascension to the team's go-to guy and All-Star. As Mullin faded in the background, Sprewell's game grew louder and more intense.

"I owe a lot to Chris," he said. "I learned so much from him, in terms of defending, getting steals, and playing smart. We really didn't hang out a lot, but we never got into any altercations. We always respected one another. We were always there if the other guy was having a difficult time. Mullie and I are real close."

Van Gundy's grand plan had backfired for a game. The Knicks had given back home court advantage, and the head coach was again taking it on the chin for overmanaging his roster. The same columnists who were baying for Sprewell to start suddenly had a convenient change of heart. They seized the chance to blast Van Gundy again.

"When you make changes, you're susceptible to second-guessing," he said. "I don't worry about that. I know this is the way we have to go to have a chance to win the series." Van Gundy blamed the loss on his team's inability to defend and rebound, and he drove that notion home during a verbal tirade the next day at practice.

"We're right back to where we were in the regular season," he told his players. "If we think we're going to win a series against this team by not guarding, we're mistaken. They could start the assistant coaches and it wouldn't matter if we don't guard."

The Knicks headed back to Indianapolis for Game 5 needing to win at least one more game at Market Square Arena to take the best-of-seven series. They had awakened a sleeping giant, giving Indiana new life on its home floor. Back in New York, a familiar refrain could be heard: Those knuckleheads still didn't know how to deal with prosperity.

Market Square was filled with Pacer crazies, howling insults at the Knicks from pregame warmups to the end of the game.

In the first two games, the Knicks bench got into several shouting matches with irate fans behind them. Johnson had a beer dumped on him after Game 2 as he headed to the locker room. Checketts demanded increased security for Game 5, and even Spike helped the cause. He chartered a plane with about a dozen Knick zealots. Clad in orange and blue jerseys, they took their position a few rows behind the Knick bench and slapped hands with the players as they arrived.

The Knicks were nearly blown off the floor in the opening minutes, falling behind 9–0 before scoring 10 straight points.

Indiana closed out the period with a 19–4 run and led 28–14. New York was reeling, in search of any kind of energy or enthusiasm. But just minutes later, the Gen-X factors materialized, and Game 5 was never the same.

Camby and Sprewell put their athletic stamp on the game, blowing past the Pacers and jumping over them. Sprewell scored 10 points in the second period, but Camby was flat-out awesome. He scored nine points, including two baskets off of offensive rebounds and a dunk. By halftime, the teams were tied at 42.

Camby had picked up three fouls, and Van Gundy took his second monstrous gamble in the series, keeping his most active player on the bench for the first 10 minutes of the second half. The Pacers, behind Miller, seized a 69–65 lead heading into the fourth. Van Gundy was saving Camby for the fourth quarter, and felt he was more aggressive when he wasn't in foul trouble. The last thing the coach wanted was to enter the final period with Camby on the bench, saddled with five fouls.

But had he waited too long? The Pacers had momentum, and Miller was going off en route to a 30-point night. Had Van Gundy stubbornly overlooked Camby's contributions? What game was he watching?

In fact, the move turned out to be a stroke of genius.

Inserted with 1:57 left in the third quarter, Camby gave the Knicks a rested, agile twenty-five-year-old with three fouls to give. He paid immediate dividends, drawing two quick fouls and hitting three free throws. In the fourth, with the series in the balance, he took over: Changing shots with his wingspan, suddenly appearing along the baseline to throw the ball down with two hands, Camby was everywhere.

His dunk with 5:55 left put the Knicks ahead at 81–80. Moments later, he and Johnson turned the building into a morgue. Johnson buried two 3-pointers, and Camby followed with a dunk to give the Knicks a 91–84 lead with 2:15 remaining. Sprewell added insurance, making seven of eight free throws in the final 1:44.

Two days after he was crucified for falling short as a starter,

Sprewell finished with 29 points. Camby, in the watershed game of his career, erupted for 21 points, 13 rebounds, and six blocked shots.

"He dominated the game tonight," said Bird after the Knicks' 101–94 victory.

Van Gundy, raked over for starting Sprewell and about to be condemned for leaving Camby on the bench, pumped his fist as the Knicks left the floor and headed back to New York with a golden chance to close out the series.

For different reasons, all three men felt vindicated.

"You need to be a risk-taker to be a good coach and a leader," Van Gundy said. "You can't be paralyzed by criticism."

Meanwhile, some of the Pacer faithful showed off their wonderful Midwestern sportsmanship. A year after a gap-toothed, red-faced man of maybe forty-five hollered, "Hey, psycho boy!" at Starks from behind the team bench, the same creep had found a new target: "You're a real role model for society, Latrell! You're just what our kids need."

Sprewell seemed oblivious to the ruckus. He walked off the floor after a postgame interview and headed to the locker room, where his teammates were laughing and smiling. The Knicks, fresh off one of the great road wins in franchise history, were going home.

"We have to win one more game to be in the Finals," Sprewell said. "We know it's right there."

The next day in the Indianapolis airport, Miller's wife, Marita, was waiting for a flight to New York. Speaking on her cell phone, she was having an animated conversation with a friend.

"We don't have any thugs on this team!" Marita Miller said. "We have too many nice guys. We need a thug or two. That's the only way we can beat them."

Beyond his on-court exploits, Camby was also drawing attention for the two large Chinese characters tattooed on his right arm. Now that Camby was proving his worth as a player, the question on all Knicks fans' lips was, what did those eclectic-looking tattoos mean, and how did they relate to the Tao of Marcus?

A humorous *Wall Street Journal* article finally cracked the mystery. Through a spokesman, Camby gave the *Wall Street Journal* translations from a book of Chinese characters published in the United States. He said the top character meant "I strive to be the best" and the bottom one, "I love my family."

In fact, as the *Journal* reported, the first character, *mian,* most commonly means "to inspire," and the second, *zu,* means "race" or "nationality." But taken together, which is the way the Chinese read two characters stacked on top of each other, they have no meaning—at least, not to the native Chinese speakers interviewed by the *Journal.*

"Maybe it's the name of the team," said Zhang Xiaomei, a young woman working at a clothing shop in Beijing, after puzzling over a photo of Camby. "But that's just a guess."

While this was somewhat embarrassing for Camby, it was probably an appropriate end to the search for the deeper meaning. After all, Camby's reason for selecting these tattoos was not his study of imperial China but rather a love of Chinese culture that was inspired by "watching kung-fu movies."

On the morning of Game 6, Van Gundy rose early and wandered around his Chappaqua, New York, home in the best of moods. At thirty-seven, he was one win away from the NBA Finals. San Antonio had swept Portland in the Western Conference, and Tim Duncan and David Robinson were almost growing bored waiting for the East to crown a champion. Van Gundy wanted to speed up matters.

The last two months had been a dizzying experience. After all the distractions, the coach thought, his team, the town, everyone, could concentrate on basketball. But by the time he arrived at Purchase College, the mood was spoiled.

The front page story in the *Daily News* detailed how Van Gundy was about to become a rich man if his Knicks could win one more game. The $6 million contract extension he had signed in 1997 was paltry by Rick Pitino and Pat Riley standards, but it did contain several incentive clauses that enriched the deal.

For making the NBA Finals, Van Gundy would receive a $500,000 bonus. Also, the option year of his contract in 2000–2001 would be automatically guaranteed at $3.5 million. Even if Checketts somehow still decided to fire him, Van Gundy would be walking away with a $4 million parting gift.

The story hit newsstands the same day a report surfaced that Phil Jackson had had preliminary talks with the Los Angeles Lakers. Van Gundy's leverage and his bank account were increasing by the day. But he was outraged that his contract status would become more of a story than the Knicks' astonishing playoff run.

"It's a joke," he said. "It's about winning. You can't buy your way into something worthwhile. It's like, I'm the first coach to have an incentive clause in his contract? The thing is, because of this job, I'm fine financially. Believe me, wanting to win has zero to do with money."

Houston had his own priceless reasons to want to end the series. Tami's due date was a week away, and Houston was determined to be in the delivery room to see his firstborn. The couple had talked about inducing labor if the Knicks advanced to the Finals.

Never had the Garden been more electric in the past decade than it was on the night of June 11. During the playoffs, the Knicks had begun showing a video montage of great postseason moments in franchise history, updating it with each playoff win. From Willis Reed limping on the court in 1970 to Starks's left-handed dunk of the ages against the Bulls in 1993, the video peeled back layer after layer of emotion leading up to each game.

By the time Camby was shown dunking on Indiana in Game 5, the Garden was frolicking. Every major celebrity who had ever followed the team showed up to take their seats: Jerry Seinfeld. Puff Daddy. Billy Crystal. Matthew Modine. Matt Dillon.

Among them was the well-groomed, handsome publisher of *George* magazine. John F. Kennedy Jr. took his usual, inconspicuous seat along the Eighth Avenue baseline, ten feet from the Knicks bench. A frequent visitor, he had an unassuming dignity about him and lent a special aura to the building. More so than ever on this night.

They came out with stage fright, missing 13 of their first 14 shots. Indiana went up 13–4 in the opening minutes. Behind Houston and Sprewell and Johnson, the Knicks used a 15–3 binge to take a 24–18 lead. Johnson had six points in the quarter, and was looking spry around the basket. As the Knicks' only low-post scoring threat, he would have to have a big night.

But with 6:08 left in the second quarter, Johnson's night was over and the Knicks were staring hard at a Game 7 in Indiana. It began as a routine play, with the Indiana backup point guard Travis Best darting into the lane. Colliding with Camby, Best rolled awkwardly and clipped Johnson's right knee. Johnson went down in a heap under the basket, screaming, "My knee! My knee!"

For several minutes, Dr. Scott and trainer Mike Saunders administered to him. The longer he stayed down, the worse the injury appeared. When he finally rose, Johnson could not put any weight on his right leg. Herb Williams and Chris Dudley helped him off the floor and carried him to the locker room. In one freak instant, the Knicks' emotional leader was headed to the hospital with a sprained medial collateral ligament.

After everything they had gone through, now this. The Knicks would have to go the next 30 minutes without Johnson or Ewing, their two proven scorers in the post. The Seventh Avenue baseline basket had betrayed them again. You thought about Charles Smith having all those shots blocked by the Bulls, Ewing's Game 7 finger-roll against the Pacers that bounced off the back of the rim, and now Johnson lying there in agony, his team one half away from the Finals and not a damn thing he could do about it.

The curse of the 1990s was alive and well. The Garden crowd was barely audible.

After gathering themselves, the Knicks went into intermission with a 41–35 lead. But they had looked flat in the remainder of the second quarter, and the Pacers finally found their resolve after halftime. They went on an 11–0 run and led 48–42 midway through the third quarter. The only thing that kept them from pulling away was Houston's sweet stroke.

He began heating up at the end of the third, scoring nine in the period on a buffet of medium-range jumpers from the left wing. Miller and Jalen Rose kept flailing their arms and trying to grab him as he fought through screens, but their defense didn't seem to make much difference; he was feeling it, and he wanted the ball.

They were knotted at 59 after three quarters, and when Childs buried a 3-pointer to start the fourth, you knew the Knicks would hang tough. Camby came to play again, putting back missed shots with authority. The Davises were grounded and outmaneuvered.

Houston was the most brilliant of them all. He kept repelling the Pacers, hitting a jumper to put New York up two points with five minutes left. His three-point play with 3:23 remaining made it a six-point game at 79–73. He went by Rose on that play, shaking him and then exploding along the baseline for a layup and the foul.

At one juncture, Miller was talking to him, trying to get him out of his game early in the fourth quarter; Houston simply smiled at him, put the ball on the floor and drove by Reggie as if he didn't exist.

The decibel level kept rising in the arena with each made shot. Houston hit eight of his nine shots in the second half, his confidence buoyed by the loud mob exhorting him on. The Pacers got to within 78–76, but Camby soared over the Pacers' front line to tip in a Childs miss and then hit two free throws a few moments later—82–76. This crazy dream was starting to look real. Down to a seven-man rotation, the Knicks were a few possessions from knocking off Bird's team.

The defining moment came when Rose missed a 3-pointer from the left baseline with less than a minute left. Dale Davis appeared to grab the rebound, but Camby swatted it away. As the ball came free by the Knicks' bench, Dudley dove for it. The Garden was already rocking as he passed the ball to Houston while still on his back. Childs and Van Gundy began motioning desperately for a timeout, but Houston passed to Sprewell at the foul line, and he spurned convention once more. Dribbling to his right, Sprewell blew past Rose and Jackson at half-court. With his team only leading by six, he was going for the knockout.

Miller was waiting for him five feet from the basket, but Sprewell ignored him like a yellow traffic light and sped up. Having gone through the entire Pacer defense, he converted a breathtaking finger roll with 39.9 seconds left. The noise was deafening.

It was the classic sequence in which the coach and the fans yell, "No, no, no. Work the clock. Hold it." Followed seconds later by, "Yes! What a great play!" Sprewell may have been the only guy in the league with enough cojones and talent to pull it off. That coast-to-coast sprint was the perfect symbol for the series: Sprewell and Houston flying downcourt, the Pacers back on their heels. Bird's team suddenly looked awfully old.

Camby ended with 15 points, nine rebounds, and three blocks, and Sprewell scored 20. Miller shot 3-for-18 in the final game, 1-for-8 on 3-pointers. Houston, who outscored Miller for the series, finished with 32 points. In the end, it seemed like simple geography: To get to San Antonio, the Knicks went through Houston.

When the buzzer sounded, and the Knicks had accomplished the near-impossible with a 90–82 victory, the sweetest scene of the season followed. The Knicks raised their arms in triumph, and Childs flung the ball into the crowd, over Jerry Seinfeld and Puff Daddy on Celebrity Row. Van Gundy raced onto the floor and embraced Houston.

Sprewell, his engine still revving, began taking laps around the Garden court, touching the hands of fans and thanking them for their season-long support. Ewing, dressed in a suit and wearing a hat that read "Eastern Conference Champions,"

was telling NBC's Jim Gray how proud he was of his teammates.

"We're going back to the Big Show," he said. "We're going
back to the Big Dance."

In Ewing's absence, Camby changed the course of the series.
He averaged 14.3 points, 10.7 rebounds, and three blocks in the
six games. Sprewell averaged 17.7 points, Johnson contributed
16.5 points and nine 3-pointers—the most by any player in the
series. Houston was as clutch as ever. He led all scorers with a
19-point average.

What's more, Miller never emerged. He scored less than 17
points per game and shot a horrid 36 percent from the field.

For several minutes, the players stayed on the court and celebrated with the Garden crowd. Kim Van Gundy was weeping
again. A fan held up a directional sign that read, "San Antonio,
1,856 miles."

After the pandemonium died down, Houston began scan-
ning the seats for Tami, who had vowed to attend Game 6 if she
did not go into labor. He looked hard, but could not find his
wife anywhere in the arena.

The next evening, Houston was in the delivery room of a
Connecticut hospital, clad in a shower cap and scrubs. He
signed autographs for some hospital personnel before helping
Tami perform another miracle.

Remie Jean Houston weighed six pounds, seven ounces and
had her dad's sense of impeccable timing. In nineteen hours,
Allan had attained Garden immortality and fatherhood.

"Basically, it's the happiest day of my life," he said. "To have
those things happen back to back is amazing. God just put his
blessings on me, all at one time."

At peace with his game and himself, he would get on a plane
in four days to play in the NBA Finals against the San Antonio
Spurs.

12
LAST STAND

Latrell Sprewell remembered the Alamodome. His last visit to the home of the San Antonio Spurs came on November 19, 1997, twelve days before the incident that made his one of the best-known names in sports. With Golden State losing badly to the Spurs, Sprewell looked over at Gregg Popovich on the San Antonio sideline and called out, "Yo, Pop, get me outta here. Pull the trigger." He was asking the San Antonio coach and general manager to trade for him. Right there. In the middle of the game.

After the choking incident, more stories of Sprewell's bad behavior began to surface. He had been denigrating the game daily, it seemed, on a one-man crusade to become the anti-Jordan.

Less than two years later, here he was, rehabilitated as a player, leading an undermanned Knick team against the tall and mighty Spurs. The makeover was something to see. He had his endorsement contract with AND 1, and had started wearing designer glasses even though there was nothing wrong with his eyesight; Sprewell was going for the Distinguished Latrell Look in the hope that another advertiser might take the bait.

Standing coolly under the basket during media day prior to Game 1, Sprewell answered every tough question posed. His three months in New York had prepared him well for the international media onslaught. Charming and accommodating,

he was not the scowling, threatening man everyone had perceived.

Even Carlesimo was starting to come around. "Not to be critical, but I thought he would have a much better regular season,"
Carlesimo said during an interview on WFAN radio, but he
added, "Spree's a great player. It took him a while to get comfortable. It took them a while to get used to playing together.
But Spree is this good. People shouldn't be surprised when he
plays this well."

Yet no matter how you dressed him up, he was still the
enemy. The public, in search of a post-Bulls story line, demanded this.

Sprewell was the bad guy, representing the team and the city
most of the country loves to hate. He and the Knicks weren't
merely going up against a balanced and deep team that had
won eleven of twelve playoff games and swept through the Lakers and the Trail Blazers; they were going up against everyone's
favorite young player, Tim Duncan, and his humble teammates.
Saint Tim and the choir boys vs. Spree and the hooligans. NBC
had little else to hang its hat on for ratings.

The 7-foot Duncan had personally ousted all the charisma in
the West. Kevin Garnett of the Minnesota Timberwolves lasted
four games. Same went for Shaq and Kobe in the semifinals,
and Rasheed Wallace and Isaiah Rider in the conference finals.

In only his second year out of Wake Forest, Duncan was
clearly the league's best big man and arguably its best player,
though he somehow lost out to Karl Malone for the MVP
award. He was playing the game that time forgot: He used
power dribbles to move closer to the rim, faced up his defender
from eighteen feet away on the wing, and banked shots in off
the glass. He used his reach to pass to teammates cutting
through the lane. And he had this pretty little jump hook that
was beginning to look downright Waltonesque.

He offered an interesting dichotomy, an old-school mind
controlling and nurturing a Generation X body. There were no
frills to Duncan's game, no death stares after a blocked shot and
no scowls after a monster dunk. He used an economy of move-

ment and emotion. In college, this had led Duke's ever-creative fans to dub him "Spock."

Through circumstance and constant work, in two remarkable years he has become the game's best player. It is the kind of achievement that would normally establish a player as the example to emulate, the strapping twenty-three-year-old kid from St. Croix, Virgin Islands, who elected to stay at Wake Forest for four years and graduate instead of entering the NBA draft early. And yet, at a time when Commissioner David Stern was considering an age requirement for players entering the NBA, Duncan is increasingly an anomaly.

Teenagers want the money they've been told is owed to them by their needy support groups and families, and they want it now. The rookie salary cap lets agents argue that players should get into the pros fast to get those lower-earning years out of the way. Duncan and Grant Hill are examples of the benefit of growing and maturing through four years in college. Still, more and more high schoolers were opting to enter the draft, believing that the chance to be a celebrity today outweighed the patience and reward of being a champion tomorrow.

The single largest problem in the NBA today is young kids entering the league with a sense of entitlement, the idea that they are owed something because their university used their number on a jersey at the campus bookstore and they were not compensated for it.

Unlike the vast majority of NBA players, Duncan did not attend an Adidas or Nike camp for gifted basketball players when he was fifteen years old. He did not participate in the cattle-call that most American kids are a part of each summer for the college and pro scouts salivating for their talent. He was not treated better than most kids his age because he played basketball well.

He swam in high school, took up basketball in his late teens, and decided to enjoy the fruits of college rather than go to work right away. And when he did finally enter the NBA, he worked harder on his game than on his image. "He seems to be very grounded," his teammate Will Perdue said. "I've been with him for over two years now, and he never seems to get overjoyed about anything—except about maybe kicking somebody's ass in Sony PlayStation. He does take a lot of pride in that."

Besides all their obvious matchup problems, the Knicks didn't have a good leg to stand on. Ewing's left foot still had a walking boot attached and, contrary to a published report, he would not be playing a minute in the Finals. Johnson could not put weight on his right knee the day after the Knicks eliminated Indiana, and his status for the first two games in San Antonio was in serious jeopardy.

"I like to use my strength and quickness and this is definitely taking away from that," said Johnson, who had watched the Knicks celebrating their Eastern Conference title from a hospital bed. "Even when I do come back . . . the bulky brace, five, six days off, out of rhythm, a little out of shape. It's tough, but this is the Finals. No excuses."

On the eve of Game 1, Johnson was optimistic that he would play, but it wasn't until two hours before tip-off that Van Gundy announced that Johnson was available and would start. Still, Johnson, who was assigned to defend Duncan, was nowhere near 100 percent healthy.

The Knicks were installed as a nine-to-one underdog to win the championship, which was vastly better than their 25,000-to-1 at the start of the playoffs. Still, the Spurs would enter Game 1 as the most prohibitive favorite in Finals history.

"We can't just be satisfied with being here," said Ewing, because that's what he had to say. "Our goal is to win it. When this whole thing started, I told everybody back in New York that I didn't see any team that I feared and I still don't."

Mario Elie, the only true New Yorker in the series—he grew up on 97th Street on Manhattan's Upper West Side—was popping off about the Knicks' inferiority. He said New York was the weakest of the four teams San Antonio had faced, and was looking for a quick end to the season.

Seven-foot-one-inch David Robinson had sacrificed his of-

fense and become an awesome complementary player alongside the 7-foot Duncan. They were a formidable combination,
and they literally stood head and shoulders above the Knick
starting front line, which averaged 6-7. The Knicks had Sprewell and Houston on the perimeter, but getting to the basket
was going to be a monster chore.

San Antonio's point guard, Avery Johnson, was as religious
as Charlie Ward and more talented than either Knick point
guard. Portland's Damon Stoudamire had said Johnson would
never lead a team to a title, but he amended the statement after
Johnson blew by him in four games. Elie, the starting shooting
guard, had won two rings with Houston and was credited with
giving the historically soft Spurs a hard edge. Their backup
shooting guard, Steve Kerr, was the beneficiary of Jordan's second coming; he won three rings with the Bulls. Kerr's college
teammate, Sean Elliott, was San Antonio's starting small forward. Elliott had forever been characterized as a finesse-
oriented West Coast player, but the truth was that injuries had
limited him for much of his career.

Herb Williams led the procession out
to the floor for Game 1 of the Finals. He and the Knicks soaked
up the boos and were feeling good about their villain status in
San Antonio.

As the jeers grew louder, the forty-one-year-old veteran
began the pregame warmups by looking defiantly at the crowd
and then ricocheting the ball hard off the backboard to Charlie
Ward for a layup.

"This is the Finals, baby!" Williams yelled. "Get hyped!"

A record Alamodome crowd of 39,514 watched the Knicks
trade baskets with the Spurs in the first quarter, eventually taking a 27–21 lead. Sprewell was going hard to the hole, scoring
inside and drawing fouls. Houston hit a few tough pull-up
jumpers, finishing the quarter with 10 points.

But lost in their solid play was the inescapable fact that
Johnson had to guard a 7-footer. He was having trouble moving

around Duncan and already had two fouls in just two minutes, 11 seconds into the game. The Knicks led 35–31 with four minutes left in the half when the Spurs found their bearings; with Camby and Johnson both on the bench with three fouls, Duncan scored nine points in a 14–2 run, putting San Antonio ahead 45–37 at halftime. The foul problems eventually forced Van Gundy to play Chris Dudley and Herb Williams together over the final 1:51 of the half.

With 1:24 left, Houston's third foul earned him a seat on the bench, leaving Sprewell on the floor as the Knicks' lone scoring threat. The Spurs double-teamed Sprewell when he had the ball, and the result was Dudley and Williams missing jumpers in the final minute of the second quarter. This was not exactly Showtime, and to add insult, the Knicks' injury list was growing. Dudley hurt his right elbow in a collision with Duncan, hyperextending the joint and forcing him to contemplate shooting free throws left-handed.

In the second half, New York never closed the gap to fewer than six points. A CBA refugee named Jaren Jackson, another Georgetown Hoya, had five 3-pointers in the game, three of them in the fourth quarter when San Antonio pulled away and won 89–77.

Duncan had lived up to his advance billing, putting up an amazing line (33 points, 16 rebounds, and two blocked shots in 44 minutes). Johnson, Camby, Kurt Thomas, and Dudley could do no right against the game's preeminent center.

"At full strength our margin of error would be small against this team," Van Gundy said.

Near the end of the game, Ewing's dejected mug was shown on the scoreboard, much to the delight of Spurs fans. "This is killing me," he said. "It's hard to sit there and watch, but that's my fate. This is something I've worked for my whole life. So it isn't easy to sit by and watch it happen without me."

Van Gundy contemplated making some changes in the lineup, but he figured it was only Game 1 and that he had no reason to panic. And he didn't even blink when a one-paragraph item in *Sports Illustrated* came out, contending that

Sprewell had confided to a teammate that he would demand a trade if Van Gundy returned as coach. Van Gundy thought the story was about two months old, and had little to do with his current relationship with Sprewell, who denied ever telling teammates that "Either the coach goes or I go."

"If they can't get you on results, they get you on relationships," Van Gundy said of his friends in the media.

The most significant change under discussion was using a big backcourt featuring Houston and Sprewell with a conventional front line. Sprewell wanted to play with Houston, but Van Gundy didn't believe they handled the ball well enough to make that lineup work. At any rate, the Knicks still didn't have anyone to guard Duncan, which was the biggest problem before them.

In Game 2, it was Sprewell, Houston, or bust. They combined for 45 points, but their teammates only scraped together 22. Sprewell was intent on attacking the basket, an aggressive strategy that produced several spectacular moments in the first half. Robinson rejected one drive, and Duncan should have been called for goaltending when he swatted a Sprewell dunk that was already over the rim. But Sprewell got his revenge with two scintillating dunks midway through the period to give the Knicks a 13–12 lead.

"I'm going to bust your ass," Sprewell shouted at Sean Elliott. "I'm coming right at you."

San Antonio still led by five at intermission and was up by 11 early in the second quarter before the Knicks used an 11–3 run to close to 52–49 with 2:41 left in the third quarter. But then New York self-destructed. Elliott drove past Kurt Thomas for a layup and a foul with 2.5 seconds remaining in the quarter, and when Elliott missed his free throw, Duncan beat Camby to the rebound and converted an uncontested tap-in to make it a seven-point game. Sprewell got the Knicks to within 63–57 with eight minutes to play, but Robinson scored five points during an 11–4 spurt to put it away.

Duncan and Robinson feasted near the basket. They went off for a combined 41 points, 26 rebounds, and nine blocked shots, some of which featured Sprewell and Houston wondering where the ball went. Was there any reason to go on?

The 80–67 loss represented an all-time franchise playoff low and was the second lowest point total ever in a Finals game in the shot clock era. One year earlier, Utah set the mark with 54 points in Game 3 against Chicago; the Knicks still had at least two more chances to break it.

"This is only two games, we're not dead," said Houston. "We've been in worse situations."

Larry Johnson's frustration was mounting. His knee throbbing, he had scored just 10 points, grabbed seven rebounds, and was being dominated by Duncan, who had four inches on him, not to mention two good legs. Plus, he was still ticked off that the NBA had fined him $10,000 for not talking during mandatory media sessions before and after Game 3 of the Indiana series.

He was in no mood to chat up reporters the day before Game 3 of the Finals. As the series shifted to his city, the last thing he wanted was to be told by an NBA public relations official that he had to make himself immediately available for the thirty-minute session instead of continuing to shoot jump shots at the Garden and bullshit with teammates.

"Get the fuck away from me," he yelled at the NBA's Teri Washington. "I've got a job to do." When league officials finally convinced him to talk, he got himself into further trouble.

"My knee's not affecting me mechanic-wise. It's affecting me that I haven't practiced. Just like now. I can't even get shots off . . . motherfuckers bothering me."

Never a big media guy, Johnson felt there was a double standard working here. Ewing was injured and was hiding out in the training room and avoiding the press, yet he was not being afforded the same courtesy. He has long thought the league had a vendetta against him for having embarrassed Brian McIntyre, the league's general manager and vice president of communications, at the 1994 World Championships in Toronto. Beyond grabbing his crotch after dunks and spewing profanities at inferior players from smaller nations, Johnson also went on a profane tirade when McIntyre asked him to do an interview.

"They don't like me," Johnson said on the eve of Game 3. "Like I give a shit. They don't pay my fuckin' rent. I don't give a fuck if they like me or not."

Before nightfall, the league had hit Johnson with a $25,000 fine and the Knicks with an additional $25,000 fine.

The Knicks' only chance to stay in the series was to win Game 3. In the 2-3-2 finals format, they had the next three games at home. No home team had ever swept the middle three games. Most of the luster of their stunning Game 6 win over the Pacers had been stripped away by the time they took the floor on the night of June 21.

But the city pulled out all the stops for their team's first Finals appearance in five years, painting a giant Knicks logo next to the words, "I Still Believe," on Eighth Avenue at the entrance to Penn Station. Banners featuring the NBA championship trophy and "I Still Believe" hung on each side of the Garden. The Finals were back in New York, and the town was going to enjoy it.

Down 0–2, Van Gundy inserted Camby into the starting lineup for Dudley, who could barely straighten his right arm. The Knicks got the Garden back into the series quickly, going up 11 points in the first quarter.

Houston was uncanny, delivering jumpers from all over the floor. New York led only 49–46 at halftime, but Houston went on a personal 7–0 run to nearly knock the Spurs out at the beginning of the third quarter. San Antonio came back to tie in the third, behind Robinson, but Kurt Thomas helped give the Knicks the lead for good moments later. Going to the floor for a loose ball, he flipped it to Houston for a 3-pointer that shook the building.

Sprewell scored 10 of his 24 points in the fourth quarter, but the signature play of the game belonged to Camby. Soaring over the Spurs' front line, Camby in one motion rebounded a Houston miss and threw it down maliciously with his right hand. The Knicks, for one night, had scaled Mount Duncan and Robinson 89–81.

Houston had a career playoff-high 34 points, and Johnson rebounded from his atrocious first two games to score 16 points and hold Duncan scoreless in the final period. "I think you saw the true character of the Knicks," Van Gundy said after his team's 89–81 victory. "We hung in there. We were very resilient."

Popovich and Elie both were hit with technical fouls in the game, and Elliott criticized the officiating and hinted that the league wanted to keep the Finals competitive because of NBC's slumping ratings. In Indiana, the Pacers and their fans echoed the same charges during the Eastern Conference finals, that somehow the peacock was pulling strings behind the scenes.

"They got the series they wanted," Mark Jackson said.

"The only reason we ever win is because of a conspiracy theory," Van Gundy said. "It's going to be a new sequel to that movie Conspiracy Theory. It's going to star the Knicks. The only way we ever win anymore is because of officiating. Game 3 against Indiana. Game 6 against Indiana. And now against the Spurs."

The conspiracy argument was always out there for public consumption, but there was no truth and little sense to it. Though the New York market share was supposedly helpful, NBC's two lowest-rated Finals in the 1990s showcased the Knicks. Jordan's retirements in 1994 and 1999 had much to do with the decline in ratings, but the Knicks had not exactly endeared themselves to the rest of America; they were too brutish in '94, and—Game 3 notwithstanding—in '99 they seemed too overmatched.

Elliott had a miserable Game 3, going 3-for-9. All the old labels began to creep up again. "Absolutely," he said when asked if players had tried to capitalize on the unfair reputation he had as a soft player. "I had plenty of guys that tried to get into me physically and lost that battle."

"Are you still fighting the battle?"

"Not really."

Elliott had coped with more than just labels during his career. Before returning to form in 1999, Elliott persevered through a series of knee injuries and other physical ailments, and he was still battling a serious kidney disease that would require him to undergo a kidney transplant early in the coming off-season.

He first learned of the disease, called focal segmental glomerular sclerosis, after his fourth NBA season. Drafted out of Arizona in the first round in 1989, Elliott was traded by the Spurs to Detroit for Dennis Rodman, Isaiah Morris, and future considerations in 1993. The Pistons tried to deal him to the Rockets in 1994, but the agreement fell through when Elliott failed his physical because of his kidney condition. The Pistons sent him back to the Spurs later that year for the rights to Bill Curley and a 1997 second-round draft choice.

Elliott's greatest playoff moment had just come in Game 2 against Portland. Tiptoeing the right sideline, he fired in a 3-pointer in the final seconds, a shot that demoralized the Trail Blazers and became known as the Memorial Day Miracle.

He had played with Allan Houston in Detroit, and perhaps better than anyone understood how tough it was to shed a reputation. "I think his personality is quiet. He's not a Generation X–type player," Elliott said. "If you're not a Generation Xer, then you're considered soft, low key, and mellow. I think he plays hard. Soft guys don't go out and score 30 points in the Finals."

During the mandatory media session the day after Game 3, Johnson decided that if the league was going to make him talk, he would make them regret it. He sat down for the full thirty minutes, answered every question, talking about the teachings of Elijah Muhammad and Louis Farrakhan and comparing the Knicks to "rebellious slaves."

"We don't go with the mainstream, we don't go with the masses," he said. "We don't like you, which has been my motto my whole life growing up. I don't like that person, that person don't like me. Fine. That's mutual respect. Stay away from each other, but don't come to me and smile and stab me behind my back. I don't like you, that way we don't have to communicate. . . .

"You know what this team kind of reminds me of this year? Vegas and Coach Tark. Tark would always say, excuse my French, 'Fuck the world. Fuck the world.' We ain't got time to try to be liked by the world. We tryin' to win a basketball game. What you tryin' to do? Win a basketball game or be liked by the world? . . .

"I'm listening to Minister Farrakhan and the Honorable Elijah Muhammad and learning about who I am and where I come from and what I can be. I definitely wouldn't sit here and tell you all how I'm so great and holy. I have a whole lot to learn. I have baby knowledge."

Some thought he had gone off the deep end; others felt Johnson was getting back at the NBA by making outrageous statements. Either way, he took the focus off bad basketball for a few days. As the media were clearing out, his teammates, stretching in a circle on the Garden floor, teased Johnson for having to be told now that he would have to end the interview.

"You talked to them today, L?" Herb Williams asked.

"Yeah, I talked," Johnson replied. "But I don't think they liked what I had to say."

In Game 4, Johnson had more fouls (six) than points (five), while Elliott finally resurfaced as a third option to Duncan and Robinson. Elliott scored 14 points and hit two 3-pointers as all five starters scored in double figures.

The Knicks hung in as best they could, with Ward scoring 10 in the first quarter after having been badly outplayed by Avery Johnson in the series' first three games. Sprewell and Houston erupted for a combined 46 points, but neither scored over the final 5:40. In the fourth quarter, Sprewell spun around Jaren Jackson and seemed to have a free path to the basket; somehow, Duncan recovered, blocked the ball from behind, and started the break the other way.

It wasn't about the Knicks and Spurs anymore. It was about height vs. heart, a series in which even the Knicks' corpuscles and resolve could no longer compensate for all those inches and pounds they gave away.

In their most difficult loss of the postseason, New York crept to within one point with 5:24 left, but Ward missed a free throw that would have tied it. Robinson and Duncan answered with consecutive baskets and Elie made one free throw to put the Spurs ahead 86–80. Camby's three-point play with 4:09 left cut the deficit in half, but the Knicks' next four possessions resulted in three errant jumpers and one Johnson free throw.

Ward also returned to reality in the final minutes, committing his lone turnover and misfiring on a 3-pointer before the Knicks grudgingly lost to the Spurs 96–89. Ward, like the Knicks, started strong but crawled across the finish line well behind the Spurs.

With Chris Childs limited to seven minutes due to a left knee he sprained late in Game 3, Van Gundy had Ward on the floor for the entire second half, which only further exposed Ward's weaknesses.

Ward played 41 minutes—he had played 30-plus minutes in just three of the Knicks' previous eighteen playoff games—and registered his first double-figure-scoring game since Game 4 against Miami. But after making his first four shots against San Antonio in Game 4, including a pair of 3-pointers, Ward went 0-for-5 with one free throw over the final three quarters. He also lost another duel with Johnson, the Spurs' point guard, who finished with 14 points and 10 assists in 44 minutes.

"I got some shots," said Ward. "I just didn't hit them."

The Knicks had defied logic and rewritten team history during their improbable postseason. Down three games to one, a deficit no team in the finals had ever overcome, they now needed exactly three more miracles.

"This makes it more fun," said Camby. "We were 21-21 and no one gave us a shot of making the playoffs. People doubted us before, they're going to doubt us now. But we're confident."

Jeff Van Gundy had been concealing a pertinent fact since May: He wasn't going anywhere.

The day before Game 5, with his team one loss away from the summer, Van Gundy dropped a story into reporters' laps. Checketts, he said, had told him as far back as last month that he would return as Knicks coach for the 1999–2000 season.

"He made it clear to me that he wants me back, and I'd like to," he said. "The only thing we decided is that we're not going to talk about it until after the season. I don't think that's a revelation." Told that it was, he said, "I didn't mean it to be."

Van Gundy's timing of the announcement was interesting. He could have been deflecting attention away from his undermanned team. Or perhaps making sure it was out there, for the public record, that Checketts had finally endorsed him.

Some in the media felt that Van Gundy had strung them along, winning the sympathy vote and playing the martyr to the hilt. But maybe it was just another innocent slip.

He was sitting in the middle of a dozen reporters, talking about his future, when he casually mentioned the fact that Checketts wanted him back. He could not even remember exactly when, except to say the discussion took place sometime between the Atlanta and Indiana series—days after the Jackson-Checketts story broke.

Either way, the pressure had been lifted on the eve of the Finals, when Phil Jackson had agreed to coach the Lakers. Instead of figuring a way to make Sprewell and Ewing coexist he was signing on to baby-sit Shaq and Kobe.

You could not put it past Van Gundy to draw attention away from Larry Johnson, too. Johnson's media gatherings were swelling, with as many as fifty reporters and ten cameras on hand, every one waiting for the next controversial utterance. That was a reason for caution, but on this team there was always bait, and Johnson took it.

Bill Walton, the outspoken NBC commentator and Hall of Fame center, had been carving up Johnson for weeks. Disgusted with Johnson's Big L symbol, which he felt was the low-class move of a player who cared about himself instead of his team, Walton now had new ammunition.

He took aim at Johnson's "rebellious slaves" comment and fired away. "He's a disgrace," Walton said on Marv Albert's nightly highlight show for the Madison Square Garden network. "I'm embarrassed not only for the league, but for the human race." When Johnson struggled in Game 4, Walton called it, "A pathetic performance by this sad human being.

"Playing in the NBA is a privilege. The NBA has given people like me the greatest life that anybody could ever have. When I hear or see people who are putting the NBA in a bad light, I get embarrassed, disappointed, and angry."

The 6-11 redhead often said what was on his mind. To overcome a speech impediment in his first years as a broadcaster, he was told by network executives to blurt out whatever he was thinking. Walton would change his opinion midway through a telecast sometimes, but that stream-of-consciousness delivery became his trademark even as it got him into trouble.

Among Walton's favorite targets were the Knicks' two point guards, Ward and Childs. Before Game 4, Walton declared, "I'm for anything that gets Charlie Ward off the court." And when Ward had 10 points in the first quarter of Game 4, Walton's retort was, "Please, here's a guy making $30 million and all he gets is a couple of baskets in a half of a half? Please!"

Walton was one of the few broadcasters who would go into the locker room before a game. He wanted to gauge the mood of the team, talk to the players, and perhaps pick up a tidbit he could relay on the air. Some players, like Ewing, acknowledged his presence by shaking his hand and saying hello. Johnson, who had been told that Walton regularly ripped him, steered clear.

"Larry Johnson does not answer my questions and does not acknowledge my existence," Walton told reporters.

Until now.

When reporters told Johnson what Walton had said about players who disrespect the league, he replied, "Is that what Bill

Walton said? That's not the same Bill Walton that was in UCLA, smoking pot and bein' a hippie . . . not that one? If that is the way Bill feels, that is the way Bill feels. You know what? I respect that. That way, me and Bill know where each other stand. For the longest time, Bill has been killing me on TV, my family and everybody tells me. But when he sees me, he's shufflin', bucklin', and goin' on."

For the third straight day, Johnson could not help himself. He kept on going, repeatedly mentioning Walton's name regardless of the topic. "My man Avery [Johnson], we are from the same plantation. Both got the Johnson name. Tell Bill Walton that. We're from Massah Johnson's plantation. Damn Bill Walton. Tell him to trace his history and see how many slaves his ancestors had."

Johnson had begun to embrace the Muslim faith and observed Ramadan for the first time in December of '98, in which he fasted during daylight hours. The Houston Rockets' All-Star center Hakeem Olajuwon did the same during the Muslim holy month. When Ramadan began, Johnson was up at dawn and by 7:00 A.M., after weightlifting and running, he would gulp down a protein shake, inhale a Power Bar, and then wait until nightfall before eating or drinking again. "You would not believe at around 3:00 or 4:00 P.M. just how grouchy and how ready I was to bite someone's head off," Johnson said during training camp. "By 5:30 P.M., I could eat grass."

He was basically using the religion for its dietary purposes, and he arrived at training camp in January twenty pounds lighter. Now, in the NBA Finals, he was throwing people way off course, cursing up a storm and showing this nasty side that made it seem like a mid-afternoon in Ramadan all over again.

Teammates and coaches didn't think the world was seeing the real Larry Johnson. "He's guarding a guy who is a lot taller than him," Chaney said. "He's half hurt, and he's not handling it very well. I think it's getting to him mentally."

Johnson was, after all, the poor kid from South Dallas who came back to the neighborhood. He donated $1 million to build

a recreational and educational center named after him on
the land where the demolished apartment complex he once
lived in had stood. Yet even though he was earning $9 mil-
lion per season, the persecuted black man in him would not
go away. He felt he had a message that needed to go out,
however un-mainstream it appeared or how inappropriate the
timing.

"This is a beautiful country, the best country," Johnson
said. "But it is not holy, it is not righteous. We talk about
what's going on in Kosovo and Nigeria. What's going on here?
Here, the NBA is full of blacks. There are great opportunities.
They've made beautiful strides. But what percentage of black
people have made similar strides? I'm the only one who came
out of my neighborhood. Everybody I know is dead, in jail, on
drugs, selling drugs, or poor. So am I supposed to be honored
and happy by my success? Yes I am. But I can't deny the fact
of what's happened to us over years and years and years, and
we're still at the bottom of the totem pole. I can't turn my
head to that. That's my point. That's what you can tell Bill
Walton."

Walton's words had put Van Gundy in an uncomfortable position. On one hand, Johnson was one of his favorite players; he
felt he had to support him, even when he erred in judgment by
spouting obscenities. On the other, Van Gundy had forged a decent relationship with Walton over the past few years, and Walton represented a link to Van Gundy's favorite team as a kid,
John Wooden's UCLA Bruins.

One of Van Gundy's most vivid memories as a child was of
his father, Bill, taking him to the Final Four. At the 1968 national semifinal, six-year-old Jeff waited for the Bruin players
by an escalator at the Los Angeles Sports Arena. Besides the
Bruins, he had just watched his future assistant coach, Don
Chaney, play for the Houston Cougars. Lew Alcindor [as Ka-
reem Abdul-Jabbar was known then] acknowledged little Jeff by
softly raking his hand across Van Gundy's head before he
walked up the escalator.

In the most surreal of ways, it seemed like everything was

coming full circle in his life. Before Game 4 of the Indiana series, Van Gundy was about to conduct an interview with NBC Sports when he spotted Walton, who was talking on his cell phone. Told it was Wooden on the other end, he said, "That guy's my hero." Walton handed him the phone, and the eighty-six-year-old Wooden dispensed his wit and wisdom for about two minutes.

"He told me, 'Quit all the isolations and play team basketball,'" Van Gundy recalled, smiling. "Well, everyone knows he hates the NBA. So I was kidding him about it. I told him we're going to run forty isolations for Allan Houston. He said, 'Oh, please have him face the basket. They're so much more effective facing the basket.'"

Wooden on their meeting of minds: "Well, I told him adversity brings out character. Seems like so many people back there wanted him fired. The way he has brought the team along, I certainly think he deserves to be congratulated. That's not an easy group to coach, from what I understand. I noticed the comments he made to his team, 'We've lost some players, but we'll carry on.' I admire that type of attitude."

Three hours before Game 5, Van Gundy heard noise from the Garden floor and strolled out of his office to see what the fuss was about. The NBA championship trophy had arrived, and the dress rehearsal for a possible presentation at center court was in full swing.

A supervisor was yelling at a group of ushers. "You got to get down here with one minute to go! You got to get on one knee, facing the audience, and hold that rope."

The NBA was trying to see how fast it could put together a makeshift podium in case the Spurs won. The whole idea of San Antonio celebrating on the Garden floor angered Van Gundy, who stood in the tunnel that led to the floor for nearly thirty minutes, his piercing gaze taking it all in.

He knew Johnson could not stop Duncan, and that Camby was no match for Robinson. The Spurs had not lost consecutive games since February and had not lost three straight games all season. But he was hoping beyond hope that the Knicks could somehow take the series back to San Antonio for Game 6 and—who knew in this wild season?—a monumental Game 7. If there was any team that could challenge history, his had a shot.

"We can win the series," he told them the day of the game. "We're only bound by what we think we can accomplish. No eighth seed has ever made it here, either. So history doesn't have to hamper us. All we have to do is win one home game. Then we can go down there and get one road game. And then you're playing the ultimate game."

New York was as desperate as its team. Callers flooded WFAN radio, wondering whether Ewing would play with the season on the line. He was still wearing his walking boot and undergoing daily treatment.

"Willis Reed has a better chance of playing than Patrick does," Van Gundy said, ending the speculation.

In the summer, a Friday evening is always a heavy-traffic night in Manhattan. Commuters leave town and head up the New York State Thruway; people cross the George Washington Bridge, heading out to the Poconos; cars are backed up everywhere. Getting to the Garden from where the players live in Westchester County and just over the border in Connecticut can be awfully brutal. Sprewell was one of a handful of Knicks who experienced a logjam driving to Game 5.

He still had time to warm up and stretch when he arrived at 8:00 P.M., but by the time the ball was tipped at 9:16 P.M. his shot had no rhythm. Over the first 30 minutes, he would miss nine of 12 field goal attempts.

In perhaps their last game of the season, the Knicks were suddenly flat. The Garden crowd they had enchanted for the past two months was watching the dream end badly.

They waited and waited for the Knicks to make a genuine run. And waited.

Meanwhile, Duncan was taking over inside and leading the Spurs to a 40–38 halftime lead. San Antonio opened with a 7–0 run to start the third, and looked on the verge of blowing the Knicks out on the way to the franchise's first title.

About that time, Sprewell woke the Garden, making five straight shots; by the time the fourth and fifth left his hands the crowd was already standing and waiting for the ball to go through the net.

Duncan was up to the challenge. Drop-stepping inside, throwing up jump hooks from fifteen feet out, he scored seven straight in the period and began waging a mano-a-mano duel with Sprewell. During one incredible six-minute span beginning in the final two minutes of the third quarter, Sprewell and Duncan accounted for 28 of the game's next 29 points. They scored 14 points apiece, and were trading blows like two prize-fighters. It was reminiscent of the way Dominique Wilkins and Larry Bird went back and forth so famously in Game 7 of the 1988 Eastern Conference semifinals. "He was on, I was on, I'm sure it was a fun game to watch," said Sprewell.

With less than 10 minutes left, Sprewell nailed a 3-pointer and then followed on the next possession with a short jumper that gave the Knicks a 68–65 lead. He was waving his arms, motioning for the crowd to scream along with him.

He had just completed one of the most mesmerizing stretches in Finals history, scoring 21 of his team's 25 points during a 15-minute binge. "He kept hitting shots," said Duncan. "He was out there, eighteen or nineteen feet, hitting them."

When Sprewell sank two free throws to put the Knicks in front 77–75 with 3:12 left, one more road trip seemed likely.

No matter what happened now, this would be the last home game of the 1999 season. And Sprewell was going out just as he came in during an exhibition five months earlier: draining 3-pointers. Exhorting the crowd. Playing the game the only way he knew how—on raw instinct and desire.

It was better than Sprewell, Checketts, Van Gundy, and even Grunfeld could have imagined back in January when they first met in Milwaukee. They all had accomplished something: Checketts's image had taken a beating, but he delivered the bottom line by giving his bosses at Cablevision ten of a possible eleven home playoff dates, worth more than an estimated $20 million; Van Gundy had saved his job and was now in line for a big raise; Grunfeld had lost his job, but had achieved his own vindication as the architect with enough foresight to build a conference championship team; and then there was Sprewell, who had used the game as a tool to salvage his career, repair his image, and prove that he could elevate a team to the Finals.

Sprewell's two free throws with 3:12 to go gave him 35 points on the night, a career playoff-high. Duncan, the Finals MVP who finished with 31 points, hit a free throw. With 47 seconds left, Avery Johnson squared up in the left corner and hit the biggest shot of his career to give the Spurs a 78–77 lead.

Sprewell and Avery Johnson both missed jumpers on each end, and suddenly New York was down to its last possession.

With 2.1 seconds left, Van Gundy diagrammed a play. It called for Ward, who was inbounding the ball, to pass either to Houston coming off two screens or to Sprewell breaking toward the basket. Ironically, it was a play Van Gundy saw San Antonio run several years earlier before deciding to insert it into his own playbook.

Sprewell slipped past Elliott quickly, and Ward saw him out of the corner of his eye. His inbound pass from midcourt hit a streaking Sprewell under the basket. At the end of this five-month sprint, he had nowhere to go.

Trapped underneath with Elliott on him and Duncan closing fast, he took one dribble away from trouble only to find more waiting for him on the left baseline.

"Charlie threw an excellent pass," said Sprewell. "I was just too far under the basket. With their size coming down on me, I didn't have the layup like we had planned on."

The twin towers were closing in on Sprewell the way the Spurs were closing in on a title. With time expiring, Sprewell launched a fade-away twelve-footer over the outstretched arms of Duncan and Robinson.

It went eleven feet.

At 11:50 P.M. Eastern Standard Time, it was over. The Spurs mobbed each other on the Garden floor. The well-trained ushers were flawless, kneeling down and holding the rope just like they were told. The podium was erected as the Green Day song "Good Riddance" blared through the Garden sound system.

It's something unpredictable, but in the end is right . . . I hope you had the time of your life.

Sprewell's shoulders slumped as he walked with his head down amid the sea of commotion around him. He untucked his jersey and shook his head in disbelief. Rick Brunson tried to console him as the Knicks huddled for a postgame prayer at midcourt, but it was no use.

"It was all for naught," he said. "It's disappointing once you know it's finally over. It's all for nothing at this point."

He felt empty, like he had let his team down. But the men who had been in his living room on that January day—along with 19,763 at the Garden that night—knew differently.

Who knows what would have happened had Houston's shot against Miami bounced out? Sprewell probably would have taken his share of the blame for a season gone terribly awry. The moves of Grunfeld and Checketts would have been viewed as failures; for the first time since 1991, the Knicks would have failed to advance to the second round. Van Gundy would have surely lost his job, his team sandblasted in the off-season.

But winning is a great deodorant. The ball bounced in, and the Knicks were suddenly viewed in a different light. They rolled through Atlanta and caught lightning in a bottle against Indiana before falling to a superior team in the Finals.

In five months, the most notorious villain in sports had become the most unlikely hero in the post-Jordan era—at least in New York. And in their own way, the Knicks became a small preview of how the new NBA might be viewed.

Were you willing to love the song even when you have questions about the singer? As the only eighth-seeded team to make the Finals, a Knicks team that many people had trouble rooting for had accomplished something that was impossible to dislike.

Sprewell had been seen as the antithesis of the team player, of what the beauty of basketball and sport are all about. But as he kept pulling the team along in his wake, he suddenly seemed redeemable on all fronts.

When they were falling on their faces in March and early April, the Knicks were Gen-X rebels without a clue. When they took off on their thrilling playoff run, they became the protagonists in a saga about heart and character, quickness and youth.

Somewhere in between, the Knicks laid waste to the whole character-analysis game. They forced us to confront the gritty truth: The sporting public today accepts anyone who wins for their team, even a guy marketed as America's nightmare.

Nowhere was this more evident than in the new NBA, a league where fans find it increasingly hard to worship the men on the court because we know so much about what they do off it. Maybe the sports star of the new millennium is less the embodiment of some unrealistic ideal and more just a person who puts the ball in the hole.

Two months after their implausible run through the playoffs, it's clear that the Knicks' story was a tale of redemption on the floor and nothing more. In the end, they were all just ballin', playing their games the only way they knew how, trying to stay on the court as long as they could.